Dance of the Vampires
&
Six Other Plays

Bole Butake

Langaa Research & Publishing CIG
Mankon, Bamenda

Publisher:
Langaa RPCIG
Langaa Research & Publishing Common Initiative Group
P.O. Box 902 Mankon
Bamenda
North West Region
Cameroon
Langaagrp@gmail.com
www.langaa-rpcig.net

Distributed in and outside N. America by African Books Collective
orders@africanbookscollective.com
www.africanbookcollective.com

ISBN: 9956-790-39-7

© Bole Butake 2013

DISCLAIMER
All views expressed in this publication are those of the author and do not necessarily reflect the views of Langaa RPCIG.

Table of Contents

Preface One v

Preface Two ix

Part I: Dance of the Vampires 1

Part II: Family Saga 59

Part III: Lake God 111

Part IV: Betrothal without Libation 195

Part V: And Palm-wine will flow 243

Part VI: The Rape of Michelle 285

Part VII: Shoes 331

Preface One

Tribute to Bole Butake, A Literary Luminary
By Francis Wache
Editor-in-Chief, The Post

The Post print edition no. 01354, Sunday, July 01, 2012 CameroonPostline.com -- Growing up in the 50s in the verdant valleys of Noniland, chances were stacked more on the side of Nazarius (a name he dropped) Bole Butake becoming a tapper of frothy palm wine or a farmer a la Achebe's Okonkwo, levelling the hillocks and mulching the valleys.

He did not choose those paths.

Instead, he heard about the Golden Fleece and, because he was highly intelligent, he convinced his uncle to send him to Sacred Heart, a leading Catholic College. He had lost both parents in babyhood. He will later attend the prestigious CCAST Bambili, the lone High School in West Cameroon before moving to the University of Yaounde. On graduation, as one of the "Mbassi Manga Boys" (Mbassi Manga was the all-powerful and influential Dean of the Faculty of Arts), he left for Leeds from where, on his return, he taught at the University of Yaounde until his retirement this June.

More than an academic, Butake distinguished himself as a playwright. His repertoire of plays includes, The Rape of Michelle (1984), Lake God (1986), The Survivors (1989), And Palm-wine Will Flow (1990), Shoes and Four Men in Arms (1993), Dance of the Vampires (1995), Zintgraff and the Battle of Mankon (2003), Family Saga (2005, Betrothal Without Libation (2005), Cameroon Anthology of Poetry (2010).

In all his plays, Butake takes sides with the downtrodden, the wretched of the earth, the deprived and the underdogs. His jabs and jibes, aimed at the rulers, are scathing, at times vitriolic.

Butake will be remembered for starting The Mould, a literary magazine considered as a nursery for budding University students with a creative instinct. Although nobody has become a Nobel laureate from that nursery, it undoubtedly contributed enormously in enriching the Anglophone Literature that we have today.

A Fonlonian disciple, Butake insisted that teaching Literature, ultimately, was futile if it did not lead to making the student, herself, a producer and not only a consumer of literary classics. Buoyed by this conviction, Butake, alongside Hanzel Ndumbe Eyoh, created the Flame Players, a drama troupe at UniYao. Over the years, they staged and thrilled Anglophone drama aficionados.

In the 90s, as the nation writhed with the throes of the birth democracy, Butake burst on the political arena when he was appointed to accompany a delegation of CPDM stalwarts to Muanenguba Division in the Southwest Province to drum support against multiparty politics.

Terrified, Butake penned a rebuttal. He would never–NEVER – join the ranks of the oppressors, he argued. He would, he insisted, stay in the amphitheatres and share knowledge with his students.

Up till today, controversy still rages about that act. Some opinion, still peddled, particularly in Noni circles, bears a grudge against Butake for depriving them of a Ministerial portfolio. According to this school, Butake's trip to Muanenguba was intended to immerse him into the CPDM baptismal waters. He was to emerge from the boiling bowels of the Twin Lakes with the halo of Minister of, guess…, Culture, of course!

That is not true. What happened was a typical CPDM error. Bole, Dr Butake's first name, is a common Bakossi name. When the CPDM ngomba went into conclave and decided that they should pacify dissident lecturers who were fomenting riots at the University, a CPDM big shot proposed that there was this Bole…Somebody who was writing anti-regime plays and needed to be gagged by, he said, "getting him on our side." He tried to capture the elusive name again: "Bole…Bole…Bole…" The other name did not just come. Another inspired comrade chirped in, "Butake." The speaker glowed: "That's him!"

And that is how, Bole Butake, a blue-blooded Noni notable was almost transmogrified into a Bakossi CPDM rabble-rouser. All in the name of dimabolaing (fighting against) multiparty politics.

Be that as it may, Butake did not join the beleaguered CPDM bandwagon. Instead, he dipped his pen in his inkpot and wrote: "I refuse to be lapiroed".

Let Butake, himself, tell the tale: "My troubles really began in 1992 when in early February I was appointed, without being consulted, as 'chargé de mission' for the ruling CPDM party during the first multi-party legislative elections to some part of the country. I wrote a damning disavowal… A week later I was replaced. A year later I would begin living the consequences of my deed because the new Chancellor of the University banned all theatre performances on campus and unleashed a war of harassment against my person."

His numerous ordeals notwithstanding, Butake has been an outstanding scholar, a genuine intellectual, a path-finding playwright and a gadfly for an anaesthetised society.

Although he has stopped formal work at the University, a new life opens for him: a supervisor of Doctoral Theses; a farmer, the first job he had as a kid, chasing monkeys and birds from the cornfields. Thankfully, the Prof (Rtd) will not have to mount any podium or climb any rooftop to sing alleluias to any party before getting access to the vast arable ancestral farmlands in his native Noniland.

Naturally, he will continue to write and direct plays. In fact, I would suggest that he should write a play entitled "The Professor Who Almost Became Minister." You have the Noni people as background. You have the young Noni gendarme officer who would have become your bodyguard; there is the High School teacher who should have become your Private Secretary; your orphaned house helps (Nya and Bofa) rescued from grinding village poverty; and party visits (especially on 6 November: the date of the coming of the Messiah; and May 20: the day water and oil had an unprecedented mix) and sporadic bags of rice and cartons of soap for the bamboozled electorate, every time an election rolled around. And so on. And, above all, don't fail to paint the scene of the Eldorado that you selfishly refused to give the Noni people...Never mind. And, in the background, the bewitching throbs of the njang dance.

Prof. Butake couldn't have been that kind of Minister because he argues in Home or Exile that: "It is really disgusting how people can abuse their consciences and allow themselves to be manipulated by Machiavellian political leaders because they want to be appointed to high administrative offices where they will be in control of budgets and so can serve themselves generously from the tax-payer's sweat."

One thing I wish you, though, as you formally depart from the raucous lecture halls, is this: Let the ink continue to flow!

First published in The Post print edition no. 01354

Preface Two

Bole Butake – And The Playwright Retires: Cameroon's ace playwright and actor, Prof. Bole Butake talks on his university teaching career as he prepares to retire at the end of this month.
By Kimeng Hilton Ndukong, 12 July 2012, Cameroon Tribune, 12 July 2012

The mention of Bole Butake's name will most likely ring a bell – especially among those familiar with Cameroon's literature in English. This is especially true for students who have had occasion to study or perform some of his plays. After more than 40 years of teaching in the then University of Yaounde (now University of Yaounde I), Prof. Butake is retiring at the end of this month a fulfilled man. Beginning as secondary school teacher of English language to Francophone university students, the don – who lost both his parents within a week when he was only four – would later rise through all lecturer ranks, becoming Professor of Performing Arts and African Literature in 2000. He was also Vice Dean for Programming and Academic Affairs and Head of Department of Arts and Archaeology in the same university.

You're going on retirement at the end of this month after more than three decades of teaching. What has it been like?

I have actually been working for over 40 years. I began in 1972 when I was posted to the university as secondary school teacher to teach English to Francophones. Two years later – in 1974 – I became an Assistant Lecturer. I've had an interesting time, rising through all the grades to become a professor.

Would you say you had a fulfilled career?

I feel quite fulfilled with my career because I love teaching – imparting knowledge. I'm also in cinematography. I have done workshops with people in various parts of Cameroon, beginning from Limbe and Muyuka in the South West Region to the North and

Far North Regions. So, I have visited nearly all parts of Cameroon, holding workshops with ordinary village people on techniques of theatre for development. I have taught or introduced them to using theatre in human rights activities, women's rights, early pregnancy and marriages amongst young girls, the education of the girl child, democracy... In short, we have worked in many areas.

You didn't get involved in partisan issues like some of your colleagues. What prompted such a decision?

I was very interested in teaching at the university, not in doing politics. So, I decided to concentrate on my teaching job. In fact, I was asked a number of times to go and campaign for one party or the other, but I refused because I didn't want to get involved in political matters. The way politics is done in our society is not really healthy. You have to tell lies, say things that you don't believe in. I don't believe in such things.

I decided to steer clear of politics because it was an area I found to be very slippery and dangerous. I need my sleep when I go to bed. To stand in public and promise people something and to face them tomorrow without having done it is what I wanted to avoid. That is why I decided to stay away from what to me is a dangerous game. I don't envy those who do politics, but I can't do it.

Did the decision have to do with your integrity?

Yes, definitely because I think a lot about myself, my conscience and I don't see myself standing in public and making a declaration that people will prove wrong. Generally, when I make promises, I like to keep them. For instance, when I was president of my village development committee, we promised water for the village, galvanised the people and gave them water and they have been expanding on that. I'm waiting for other people to take the baton and provide other facilities for people in the village. At least in my time, I did my best. Apart from the water plant, we also expanded the hospital, got some equipment for secondary schools and other things. Those are the types of things that I like to do and not to make empty promises which cannot be kept.

Is such concern for integrity borne out of your religious upbringing?

Religion ... and it can also be genetic. My parents died when I was still four years old. Both of them died within the same week. I cannot say it is the influence of my parents and I don't have other brothers or sisters. I have a lot of relatives, but they are all cousins, uncles, aunts etc. It is just genetic, I think. Though I am a Catholic, I go to church when I can. I believe in God but I think it is more of genetics than religion.

What, according to you, is the state of theatre in Cameroon today?

It is in a sad state. The problem is not lack of playwrights, actors or training facilities and institutions. The problem is with the people who matter – business people – who do not want to invest in theatre. Can you imagine that a big city like Yaounde does not have a theatre house where people can sit and relax on a daily bases? They have to go to the French Cultural Centre. There is no Cameroonian who has a theatre house. Can you imagine that there is no cinema hall in Yaounde and Douala today?

There was a time that all the major towns in the country had cinema halls. I know that in Bamenda, there were at least two cinema halls. In Yaounde, there was a time there were about nine cinema halls and 11 in Douala. Today, there is nothing. It is a very disturbing situation that theatre is gone down. The 70s and 80s were the golden age of Cameroon theatre.

Since then, churches and supermarkets have taken over the big cinema houses. Maybe, the people were distributing European and not African films. Today, people watch films on cable television and that is why they don't go to cinema anymore. And we have Nigeria next-door that is producing Nollywood films. With just FCFA 200, you can get a Nigerian home movie.

Though theatre has dropped, I think it is still a worthwhile investment. I will encourage any businessman to build a small hall of even 200 or 300 places maximum. And I challenge that person to give it to me and we will be able to use it well and have plays produced there practically on a daily basis.

Do you really believe such a venture will be viable?

It will be used in a more professional manner. We'll employ people on permanent basis and pay taxes to government. The day that we are not performing a play, we are showing films or having a musical concert to be busy all round.

Maybe businessmen need to be convinced that it will be financially viable?

How do you convince them when everybody is in import and export? When people talk about business, it is importing and exporting. They import the last grade of second-hand goods that have been dumped. They dump it here in the country, causing pollution instead of creating jobs. I don't see how you can convince them.

I have gone to television and radio stations and talked about this a number of times. I have even talked to some business people and one had a strategic piece of land near Obili in Yaounde. We drew up the plan for the theatre house and later, he changed his mind, sold the plot and the project collapsed.

What would you say is the state of Anglophone creative writing in Cameroon?

Creative writing is really growing and I like the way it is developing. For instance, there are two publishing houses now – Langaa Press and Miraclaire Publishers. Both of them are based in the United States of America and publish works of Cameroonian Anglophone writers every year. These books are not well known back in Cameroon because they are not properly distributed. Some of them cost between FCFA 10,000 and FCFA 20,000, which is quite exorbitant. I think this year alone, Langaa has published more than 20 books already. And I know that Miraclaire has published about 10. These are mostly works of Cameroonians.

What is the quality of these works?

The quality is very good. I have read many of them and I can tell you that the quality is very good. I trained some of the authors when they started working here in the university (the University of Yaounde I). We created a literary club called 'The Mould.' We used to meet and discuss our poems and short stories. Many of them have become renowned writers and have recently won prizes. They are doing very well as you won't be able to win a prize if you don't write well. I think they can stand their grounds anywhere in the world.

Any advice for young people who want to get into creative writing?

I will give them a lot of encouragement, but I will tell them to prepare. There is one thing with young people; they do not prepare adequately. They do not master the tenets of writing. It happens that in Cameroon you write either in English or in French. There are very few people who can read and write in their mother tongues. So, you have to write in foreign languages and if you don't master the tenets of the foreign languages, you will be unable to express yourself.

So, the greatest problem young people face is that of language. I was reading the script of one of my students in French. As an Anglophone, I still found mistakes in it, indicating that something is wrong. They should begin by mastering the language and maybe they will improve. When you have good ideas, it is better to express them because it is through communication that readers understand what you are talking about.

How do you see the future of theatre arts in Cameroon?

I think it is promising. I have said that before long, business people will realise that it is viable to invest in the cultural entertainment industry. Just look at Nigeria and see how many people the Nollywood industry is employing. They are the next employer after government. In the United States, the entertainment industry is the biggest employer and people are earning thousands of dollars out of music, dance, film etc. The future is very bright for the local entertainment industry. People who have money should be brave enough to invest in it. They will reap a very good harvest.

Part I

Dance of the Vampires

Part 1

Once of the Vampires

Dramatis Personae

PSAUL ROI	:	Monarch
SONG	:	Chief of Protocol
TOWN CRIER	:	Chambiay
FIVE MASKED FIGURES	:	Vampire cult
ALBINO	:	Emissary from Albinia
NFORMI	:	Army General
FOUR SOLDIERS	:	
VOICES OFF	:	

First Movement

Complete silence. Eerie sounds of night birds of ill omen: owls, bats etc. Orchestrated sounds dominated by deep wind instruments and shrill voices (combination of Lum and Kwifon) of Dikang and howling of Nkow. Five masked figures perform the cult dance. Psaul Roi is on his throne and the impression must be given that he is dreaming; and the forces of good and evil must be seen to be having a combat in him.

VOICE

Dance of the Vampires. They are at it again. But evil ends by consuming itself. No matter how long, evil shall always consume itself. All that has a beginning must have an end. Truth shall always prevail. And the land shall be free...free...free!!!

(Sound of orchestra rises violently subduing VOICE followed by howling laughter of mocking voice).

EERIE VOICE

The sounds will never cease! The dance will never stop! Power is in our hands. The land is in chains as the vampires dance the dance of the vampires. He that does not believe let him open his eyes and ears and watch a most spectacular spectacle- Dance of the Vampires!

Lights turned on gradually revealing a man wearing a tight-fitting safari suit (white) with white shoes and helmet to match, sitting on a throne on a raised platform. In front of him there is an exquisitely decorated low table at which he is dealing cards while swallowing mouthfuls of some local alcoholic beverage. It should be clear that he is in his private quarters although there is a working table piled high with files. There is a door which is used by actors or characters coming from outside.

PSAUL ROI

Power is in our hands? We who? Psaul Roi and who? Power is in our hands! Psaul Roi, you are a fool. You are king with only the semblance of power. Real power, absolute power is in the hands of the vampires. What to do? Psaul Roi, what to do to have absolute power? I want power! Psaul Roi wants absolute power. Absolute power even if I have to wrestle with the vampires. I want absolute power! Power!!! (*An apologetic knock at the door. Psaul Roi swallows a mouthful and then impatiently*) Who is it? Who is there?

Door opens gradually and SONG, Chief of Protocol, sticks in his head.

SONG

It's only me Your Most Royal Majesty. May I come in?

PSAUL ROI

Come. Come inside. You want a drink? Serve yourself.

SONG

(*Advancing with all humility*) I am very sorry to disturb Your Most Royal Majesty at this time of day.

PSAUL ROI

What time of day is it? I can hardly make morning from noon, day from night. All because of those vandals who won't let me sleep a wink.

SONG

No need to bite your tongue about them, Your Royal Majesty. The army...

PSAUL ROI

Watch your tongue, Mr Protocol. What impudence! Insinuating that My, Our Most Royal Majesty would bite my, our tongue!

SONG

(*Falling on his knees*) I beg royal pardon for my impudence, Your Most Royal Majesty.

PSAUL ROI

(*After very careful consideration*) All right. I will grant you royal pardon. Go right away and ask my Chief Counsellor... what is his name?

SONG

Chinkene, Your Most Royal Majesty.

PSAUL ROI

What?

SONG

His name is Chinkene, Your Royal Majesty.

PSAUL ROI

What did you say? Where did "Most" vanish to?

SONG

Again I must beg royal pardon, Your Most Royal Majesty.

PSAUL ROI

You see how you make work difficult for me? Now you go and instruct my Chief Counsellor, whatever his name is, to prepare two instruments of royal pardon in your favour for my immediate signature and royal seal. You remember the crimes, don't you?

SONG

I do, Your Most Royal Majesty. One for declaring that Your Most Royal Majesty bit Your Most Royal tongue and the other for deliberately leaving out "Most" in addressing Your Most Royal Majesty.

PSAUL ROI

Good. Two instruments of royal pardon which must be proclaimed throughout the land by sunset. Is the Town Crier in attendance?

SONG

Your Most Royal Majesty, he is in the waiting room.

PSAUL ROI

What is his business in the waiting room? His place is in the courtyard. Tell him that.

SONG

Your Most Royal Majesty, I came to announce his presence in the waiting room. He...

PSAUL ROI

(*Looking at his watch disinterestedly*) When did you come?

SONG

When I came now Your Royal Majesty.

PSAUL ROI

When you came now...

SONG

I beg...

PSAUL ROI

Not for royal pardon again. I will not grant it. Too much work for one insignificant worm I picked up from the gutter. You are all rotten maggots I exhumed from the grave. What were you before I made you...?

SONG

Chief of Protocol, Your Most Royal Majestic Emperor, I was...

PSAUL ROI
You think I am one of you pigs whom you can flatter?

SONG
No, Your Most Royal Majesty. You are...

PSAUL ROI
I can see that you are fighting hard to keep your job. What job do you even have? Coming to disturb my peace and tranquillity about one zombie or other coming to see me. Where did you say Town Crier is?

SONG
In the waiting room, Your Most Royal Majesty. He said it was urgent because...

PSAUL ROI
What was urgent? Seeing me? You are all beginning to fly places. Like the vampires that you all are. Who decides the urgency of any matter in this land?

SONG
Your Royal...Most Royal Majesty. Your Most Royal Majesty.

PSAUL ROI
The two instruments of royal pardon are they ready?

SONG
Your Most Royal Majesty, I beg...

PSAUL ROI
I will not grant. Too much work just for one rotten maggot.

SONG
Very true, I beg...

PSAUL ROI
I will not grant. Too much work just for one rotten maggot.

SONG
Very true, I beg...

PSAUL ROI
I will not grant. Too much work just for one rotten maggot.

SONG
Very true, Your Most Royal Majesty. I have been in the palace all this while.

PSAUL ROI
And what was your business in the palace?

SONG
To announce the presence of Town Crier in the waiting room, Most Royal Majesty.

PSAUL ROI
Ah! I remember. You said it was urgent.

SONG
Not me, Most Royal... Town Crier...He said Your Most Royal Majesty was due...had to...desired...would like...to address the people this ...this...this...afternoon.

PSAUL ROI
Go right now and ask the Chief Counsellor to prepare a royal instrument of destitution in favour of Town Crier. Most urgently; and the instruction takes precedence over the instruments of royal pardon in your favour. He will proclaim the destitution himself. I am in no frame of mind now to designate another. As soon as he is done with the proclamation he must be immediately put under the custody of

the army. These are royal instructions and I want them executed with maximum celerity.

SONG
(*Alarmed*) Your Most Royal Majesty, this instruction cannot be executed. I beg...

PSAUL ROI
I will not...

SONG
Town Crier has the army in his hand.

PSAUL ROI
Am I or am I not the Commander in Chief of the Royal Armed Forces of...

SONG
Your Most Royal Majesty, you are. And Chambiay is Chief Commander. He is also the High Priest of our...

PSAUL ROI
Chambiay? Who is...?

SONG
Town Crier! Chambiay, Chief Commander of the Royal Armed Forces and Chief Vampire, High Priest of our...

PSAUL ROI
And what am I? Who am I? Show him in. Bring him in right now.

(*Song exits, Psaul Roi drinks straight from the bottle and begins to pace about impatiently*).

PSAUL ROI

Commander in Chief, Chief Commander! Chief Commander, Commander in Chief! I have power. Power to instruct. Power to designate. Power to des... No. Now no more power to destitute Chief Commander. Commander in Chief, Chief Com...

(The door suddenly flies open and an army general steps in smartly and salutes Psaul Roi who is visibly stunned).

TOWN CRIER

Your Most Royal Majesty, I am highly indebted and deeply grateful for this audience. The people are already swarming to...

PSAUL ROI

Who are you? I was expecting...

TOWN CRIER

Chambiay, Town Crier of Your Most Royal Majesty!

PSAUL ROI

What is that you are wearing? Are you in the army?

TOWN CRIER

Chief Commander, Your Most Royal Majesty.

PSAUL ROI

Who made you Chief Commander?

TOWN CRIER

By Royal Proclamation No. 999/ 777/555/DOV/RME signed and sealed by Your Most Royal Majesty on April 6, 19...

PSAUL ROI

Do you have the proclamation?

TOWN CRIER

(*Pulling it out from breast pocket*) A copy, Your Most Royal Majesty. Duly certified by Your Royal Majesty's Chief of the Security Service.

PSAUL ROI

(*Examines it closely and hands it back*) This looks authentic. And... were you made Town Crier by royal proclamation under my sign and seal?

TOWN CRIER

Your Most Royal Majesty, by the same proclamation. (*reading*) Town Crier and Chief Commander of the Royal Armed Forces, Chambiay.

PSAUL ROI

Have I granted you audience before?

TOWN CRIER

This is the first, Your Most Royal Majesty. I am greatly privileged, highly honoured to be in the Royal presence.

PSAUL ROI

And I understand you are also the cult leader... the High Priest... the Chief of Vampires?

TOWN CRIER

Your Most Royal Majesty, your most humble servant.

PSAUL ROI

Why haven't I seen you before? I mean such an influential personality... Is that why you have not cared to come to me?

TOWN CRIER

Only NGUMBA knows how hard I have tried, Your Most Royal Majesty. (*indicating table piled with documents*). But always you are busy, very busy Your Majesty, Chief of Protocol said, and now I believe.

PSAUL ROI

Is that his name? I mean Chief of Protocol, is his name NGUMBA?

TOWN CRIER

No, Your Royal Majesty. NGUMBA is the name of our guardian spirit.

PSAUL ROI

Am I a member of the cult?

TOWN CRIER

A co-opted member, Your Royal Majesty.

PSAUL ROI

Am I right to think that others are initiated?

TOWN CRIER

Your Majesty, it is so.

PSAUL ROI

I want to be initiated. How soon can that be done?

TOWN CRIER

It can be done ... soon... but consultations and preparations have to be made.

PSAUL ROI

I want it tomorrow!

TOWN CRIER

Your Most Royal Majesty, the people are waiting in the market place.

PSAUL ROI

I don't care. They can wait. I will not talk to them today. Some other time. Where is Chief of Protocol? Let him tell them to go home. Psaul Roi will not give them political nourishment today. Get him for me, will you? No, wait. You must not leave this place until we are settled about the initiation. (*going towards door*) Protocol? Chief of...

TOWN CRIER

He will not be of any use. Only I know how to tell them to disperse. They can wait. They are a very patient lot, Your Majesty.

PSAUL ROI

These consultations and preparations that must be made, don't worry about money. You know the land is wealthy and we... I have money and abundant resources. What is it you want? Name your price and fix the initiation for tomorrow.

TOWN CRIER

Your Most Royal Majesty, I have to consult first. What you demand is very delicate. It will cost the land an awful lot.

PSAUL ROI

I don't care how much it costs. I just told you that the land is rich and full of resources both human and natural.

TOWN CRIER

Your Majesty, are you ready... are you prepared for the consequences... of your initiation? No monarch in this land... beginning with Kimbuwsi, the founding father, through Mungai, Nyonudfu, Nyowike, the conqueror, and Nyobome the thinker, ... no monarch in this land has ever been initiated. They have always been co-opted. That is why I fear the consequences and dread the repercussions. The people are very patient and tolerant. It will not be right to push them too far.

PSAUL ROI
Look... em... I don't want to keep calling you by your office.

TOWN CRIER
Chambiay is my name.

PSAUL ROI
Chambiay, my friend, I do not understand why this thing is gnawing at your heart. I am the monarch in this land. I own the land and all the people in it. I want to be initiated into the cult; and you dare have the effrontery to stop me?

TOWN CRIER
I do not stop you, Royal Majesty. Only that I fear for the consequences.

PSAUL ROI
Leave the consequences to me. I will take care of them. But I want this initiation tomorrow; and that is an order, a royal edict. I will instruct Chief Counsellor to prepare a royal proclamation for our signature and seal.

TOWN CRIER
Top secret, Your Majesty. Business of the cult is not for public consumption. It is top secret.

PSAUL ROI
Alright, go now and tell the people to return to their homes. I will give them political nourishment another time, another day. I have never worked so hard in any one day. You will surely need some money for the consultations and preparations. (*Goes to his work desk and pulls out stuffed envelope*) I do not know how much is in there but it

should take you a long way. Let me know in the morning if you need anything else.

TOWN CRIER

Money will not be the deciding factor, Your Majesty. Money cannot do it.

PSAUL ROI

(*Going back to table and pulling out another stuffed envelope*) Did I say money was going to decide anything? Here, take this too. You can call that inconvenience allowance or whatever. Go now and get things moving. By the way, is my Chief of Protocol one of you?

TOWN CRIER

(*Nervously trying to stuff envelopes into his pockets*) Ye... Your Royal Majesty, not even the initiated know all the other members.

PSAUL ROI

I thank you. Please, go now and begin your consultations. Please, tell my Chief of Protocol to come.

(*As Town Crier exits Psaul Roi goes to his back to his throne and begins to pour himself a drink slowly. There is a timid knock at the door and Chief of Protocol sticks in his head.*)

SONG

Your Most Royal Majesty, may I...?

PSAUL ROI

Come on inside; and drink from my glass.

SONG

Your Most Royal Majesty, I will get another glass if you insist that I must drink.

PSAUL ROI

Indeed, I do insist; and from my glass. There, we do share a lot of things together. I don't see why we can't share a glass and a drink. You are my only companion. No! There are two companions that I have, power and Chief of Protocol. Now I find that I don't have power; so I will have you. Let me drink a little.

SONG

I can get another...

PSAUL ROI

No...no...no... We shall drink from the same glass. You and I. Two companions at the helm of the land.

SONG

There can only be one monarch at the helm of the realm, Most Royal Majesty.

PSAUL ROI

If only we had power, absolute power! (*Waving in the direction of his work table*) There would be no need for all this paper work.

SONG

But you have power, absolute power, Most Royal Majesty. You have power!

PSAUL ROI

Then why can't I destitute whoever I want to?

SONG

Town Crier?

PSAUL ROI

Why can't I destitute him? He is high priest, Chief Vampire, Town Crier and Chief Commander while I am only Commander in Chief. Why? Why? Why? I am not even a member of the cult. Why?

SONG

Because no monarch has ever been a member, Your Most Royal Majesty.

PSAUL ROI

But you are a member? Otherwise how do you know my friend eh... eh...

SONG

Song.

PSAUL ROI

Song, of course. Song. Sometimes I have these little memory lapses. Song, my friend, if we had absolute power, the two of us, just the two of us would run this kingdom like a little family business.

(*Sudden sounds of explosions and gun-fire from off*)
What is that now?

SONG

It must be Town Crier asking the people to return to their homes.

PSAUL ROI

Must he use the army? Must he use force?

SONG

The people are so patient and tolerant that they must be forced to return to their homes. Otherwise they could wait for an eternity. All this for love of the monarch, Your Most Royal Majesty.

PSAUL ROI

You see what I was saying? Right now there are too many people storing away. Too many vampires. Two vampires would be ideal. Just you and me. Come. Let me show you something. (*steers him towards work desk and pulls one of the drawers*) Look. What do you see?

SONG

Envelopes, Your Most Royal Majesty.

PSAUL ROI

Ah! Song, my friend. My very good friend and daily companion; not envelopes but money. The whole palace is full of money. Take some, as many as you want.

SONG

One is good, Most Royal Majesty.

PSAUL ROI

No! Take some more, as many as you want. Hide what you have very carefully, where those other thieving vampires will not get at it.

SONG

I thank you, Most Royal Majesty. Shall I beg leave of you?

PSAUL ROI

No, my friend, you must keep me company. I will get another bottle of this wonderful stuff from the royal brewery and we shall drink ourselves to sleep.

SONG

There is a very important engagement from which I cannot disengage myself. There is a meeting and it is my turn to be present.

PSAUL ROI

A meeting? A meeting that is more important than keeping the drinking company of a lonely monarch who is also sad?

SONG

Most Royal Majesty, it is not often that one takes his turn at this meeting. It is very important.

PSAUL ROI
Since you won't stay with me, I will have to come with you. Your meeting will be graced by our royal presence.

SONG
Most Royal Majesty, you cannot. You are not...

PSAUL ROI
I am not what?... Initiated?... So the vamps are deciding on my fate this night?

SONG
I do not know what will be discussed, Most Royal, I was only just informed now by Town Crier.

(*Psaul Roi whispers into his ear and he smiles broadly as both of them walk back to low table*)

PSAUL ROI
Sit down, my friend, Song.

SONG
Most Royal Majesty, I cannot.

PSAUL ROI
You must start learning to savour power and royalty. If you agree with my plan, by this time tomorrow, there will be only two vamps in this kingdom, you and me. And all the wealth and resources shall belong to you and me.

SONG
All the money shall belong to us, just you and me?

PSAUL ROI
Just you and me; and I shall have absolute power.
(*As they smile at each other, gradual fade to black*).

Second Movement

(*Darkness accompanied by eerie sounds of night birds. Orchestra music of Kwifon and Lum with shrieking Dikang and howling Nkow. Sound sustained as lights are turned on revealing a completely masked figure in red, his back to the audience, in the middle of a white circle with black candle alight in left hand. In his right hand a staff of office dominated by human skull. As music fades gradually four other completely masked figures in red enter walking backwards. Each has a red candle which is lit from that of the figure in the middle of the circle in one of the four cardinal points.*)

CENTRE

His Royal Majesty demands initiation. What do the four pillars say? Speak, North!

NORTH

I am the pillar on which the land is hooked. My feet are wedged by the weight of a thousand solid granite rocks. The monarch's initiation is like a dead dog whose head cannot enter the cooking pot. I am the pillar on which the land is hooked. A dead dog is no good for the cooking pot. The spirit of the cross flows through my heart down to my feet, down South, down South.

CENTRE

(*turning right round*) Speak, South!

SOUTH

The blood of ten dogs is like a mere drop of water in a burning throat. Not even the blood of a thousand dogs. I cannot hear the blood of a thousand dogs barking. The monarch's thing requires two thousand. Shall we become greedy suckers of blood for the monarch's mere delight? The spirit of the cross rises from my feet, through my heart and out through my hands. Through my arms left or right.

CENTRE
We all know you bear the weight of the land on your shoulders, but two thousand dogs is a lot; an awful lot of blood which surely transforms us into suckers of blood. East, speak!

EAST
(*female voice*) I am the home of the sun that bathes the land with radiance. I am the womb that peoples the land. Two thousand is too much blood; for the spirit of fertility condones not the wanton shedding of blood. The spirit of the circle flows from my heart through my arms embracing North and South, extending West, a human spirit.

CENTRE
West, your turn!

WEST
The spirit of the West is the spirit of the wind, the wild west wind blowing down baobabs and howling for blood. The spirit of the West accepts two thousand dogs for the monarch's thing...

CENTRE
That is violent language, very violent language, unknown to the spirit of the cross and circle.

Unmask. (*As other figures advance threateningly towards him, West unmasks revealing Psaul Roi*).

VARIOUS VOICES
Abomination! Impossible! Unbelievable! Desecration! (*Then they turn towards Centre demanding explanation*)

CENTRE
Song will pay dearly for this.

PSAUL ROI
If any harm befalls him I will tell the people. I told you that I wanted to be initiated and I will be initiated.

EAST
Two thousand human beings from my loins! This is madness.

PSAUL ROI
I do suffer mental lapses from time to time. However, this is not one of those moments.

EAST
I will not stay here and see the land destroyed.

PSAUL ROI
Nobody leaves this place until I have been initiated. By the way, is it not true that anyone who stumbles on your meetings must be initiated?

CENTRE
I see Song has been telling you a lot of secrets.

SOUTH
(*to Centre indicating Psaul Roi*) What secrets does he share with you?

NORTH
Our hands are tied. We are obliged to initiate him.

EAST
I fear and I tremble for the consequences.

SOUTH
Blood, fire and destruction shall henceforth be constant visitations in this land.

CENTRE
A vampire monarch assumes the role of chief vampire. We are undone.

PSAUL ROI
What is the use being a monarch without absolute power?

SOUTH
Chambiay, I want my share of the booty before we proceed. There is nothing left to protect in this land.

EAST
I will also like my own share. What shall become of the land?

PSAUL ROI
After the initiation we shall all go to the palace in procession and I will give you money. That is what you need, not power.

CENTRE
We shall now proceed to the shrine of the circle and cross where the rites of passage shall be performed. But the consequences...

NORTH, SOUTH and EAST
Consequences...consequences...

PSAUL ROI:
Absolute power!

(*Exeunt with Centre leading, followed by Psaul Roi, North, South and East in procession to the music of Kwifon and Lum a pace slower than at beginning.*)

Third Movement

(Stage bare. However, a cyclorama dominated by military motifs is optional. There is a lectern DSC. next to which is a stand on which Song will put a drinking glass when he enters. Sound effects of a large crowd waiting to be addressed by the monarch. When lights are turned on four heavily armed soldiers storm the stage and then proceed into auditorium where they keep a stern watch on the spectators throughout the scene. Song, Chief of Protocol, now in the costume previously worn by Town Crier enters from RW.)

SONG

His Most Royal Majesty, Psaul Roi! People of this land, Psaul Roi, His Most Royal Majesty! Long live the monarch! And long may his reign be!

Crowds cheering as Psaul Roi in his usual outfit and walking stick makes entrance looking dazed but managing to maintain a certain dignity. He is clutching a bottle with some red liquid inside which he sips from time to time. He salutes the crowd before proceeding to the lectern. Song walks with deference towards him, a file in his hand but Psaul Roi waves him off.

PSAUL ROI

People of this land! My dear mothers and fathers, daughters and sons, the joy in my heart as I stand before you is immeasurable. The joy in my heart is immeasurable because of ... why? The joy in my heart is immeasurable because... because... because... (B*eckons at Song who brings him file and he reads*) because we have won an astounding victory over the forces of evil and subversion in the land. (A*bandoning file*) My dear people, we have been victims of a bad... evil, malevolent spell cast on all the land by a... a... band... a gang even of... of... a handful of very greedy people whose sole objective has been to enrich themselves and to eat like greedy little children until you, their mothers, have to rub their swollen stomachs with palm oil and make them sit by the fire so that they do not explode like an over-stretched drum. (*Laughs heartily at his own joke*) Talking about drums, my people, you know what I discovered the other day? You people say that I don't come out of the palace often, that I don't know your problems. But you are all liars. (*Song, alarmed, approaches in an attempt to make him stick to the text in vain*) I say you are all liars because I know all your problems and I have solved them. Do people who have problems spend all their time eating and drinking? Answer! What? Talk louder my friend, the soldier is standing by you for your protection. You eat to stay alive and drink to forget your problems? I thank you. But that is a foolish answer my friend. What? I permitted you to speak, didn't I? Now you sit down and learn from me because I know better or the soldier will take you out and I don't care what he does to you. Thank you. There is an obedient son of the soil. I know my people that you are patient, understanding, tolerant... What? You are not patient? Don't shout at me, friend, I can... You are not my friend? Is that why you don't respect authority? You may be old enough to be my father but the fact that I am king and you are not demands some deference... reverence even... to the institutions which I incarnate. Yes... Your Most Royal Majesty... Thank you. Yes... Why I have all these armed people standing around you? First of all, they are not armed people. Vandals are the armed people. These are called soldiers whose prime occupation is to ensure your safety and the protection of your property . Yes? How come the People's House caught fire right under their watchful eye? Whose? The soldiers' watchful eye? If there were many soldiers then you have to say under their watchful eyes. And I have never seen a Cyclops soldier although they usually take aim with one eye only. (*to Song*) Not so, Chief Commander.

SONG

Very true, Most Royal Majesty. The speech, Your Most Royal Majesty! The speech.

PSAUL ROI

My people, doesn't he look nice in that costume? Chief Commander of the royal armed forces, Town Crier, Chief of

Protocol and Chief Counsellor all by royal proclamation. You don't look at all happy as my number two. You want to be king?

SONG

Your Most Royal Majesty, I don't want to be anything other than what Your Most Royal Majesty has made me. But...

PSAUL ROI

My Most Royal Majesty am holding a free exchange of ideas with my people to whom I am giving free political nourishment and you are talking about a speech? Because you wrote it? Do you want me to...

SONG

I beg royal pardon, Most Royal Majesty.

PSAUL ROI

I grant you royal pardon. Now it is your duty to prepare the instrument of royal pardon and submit it for my sign and seal, after which you will proceed to proclaim it throughout the land. That is the best part of my job as monarch- signing and sealing instruments and proclamations. It is the only moment that I have a feeling of fulfilment. It is like having an orgasm which I have never had. My people, do you know how much I have sacrificed and suffered because of this job you freely offered to me. And then you sit back and say he has no feelings because he has neither wife nor children. What? You have often asked yourselves? If I am the subject, how can you be asking yourselves? Ask me and I will tell you. But haven't I tried? What herbal cure have I not tried? Witch-doctors, healers, fortune-tellers, soothsayers and even witches and wizards. And didn't I know it? Right from my early childhood nothing had ever tickled me down here. Nothing. I didn't even have any leanings towards the opposite sex. So I turned my energies to more useful opportunities. When you have power the rest of the land lies at your feet. But always it turned out that money was not enough. Aren't women curios beings? I have seen men who have given up their manhood in order to be wealthy. Others, like me gave it up for power. But no matter how much wealth you put at the feet of a woman she will never be satisfied until you can make her tick. And they tried to escape with my wealth since they could not get their he-goats into the palace to service them. So I had them snuffed out. You know what it means spreading a story like that? Psaul Roi is impotent. His Royal Majesty is a eunuch. What? Speak up , my friend. How many times must I tell you that the soldiers are there for your protection. What ? Why did I kill...? I did not kill anyone. Yes, I had them snuffed out, not killed. What is the difference? Semantic. Why have I told you now? So you can know that it is coming from my own mouth and that is very different from rumour which comes from below. What is going on over there? Let him in, soldier. Don't you see that he is desperate to come in? What? An earthquake? Where? In the mountains? How many people dead? Two thousand? How do you know? Rumour! Did I not warn them to leave the mountains and settle in the valleys? But they take pleasure in flouting royal authority. Serves them right. Two thousand less vandals. What? Have I no sympathy? And how can I be so unfeeling? Soldier, I command you to bring that vandal's head to the palace. Take him out now and his stubborn head shall henceforth decorate our royal and sacred altar. My people, power has no time for niceties and emotion. These only expose you to treachery and spears in the back. Your enemies will not give you rest if you are soft in the head and in the heart. That is why I have a new Town Crier and Chief Commander. (*to Song*) You will send emissaries to all friendly kingdoms and let them know that a terrible calamity has befallen us. Dramatize the situation as best as you can. Tell them we have lost five thousand dead in an earthquake and volcanic eruption and that half the kingdom has been destroyed. More than twenty thousand wounded and shelterless and foodless. We are desperately in need of aid... no...financial assistance to begin the painful and very difficult task of rebuilding our broken kingdom. After that you can send a large number of troops to the area to see if there is anything worth recuperating for the royal purse.

SONG

Right away, Most Royal Majesty. There is also news that all the important markets in the low lying regions of the land have been razed to the ground by fires.

PSAUL ROI

Send in soldiers, send in troops, my man, to rescue the goods. When they don't want to pay tribute to their monarch they set the markets on fire. Let the soldiers bring the goods to the palace. Who said that? Who dare say that I am mad? What? You will pay for this. All of you will pay for this. Soldiers, what are you waiting for? Open fire on these vandals. Shoot to kill and I don't care how much blood you spill. I have absolute power. Absolute power!!!

SONG

Quick, Your Royal Majesty, the soldiers cannot contain this crowd. Run, Your Majesty! Let us run for dear life. (*Soldiers also beat it while opening fire.*)

Fourth Movement

Same as opening scene except that there is an altar with candles burning. A human skull is placed prominently on it as well as a bloodied parcel. Psaul Roi is sitting on the throne playing cards and drinking. There is a timid knock at the door and he almost jumps out of his throne with fright. He grabs his walking stick and advances stealthily towards door.

PSAUL ROI

Who is there? Who is it?

VOICE

Song, Your Most Royal Majesty. Chief Commander, Chief Counsellor, Chief of Protocol and Town Crier by royal proclamation.

PSAUL ROI

Have you crushed the rebellion? Is the kingdom quiet now? How many killed? I ordered you to shoot to kill. I don't have any money to waste on detention camps. How many?

SONG

Calm, Your Most Royal Majesty. The army has done a very good job. The market place and roads leading therefrom are littered with corpses. The problem now is how to dispose of them.

PSAUL ROI

Requisition labour to bury them. Must I think for you always?

SONG

The survivors have all fled the land, Your Most Royal Majesty. What is the use of a ruler without the ruled?

PSAUL ROI

The best for the ruler. No headaches with vandals and no need to distribute the meagre resources. Get the soldiers to build incinerators and sizzle the bodies in them. Or dump them in the rivers and lakes. Anything, so long as the stench does not contaminate the palace.

SONG

The troops are getting restless. They want reward for putting down the rebellion in the market place the other day.

PSAUL ROI

But I gave you money...

SONG

The delegations to foreign kingdoms to seek financial assistance to begin the painful and difficult task of rebuilding our kingdom. Your exact words, Most Royal Majesty.

PSAUL ROI

They left, all of them?

SONG

Most Royal Majesty, they all left.

PSAUL ROI

How many delegations?

SONG

Fifty delegations of five people each. I understand some of them went with their wives and children. That way, they said, more impact of pity would be created.

PSAUL ROI

Any response yet? I mean in terms of cash flow.

SONG

Most Royal Majesty, the response has been very positive and spontaneous...

PSAUL ROI
How much? Tell me how much they have...

SONG
A lot of food items, especially rice, milk and flour...

PSAUL ROI
You mean I disbursed all that money just for flour and milk and rice? How am I going to reward the soldiers?

SONG
There is someone waiting in the waiting room.

PSAUL ROI
Who is it? I don't have money to distribute to people.

SONG
Albino, an emissary from the kingdom of Albinia.

PSAUL ROI
Albino from Albinia. No way I see him. Our people dread Albinians for their tight fists.
No way.

SONG
I have discussed with him a little and...

PSAUL ROI
By what royal instrument of authorization?

SONG
He has some very interesting proposals, cash-wise.

PSAUL ROI

Cash-wise? Bring him in quickly before he changes his mind. The troops must be rewarded.

Song exits and soon returns with Albino who is costumed in a collarless coat, helmet and white shoes. He has a black attaché case.

SONG

Your Most Royal Majesty, his Excellency Emissary Albino from Albinia.

PSAUL ROI

Oh my friend Albino from Albinia, welcome to our modest but, I can assure you, very hospitable kingdom.

ALBINO

Thank you, Your Excellency the Most Royal Majesty. I must begin by presenting the condolences of the people of Albinia to Your Most Royal Majesty for the great calamity that has befallen your beautiful and very hospitable kingdom. It must have been a terrible plague judging from the corpses on your streets.

PSAUL ROI

No plague, my friend. Only vandals.

ALBINO

Vandals? And they did this to your people? Where were the royal armed forces? In Albinia the valour of your army is almost legendary.

PSAUL ROI

Song, I command you to tell our august guest what happened. He should understand.

SONG

His Most Royal Majesty was giving the people political nourishment, communing with his people when news came of this catastrophe, the volcanic eruption in the mountainous region which left two thousand dead.. and twenty thousand wounded. And there was also news that some markets had caught fire. And when His Royal Majesty explained that the people in the affected areas had been warned to leave, they became very angry and started throwing stones...

PSAUL ROI
Lightning bolts, not stones. At me, their monarch and benefactor.

SONG
So he ordered me, Chief Commander, to order the soldiers to shoot. That is how there are corpses all over.

PSAUL ROI
Believe me Mr Albino, there was absolutely no provocation. Surely, vandals had infiltrated the market place.

SONG
And there was no other way of containing them.

ALBINO
So everyone in your kingdom is dead?

SONG
The rest escaped, ran away.

ALBINO
A kingdom is none unless there are people. What is the use being a ruler without the ruled?

PSAUL ROI
No headaches with vandals and no need to share the meagre resources.

ALBINO
Your Most Royal Majesty, the people of Albinia are willing to give you financial assistance so long as you are disposed to do business. We do not distribute money for nothing.

PSAUL ROI
Song, have any of the delegations reported back to you?

SONG
Your Most Royal Majesty, no. The house is on fire and they have all fled.

ALBINO
Your Majesty, we must bring the people back...coax them to return. But first we must clear the land of the already decomposing bodies. But only on condition.

PSAUL ROI
What is the condition?

ALBINO
Business. Albinia cannot do business with a king who has no subjects because it is they who provide labour and consume goods. So your kingdom must be peopled again.

PSAUL ROI
That is easy. (*to Song*) You can prepare a royal instrument of pardon in favour of all those who want to come back. But no vandals. Otherwise I will give royal instructions to the army to shoot to kill. (*to Albino*) Before the end of the day he will proclaim the royal instrument throughout the kingdom. The people will be back tomorrow.

ALBINO

Can't you see that he will be making the proclamation throughout an empty land? Can't you see that no one will hear your royal whatever?

PSAUL ROI

Talk polite to me, Mr Man. I am monarch here.

ALBINO

Then think like one. I thought Albinia could help but it looks like the monarch thing has gone into your head. I must be going.

SONG

Wait a little, Mr Albino. Your Most Royal Majesty, if he leaves now then we are finished. The soldiers are marauding in the land spitting fire and spreading death everywhere... looting and raping because they have not been rewarded. Most Royal Majesty and Commander in Chief, can you imagine what will happen when they turn their weapons against the palace and demand reward? Can you trust a dog that is hungry even if that dog has been your faithful companion for years. Think again, Your Most Royal Majesty and reconsider the proposal of Mr Albino. We cannot miss this occasion. I don't even know how Chambiay used to manage...

PSAUL ROI

Don't pronounce that name in our royal presence or I will lose my mind.

SONG

(*suddenly furiously*) May lightning shrivel his legs and thunder blow up his private parts! May elephants ravage his farms and gorillas and baboons devastate his crops! May leopards prowl among his sheep and lions devour his offspring! May these and many, many, many more calamities befall him!

PSAUL ROI

Who?

SONG

Cha... the disgraced former... I dare not pronounce the name, Most Royal majesty.

ALBINO

Can I go now? I am a businessman. Time is money. Where I come from, we don't have time for aimless words.

PSAUL ROI

What do you want, Mr Albino?

SONG

Give him a chance, Most Royal Majesty. I have heard of the prosperity of Albinia.

PSAUL ROI

And how do you intend to proceed?

ALBINO

First, we must clear the land of the decomposing bodies. For this to be done efficiently and efficaciously, we need the services of the royal armed forces. They will have to clear the mess they caused.

PSAUL ROI

They are still waiting for their rewards; and my purse is empty.

ALBINO

I will just have to coax them to do it; if you give me leave.

PSAUL ROI

Song is Chief Commander. He knows them better. But can I trust you?

ALBINO

Your Excellency the Most Royal, there is no business without trust, without goals. Your goal is your throne, power. Mine is gain. Shall we seal with a handshake? (*as they shake hands*) Done!

Blackout.

Fifth Movement

Several days later. Albino's sparingly furnished office. Lights turned on gradually revealing Albino, Song and Nformi in a working session. Albino's attaché case is placed prominently on the table).

NFOMI
Man, you make us work like we have never done before. We are predators not vultures. And the heat from those incinerators is only comparable to a volcano. That is why my men want more compensation.

ALBINO
What wonderful predators you are! Preying on your own kind. Don't you see the consequences of your own folly? I have had to bring in specialists from Albinia to build the incinerators and to fell trees for wood and transport it to the various locations. And here you are asking me for more compensation. You can ask your Chief Commander here, or your Commander in Chief who has barricaded himself in his palace and is drinking himself to certain death, what the real situation of your beloved kingdom is. By the way, His Royal Majesty is thoroughly frightened of his great, royal army. You know why? Chief Commander, you tell him.

SONG
Because...because...

NFORMI
There is no money for our rewards?

ALBINO
Exactly! The great monarch is broke and Albinia has sent me to rescue the land.

SONG

The monarch! To rescue the monarch!

ALBINO

In Albinia, we do not think individuals, we think people.

NFORMI

I like that.

SONG

What?

NFORMI

What he said. Here we think only His Most Royal Majesty because we are frightened of his royal edicts, instruments and proclamations. Now I have discovered his real strength and I am ashamed to be making the discovery only now.

SONG

What discovery?

ALBINO

Too many words. That is the problem with you people. Song, you will kindly tell his royal majesty that I have received his request for cash and that it is receiving the very serious attention it deserves. However, the final decision rests on the ruling council of Albinia. So don't come back here tomorrow, or the next day, or next week or the week after to ask for money. You may now return to your monarch.

SONG

(*to Nformi*) Don't let him fool you. Please, don't let him. (*exits*)

NFORMI

What did he mean?

ALBINO

Didn't you see the frightened look in his eyes? And the nervousness in his voice? He is scared out of his senses. And you, you are a very smart soldier.

NFORMI

Do you know that Song has never been in the army? Yet he is Chief Commander, whatever that means.

ALBINO

Well, it means privileges and honours which regular soldiers like you don't have and will never dream of having. Yet he and the monarch are completely dependent on the army, on you, to do their dirty job of keeping the people under an iron heel.

NFORMI

What are you talking about? What are you trying to suggest?

ALBINO

We are talking about the plight of your people. The manipulation of you soldiers by one man, an alcoholic who happens also to be drunk with power even if he doesn't know what to do with it.

NFORMI

So?

ALBINO

How do we get the people back. The volcano took a terrible toll but the army did worse. I could never have believed that there are intelligent people like you in there.

NFORMI

I have already said to myself 'shame on you and your likes'. The royal instrument of pardon has made no impact. And many intelligence sources report the refugees as saying that until the monarch leaves they will remain refugees. They have never been ruled by a vampire king, they say.

ALBINO

What is that, vampire king?

NFORMI

You don't know? Song did not tell you? The cunning, fawning monkey! Well, our monarch is a vampire king. There is... there used to be a vampire cult in this kingdom whose main function was to maintain some kind of balance of power between the king and council. Our monarchy is rotative so that no family in the land should feel alienated or marginalised.

ALBINO

Very interesting system of governance

NFORMI

When it was the turn of the present king's family to rule, they gave us this phenomenon. So long as tradition was maintained there was no serious problem because the excesses of the king could be curbed by the council of elders through the Town Crier and the Chief Counsellor who was also high priest and chief vampire of the vampire cult. There was really no problem so long as the king lived under the illusion that he had absolute power. So, he was Commander in Chief and signed instruments of pardon and appointment and destitution at will until the day he wanted to destitute Town Crier and found that he could not do it. I don't know the exact details of what happened thereafter, but it seems that the king corrupted Song with money and the promise of power and got himself initiated. So he became high priest and chief vampire. That did not only signal the end of the vampire cult but also the beginning of a long list of calamities which ended with the massacre in the market place and the fleeing of the people to foreign lands. And now his royal majesty is reigning over the forests and sands and the grassfields.

ALBINO

Has your family taken its turn? Has it already ruled this land? I never saw such degeneracy, such baseness, such bestiality and nonchalance all combined in one man. And yet you.. soldiers... as intelligent as you are... carried out his bestial orders to kill your own people. I don't believe it. Absolutely unbelievable! A whole crowd of soldiers with arms allowing themselves to be manipulated by one demented man, even if he is king. Unbelievable!

NFORMI

There were the rewards, the royal edicts and instruments and proclamations. You lived under the illusion that the king had special concern and confidence in you. In the army we had a lot of material advantages and benefits which the rest of the people could never dream of. So whenever they gathered in the market place to listen to someone bent on opening their eyes so that they could see the wretchedness of their lives in spite of the great wealth of the land, the army immediately saw this as a great threat to their privileges and so reacted with extreme brutality. And there were also the spies. You never could tell who was spying against you and making reports to the hierarchy. No one wanted to find himself in the desert camps or his body all mangled up, and money thrown carelessly about. You heard him, didn't you? Don't let him fool you. Please, don't let him.

ALBINO

For sure, I heard him. But you also saw the frightened look in his eyes. I could hear his voice shaking with fright. And you are a smart soldier. Has your family taken its turn?

NFORMI

On the throne? What does it really matter now? Anyone who becomes king now has the most arduous task in front of him- how to rebuild what has been destroyed and regain the confidence of the people. What people even? The land is empty.

ALBINO

It can be done. The king no longer has any illusions about the loyalty of his royal armed forces. He cannot find the money to give you people rewards.

NFRORMI

So what do I tell my men? That we now have to depend on you? And so must switch loyalties?

ALBINO

Nothing about switching loyalties until we put the king away.

NFORMI

Killing him will be doing him a favour. The people need to see him naked to be convinced. We will have to make him sign a royal proclamation destituting himself as king.

ALBINO

Just get a few men whom you can trust, some of your family members, I guess. And we can launch the operation.

NFORMI

That is what has destroyed the land, this family thing. I will not fall victim to it. And Mr Albino, before we go deeper into this thing, let me warn that I might not be the type of person because I will not allow the things you people are doing to this land.

ALBINO

What are we doing?

NFORMI

Don't tell me you are blind to the destruction of our forests. You people are transporting our forests to Albinia. And behaving as if our land belongs to you. You have turned sons and daughters of this land into your slaves. You think you own our land and everything in it? I will not allow that to continue.

ALBINO

I like your frankness. That can only come from a shrewd business man. We will do business. Here, take my hand. We will make good partners. Done!

NFORMI

Done!

Blackout.

Sixth Movement

Same as opening scene. Lights are turned on revealing Psaul Roi and Song in heated argument. Psaul Roi is thoroughly angry and dishevelled.

PSAUL ROI

He said that? It must give you a lot of pleasure coming to report to me.

SONG

On the contrary, Your Most Royal Majesty, it grieves my heart.

PSAUL ROI

A stranger in your land insults your king right in your face; you, Chief Commander and the many other chiefs that I made you, instead of punching him in the face and putting him under military custody, you come to report to me. So that I can dance, not so? Alright, let me dance for your pleasure. I am dancing.

SONG

He is the emissary of Albania and the soldiers have discovered that their rewards are coming from him.

PSAUL ROI

I knew it! The squinting, foxy tortoise has turned the royal armed forces against our royal person.

SONG

I warned him, pleaded with him even, not to allow himself to be fooled.

PSAUL ROI

Did he listen? Did Albino listen?

SONG
Nformi, Your Most Royal Majesty. Not Albino.

PSAUL ROI
Who is that one now? Each time I think that I have finished with one person another one shows up some place.

SONG
He is the general of the royal armed forces and... and...

PSAUL ROI
And... and... what?

SONG
It will be the turn of his family next...

PSAUL ROI
What turn? Whose family? Where?

There is a knock at the door and both characters recoil with fear.

SONG
Who is it? Who is there?

VOICE
Albino of Albinia. I will speak with the king.

SONG
He wishes to speak with the king.

PSAUL ROI
Unbolt the door. Let him in.

Albino, without attaché case enters.

SONG
He hasn't brought money, Your Most Royal Majesty.

ALBINO
Your Excellency, the Most Royal Majesty, you must forgive my impudence. But I was waiting and no one to announce my presence.

PSAUL ROI
Have you come to remove me from the throne?

ALBINO
My assignment as emissary to your kingdom was to explore the possibility of doing business with your people. After my brief stay here, there is no doubt that business opportunities abound. Even the insignificant but humanitarian affair of the incinerators has yielded and is still yielding a lot of dividends. Just as a ruler without the ruled is no ruler, so is a land without people, no matter how rich it may be. Your Most Royal Majesty, you turned against your people and now they won't come back in spite of your instruments and proclamations urging them to do so.

PSAUL ROI
And since you can't do business in an empty land...

There is a deliberate knock at the door and Song looks apprehensively at Psaul Roi.

PSAUL ROI
My palace has suddenly become the market place. Song, go and see who it is and what he wants.

ALBINO
Where I come from the palace is a market place where the people converge to dialogue with their king. But here, the palace, like the land, has become the evil forest where people fear to tread.

SONG

Who is there?

VOICE

Nformi, the general.

PSAUL ROI

(to Albino) Your new found friend.

SONG

What do you want?

ALBINO

(*to Psaul Roi*) Very smart soldier and shrewd business man.

VOICE

I will speak with Psaul Roi. Open up or I will smash the door!

ALBINO

(*to Song*) Open the door. We should avoid destruction. Not good for business when you are still learning. (*Song opens the door and Nformi storms in with four soldiers.*)

PSAUL ROI

Nformi, my friend, I know the royal armed forces have been waiting for their rewards. I have just been telling this man, Albino, how important it is for the soldiers to get their rewards. But he is only thinking of profits for himself and his people. He is a real menace to our land, exploiting and exploiting. He is...

NFORMI

(*indicating Albino*) Arrest him! He has done real damage to our land, exploiting and exploiting.

ALBINO

How dare you! Biting the finger that pays you. I am emissary of the kingdom of Albinia and you dare not lay your filthy hands on me.

NFORMI

Albinia and their emissary, Albino, are only interested in sucking the wealth of our land. While Psaul Roi and Song are sucking the blood of the people.

SONG

Nformi, please, I have never sucked any one's blood. I was only acting on his Most Royal Majesty's instructions.

NFORMI

While enjoying the privileges nevertheless.

PSAUL ROI

By royal proclamation, Chief Counsellor, Chief Commander, Town Crier and General of the royal armed forces, Nformi.

NFORMI

(indicating Psaul Roi and Song) Arrest them! These are the vampires who have ruined our land and brought calamity upon our people.

PSAUL ROI

You are the same dogs who used to run around me wagging your tails and licking my fingers. And now you dare to lay your hands on our royal person? Madness has entered the land.

SONG

I was only acting on instructions, Nformi, please.

ALBINO

There is more madness in you and your acts than in the land, Royal Majesty. And, Nformi, you are a very smart soldier and shrewd businessman.

NFORMI

Shut up your mouth, Mr Albino. You have no business in our land. Our people have suffered too much in the hands of exploiters like you. *(to soldiers)* Chain him up. We shall expel him and all the other Albinians whom he brought to our land to rape and loot our wealth. People who enter our land without authorisation and become masters while sons and daughters of the soil are enslaved, impoverished and exiled. This land was cursed, indeed with the cult of the vampires. Never again shall that happen in this land.*(to Psaul Roi and Song)* Strip now before you are bound in chains.

PSAUL ROI

Kill me. Kill me, please, Nformi. I prefer to die than to fall so low.

NFORMI

If you die the people will not come back. They want concrete proof that you destituted yourself. I am going to give it to them.

Nformi snaps his fingers and two of the soldiers exeunt but immediately return bearing an iron cage with a bunch of bananas suspending from the middle of it.

NFORMI

Now, Song, as Chief of Protocol, you have the honour and duty to precede your king into your new palace. *(Song is pushed into cage)* Your Most Royal Majesty, your turn. Bear the cage to the market place where these monstrosities shall be exposed to the wrath and glowing vengeance of the people they were supposed to serve. They will spend the rest of their days counting their guilt on the faces of their victims; and so measure the consequences of the macabre dance of the vampires. Away to the market place! Away!

Exeunt bearing cage.

Blackout

END

Part II

Family Saga

*(For all those with whom I have laboured
In pursuit of dialogue in conflict resolution)*

Dramatis Personae
(in order of appearance)

Kamalo: Supposed brother of **Kamala** and self-appointed theoretician or conceiver of the family estate, who pays absolute allegiance and obedience to **Fiekafhim**, his Papa. He will later play **Yaman.**

Kamala: Manager of family estate, brother of **Kamalo** and father of **Ngong** and **Sawa**. He will later play **Baakingoom.**

Baakingoom: Supposed father of **Kamala.**

Sawa: Daughter of **Kamala** who believes that **Kamalo** is her uncle. She will later play **MC, Impresario** and **Kamanda.**

Ngong: Son of **Kamala** and **Sawa**'s brother. He will later play **Yaman** and **Story teller.**

Two Bodyguards: Bodyguards of **Kamalo.**

All through the play the set is dominated by a cyclorama with the portrait of a grand, old and senile lady in traditional dress with a sparkle in her bearing. She should be depicted with a lot of jewels decorating her body thereby emphasizing her beauty and wealth.

First Movement

Kamalo, big and fat and wearing a three piece suit is lounging in an easy chair, drinking and smoking and listening to a Bikutsi tune which is playing very loud. Kamala, a diminutive man in a workaday jumper, enters from backstage. He is thoroughly angry. He turns down the volume of the music.

KAMALA: Kamalo, why are you so greedy? What happened to my share of the provisions? Why can't you ever be considerate? How many times must I remind you that there are two people living on this estate?

KAMALO: My Papa came.

KAMALA: Which Papa? You think you are the only one with a papa? Why must your father pest us every time and always taking what belongs to me? And you won't even sweep out the barn and repair the shelves in readiness for the next harvest.

KAMALO: Me? Sweep the barn and repair the shelves for what? That your work is what?

KAMALA: Kamalo, why can't you try to be reasonable by being useful to yourself and both of us? What do you ever do in this estate except lazy around in a three piece suit, drinking and smoking and… Why can't you even make your offspring do some work for our community? For instance, Redone is constantly drunk. Either he is drinking or he is already drunk and sleeping under a tree. Someday he is going to shoot someone with the gun he is always carrying. And the day that happens…

KAMALO: Redone is there to ensure the security of the estate. He, my other offspring and I, are already too busy working for the community. You think it is easy to think? And do I need to tell you that there is division of labour on this estate? I conceive, you execute. Period.

KAMALA: 'I conceive, you execute. Period.' Who made that rule? Who gave you the right to conceive thereby transforming me into your slave? You take what is mine and I have to do the cleaning and repair work? Who gave you the right to take what is mine?

KAMALO: I said my papa came. He took the provisions. He gave me the right.

KAMALA: What right?

KAMALO: The right to conceive.

KAMALA: Thus transforming me into your slave? Answer me, Kamalo.

KAMALO: Your own very mouth said it; not mine.

KAMALA: Do you ever look into the mirror? Do you ever notice how fat you have grown in the few years we have lived together, Kamalo?

KAMALO: Jealousy. Because I live my life and do my work. Jealousy.

KAMALA: Yes, of course. Your work is eating, drinking, smoking and making merry at my expense. Work indeed. If my own father were also pestering us in the same manner?

KAMALO: Is it my fault that your own papa has abandoned you? You are not even grateful that I took pity on you and brought you into this beautiful estate. Ingrate! Always complaining. Always asking questions. According to the deed... according to the agreement...

KAMALA: Every community of human beings is regulated. Without rules and contracts there is total chaos resulting in disagreements and unnecessary squabbles which will result in the wasting of our resources. Can't you see that? *(No reaction from Kamalo)*. What makes you think my father abandoned me? And who is the ingrate between the two of us? This estate belongs to who?

KAMALO: To me. That's what my papa says. I took pity and brought you into this beautiful estate. That's what my papa says. That's why I conceive, you execute. Period. That's what my papa says. KAMALA: That's what my papa says. That's what my papa says. Are you a Ngorna record with scratches on it? And what do you say?

KAMALO: What my papa says.

KAMALA: And what do you conceive?

KAMALO: What my papa says.

KAMALA: And I execute?

KAMALO: What my papa says.

KAMALA: You're a fool. A real, confounded fool. No wonder you're so fat!

KAMALO: A fool, a confounded fool, does not conceive. That's what my papa says.

KAMALA: Why does your papa only sneak in like a thief when I am toiling in the fields to steal my provisions and disappear again? *(Removes his jumper and throws it at Kamalo).* For once we will change roles. You go to the fields. I will stay here and conceive. Let me have your silly suit. Do you know how silly you look in that nonsense? Sweating, always sweating. Why don't you take it off for once? I am sure you will feel more comfortable without it. Like me, even without my jumper.

KAMALO: (Picks *up the jumper and sniffs it).* It stinks so. We cannot change roles. This suit is the insignia of my role just like the jumper is the insignia of yours. That's what my papa says. My papa does not steal. He takes what belongs to me. Here, take your jumper. We cannot change roles. That's what my papa says.

KAMALA: *(Wearing jumper).* My resources belong to you?

KAMALO: Yes. You belong to me.

KAMALA: My resources belong to you?

KAMALO: Yes.

KAMALA: I belong to you?

KAMALO: You belong to me. That's what my papa says. If you don't like it here, you can go elsewhere. That's what my papa says.

KAMALA: All right. I don't like it here. I am taking my things and going elsewhere. Kamalo, where is the deed of brotherhood which we both signed? I need my share of the resources.

KAMALO: You mean the deed of bondage hood? My papa is keeping it.

KAMALA: Keeping what? Your papa is keeping what?

KAMALO: The deed of bondagehood which you signed.

KAMALA: Brotherhood!

KAMALO: Bondagehood!

KAMALA: Brotherhood!

KAMALO: Bondagehood!

KAMALA: Brotherhood!

KAMALO: Bondagehood! Stop wasting your breath. That's why I conceive, you execute. Period. *(Removing a document from his jacket).* Here's a certified true copy, signed and sealed by my papa himself.

KAMALA: *(Reading aloud).* Deed of Bondagehood. Between Kamalo, conceiver, and Kamala, executor.

KAMALO: So, you see.

KAMALA: See what? You're a cheat. A noon-day thief and falsifier of deeds. (*He attacks Kamalo with punches which latter wards off with ease. He gives Kamala a punch which sends him sprawling on the floor).*

KAMALO: You see, might is right. That's why I am so fat. That's what my papa says.

KAMALA: I was such a fool to have trusted you. We will go back to the Court of Deeds. I didn't know you were so thoroughly untrustworthy apart from lounging around and wasting our resources.

KAMALO: My resources. I do what I like with my resources. Through the argument of force.

KAMALA: All right, all right! We are going back to the Court of Deeds. You cannot cheat me and get away with it. We are going back to the Court of Deeds. I will get back my due through the force of argument.

KAMALO: My papa is an important member of the Court. You will only be wasting precious work time and precious energy needed in the production of services and goods for my pleasure and the pleasure of my papa. In addition, my papa's dogs will not even let you leave. You have never seen any one of them. My papa's dogs are wild lions. And you now know how wild I can also be when you push me too much.

KAMALA: My father is also an important member of the Court. You're not the only one with a papa.

KAMALO: I forbid you from abandoning your job in pursuit of a useless, unequal fight. It will take you nowhere. Remember that your useless father was, like my papa, a witness to the deed of bondagehood between us. And when you return, you will have to make up for lost time. Let me warn you beforehand. Can you now go back to your job in the fields? I need time to think. That's what my papa says.

KAMALA: I am going to my father. I cannot be cheated so blatantly. There is definitely some error somewhere. I am going back to the Court of Deeds. (Storms out).

KAMALO: You will come back, bondsman. You will come back. By the argument of force you will come back. That's what my papa says. You're bonded. Bonded forever. That's what my papa says.

Blackout

Second Movement

Baakingoom, a smallish brown-skinned man with grey hair, dressed in a suit, is dozing off in an easy chair with a cup of tea on a small table by his side. Kamala comes in quietly and stands, watching the sleeping figure for some time. He coughs deliberately and the old man wakes slowly. He clears his eyes and fumbles for his cup of tea, just to make sure that it is still there. He yawns freely and mops his face with his palms.

BAAKINGOOM: Who are you? Who let you in here?

KAMALA: Father, are you so old that you can no longer recognise your own son? Or are you also blind?

BAAKINGOOM: Don't insult me, boy. I had many sons. They all turned against me saying they wanted to be free. I don't know if living under my roof and paternal love made them prisoners. There comes an age when youngsters want to explore, to experience, to savour what they call 'the good life'. At that point they begin to think that their parents constitute an obstacle. They never see it in terms of parental love and concern for them. They rather think that their father is a greedy dog who does not want to give their own share of the inheritance. Especially when they live under the illusion that they can chart their own courses in the world, judging from the talents they believe themselves to possess. So I gave them independence. I am only an old man now. The sun is setting on me. I was also a dreamer who never thought the sun could ever set. That is life. And the sons who wanted freedom come pestering me: father I want this, father, please, give me that. That's what the family reunion has become. What do you want?

KAMALA: Did you give me freedom or did you give me into bondage?

BAAKINGOOM: Say your name and I will tell you what I gave you or what you took.

KAMALA: Kamala. My name is Kamala. What did you give me?

BAAKINGOOM: Ah! Kamala, the stubborn one. I gave you freedom upon your demand. I was hesitant because you were still too young. The kind of talents you had, needed proper nurturing. But the talents went to your head and you insisted on having your freedom against my better judgement. I don't know what you chose.

KAMALA: Brotherhood! I signed a deed of brotherhood with Kamalo. Now he says it was bondagehood.

BAAKINGOOM: Kamalo, Kamala. Kamala, Kamalo. Brotherhood, bondagehood. Bondagehood, brotherhood. What's the difference? I don't know what you chose, son. I warned you when you took your freedom. You were so excited about the brotherhood

bondagehood nonsense. You refused to listen. The stubborn fly follows the corpse into the grave. What do you want?

KAMALA: Father, I signed a deed of brotherhood. Now Kamalo says it was a deed of bondagehood. Does brotherhood sound like bondagehood, father?

BAAKINGOOM: Brotherhood, bondagehood. Bondagehood, brotherhood. What's the difference, son? Brotherhood, bondagehood. I don't see the difference, son. But I warned you, didn't I? I told you that you were still too young and lacking experience in the ways of the world. Intelligence and talent do not constitute wisdom. Is that not what I told you? You are only harvesting what you sowed, son.

KAMALA: You frighten me; you shock me, father. Am I your son? Are you my father? How can you be so unfeeling, father, to your own son? Answer me, father. Am I your son?

BAAKINGOOM: Only your mother could say who your father is. Unfortunately she is not there.

KAMALA: Where is she, father? Why have I never known my mother? What happened to her?

BAAKINGOOM: Hasn't your brother told you? Go and ask him, if he is less ignorant than you are. Things are not always what they seem.

KAMALA: My brother is not my brother? Things are not always what they seem? And my mother?

BAAKINGOOM: You chose your brother against my better advice. Go and ask him about your mother. You made your choice. You take responsibility for it.

KAMALA: Yes, father. I made that choice because it was the best. Everyone in the Court said it was the best. And you stood there by me. You signed the Deed of Brotherhood as witness. As my father. You stood by me when Kamalo and I shook hands and embraced each other. You gave me your blessing. His father wasn't even there. Today he can't finish a sentence without reference to his papa. 'That's what my papa says. That's what my papa says' is the interminable refrain, like a cracked Ngoma record. BAAKINGOOM: That's why I warned you, son. You made your choice.

KAMALA: And I strode out confidently, believing in you as my rear-guard while Kamalo and I charted our new course in life. Today he is telling me that you abandoned me and he took pity on me as his bondsman whereas we signed a deed of brotherhood. Is it possible to change a deed, father? Is it possible to change the terms of an agreement between two parties without the consent of both in the presence of the witnesses?

BAAKINGOOM: Son, the world is a treacherous place where one must tread most cautiously. Life is not what it seems.

KAMALA: Look at me, father. When I left this place, I had more than half-a-dozen suitcases full of clothes. This is all I have today. I toil in the fields all day long with my offspring; and when I go to get provisions from the barn, there is nothing left because, Kamalo tells me, 'My papa was here. He took the provisions.' I have never even set my eyes on him. He sneaks in like a thief, steals my provisions and sneaks out again. 'My papa was here.' And why don't you ever come to visit me, father? Is it true what Kamalo says? That you abandoned me, your son?

BAAKINGOOM: You made your choice, son, against my better advice. When we make mistakes, we must be ready to pay the price.

KAMALA: So you abandoned me, in retaliation?

BAAKINGOOM: You made your choice, son. You never came to visit until today. I thought you were quite happy, seeing that you had intelligence and talent. The others come back once every two years for a family reunion. Although they always ended up by asking for this and for that. So I ask them what their freedom was for if they must come back to ask for alms. I have never seen you here although

I always make sure to send you an invitation. So I thought, 'That one is the exception among the crowd of irresponsibility'.

KAMALA: I never received any invitation from you, father. Or, unless, unless...

BAAKINGOOM: Unless what? What's on your mind, son?

KAMALA: What were the terms of this deed of brotherhood or bondagehood with Kamalo? He tells me that his role is to conceive while mine is to execute. In short, I am his slave, toiling in the fields from dawn to dusk in these rags while he is having air-conditioning at home in a three piece suit, eating and drinking and smoking and making merry. So he receives my invitation from you and tosses it into the dustbin. That's a dog's life I am going through.

BAAKINGOOM: Is that why you came? Your dog's life? We all have our dogs and they their lives. And we also have our own lives which we can give to the dogs, if you see what I mean.

KAMALA: I see very well, father. I have given mine to that dog called Kamalo. I have to take it back somehow, with your support.

BAAKINGOOM: How can I support you when your... is, excuse my being so blunt, the most contemptible fool who has also been hypnotized by a most Machiavellian and blood sucking parasite, a self-styled father? I could never bring myself so low down to the point of pretending to be your father just to swindle you of your talents for my selfish ends. Not me. Never. My dignity will not allow it.

KAMALA: So you are not my father? So Kamalo's papa is not his papa? My mother is not around, you are not my father, Kamalo's papa is not his papa. The likelihood is that he is not my brother. That's why you kept warning me against signing the bond with him. Tell me the story, father. Or did I fall from the sky?

BAAKINGOOM: You will have to find that information yourself, son. I am in no storytelling mood. And you might not even believe my story of you. Go and find out for yourself. I suggest you begin with Kamalo, if you can get him out of the hypnosis.

KAMALA: Can I ask you one favour, father? Sorry I can't stop calling you father. Can I come back to you if Kamalo fails to tell our story, my story?

BAAKINGOOM: I will stand by you as far as I can. Morally.
KAMALA: Only morally?
BAAKINGOOM: Morally, only.

Blackout

Third Movement

Kamalo, (same as in opening scene), and Sawa, a strikingly beautiful young lady who is wearing expensive wax wrapper material, are dancing to a Bikutsi tune. Both have been drinking and making merry.

KAMALO: You are such a charming beauty. Why did your father hide you from me all this long time?

SAWA: It's so cool and nice here na? Out in the fields na? It is hot, very hot na? The sun can even make you to melt like chocolate na? I don't know why daddy cannot also build a house as beautiful as this your own na?

KAMALO: Because there is division of labour. He only executes what I conceive. Period. That's what...

SAWA: What what? What what na, uncle?

KAMALO: Nothing, my dear. You are so beautiful. Don't call me uncle. We are not really brothers. That's what... We are not brothers at all. That's why my papa asked me to ask you to be brought here. I didn't even know Kamala had such a shining full moon in a clear sky for a daughter. Sawa, you'll kill me with your beauty.

SAWA: Uncle, why are you only flattering me na? You will make daddy to build a nice house like this your own na? Even just half as nice na? At night we cannot even sleep because of mosquitoes na? In the rainy season the whole roof is just leaking and water just pouring everywhere na? Yet the harvest is always very heavy na? I don't know what father does with all the crops we harvest all the time na? Uncle, you will make him to build our own house too, na?

KAMALO: Don't worry about that, my dear. From today you will stay here with me. Anything you want will be yours.

SAWA: But I also want my daddy and brother to enjoy too, na. We have been suffering too much in the fields for all these years na? Daddy does not even drink na? He doesn't smoke na? Only work, work, work without rest na? When I remember what Ngong goes through I can even just be crying na?

KAMALO: Who is Ngong? Who is ... ?

SAWA: My brother na? There are just two of us, Ngong and myself na? When the work is too much I will just go me and sit under a tree and daddy and Ngong will only be working, only be working. For what, I don't know na? And Redone, that your son, will only be drinking and drinking and drinking na? And when his eyes become red like those of a wild cat he will just go him and lie down under a tree and only be sleeping na? We are only afraid because of that his gun na? That one day when he is drunk as usual he can mistakenly shoot somebody for nothing na?

KAMALO: Sawa, let me tell you something. Redone can never shoot somebody for nothing. And when he shoots, no case. You people are very lucky that you are only working with your hands. Do you know how hard it is to think, to work with the head? That is my job; working with the head while your father only works with the hands. That is why I conceive and he executes. Period. That's what... Working with the head is more difficult, Sawa.

SAWA: Is dancing working with the head? Drinking, smoking and eating na? All of that is working with the head? Then I will also like daddy to be working with the head too, na? And you can take the easy work of the hands na?

KAMALO: You are just like your father. Always asking questions. Always wanting to know. Always why, why, why? Sawa, beauty does not match with wanting to know. Leave that to those whose job is to think. Leave that to me, Sawa.

SAWA: That God gave me a head for what na? If you don't ask, how will you know na? Even the Bible says that 'Ask, and you will be given. Knock, and the door will be opened. Seek, and you will find'. Mathew 7:7 na?

KAMALO: You confound me, Sawa. The Bible is a mere story book, for entertainment. That's all. That's what... Come closer, let me hold you close to my heart.

SAWA: No, uncle! It's not good na? And my daddy will be very angry to see that na? You even made me to dance with you, na? It's not good na? And the Bible is God's Holy Book, not a mere story book, na? You don't like God na?

KAMALO: There is no one who is God's enemy.

SAWA: The devil na, Satan is God's enemy na? You know that na?

KAMALO: I was talking about man, the human being.

SAWA: The devil lives in some men na? When uncle wants to hold me tight, you are allowing Satan to use you na?

KAMALO: All right Sawa, Satan is a bad man. You will stay here in this nice house and have your comfort and anything that you need. Your delicate beauty should not be allowed to melt in the hot sun like chocolate.

SAWA: I cannot stay here na? When daddy comes back he will be worried na?

KAMALO: Come back from where? He went to where? When? I forbade him from abandoning his work.

SAWA: He went to visit his father for the first time na? I have never ever seen my grandfather, na? My father was very angry. I have never seen my daddy so angry na? He said that you had insulted him. Why did you insult your brother na, uncle?

KAMALO: Just because my papa came and took a few provisions from the barn.

SAWA: That can't be all na, uncle. My daddy can't be so very angry just because your daddy took a few provisions from the barn na? There must be some other problem na?

KAMALO: I reminded him that I have my role and he has his role- I conceive, he executes. Period. That's what...

SAWA: You see na? You see na? Who made such an unjust rule na? You made that master and slave rule na, uncle? That's why you are living in a very beautiful house only eating and drinking and smoking and dancing while we are toiling in the fields for your enjoyment na?

KAMALO: Who are you talking to like that? Is that how badly your useless father brought you up? No one has never had the courage to talk to me like that.

SAWA: My daddy is not useless. You are insulting him again na, uncle? He brought us up to see injustice and recognise it na? We are working and you are eating na? That's not good na, uncle? You should come and see where we live na? Do you know that those your people who came and took me had to buy new dresses for me? These are not my clothes na? That is injustice na, uncle?

KAMALO: What do you know about justice or injustice? Is it not injustice to contest the terms of a contract that we have already signed?

SAWA: We have not signed anything na, uncle?

KAMALO: Your father signed a deed with me. Now he is contesting the terms. Is that not injustice on his part?

SAWA: You mean the deed of brotherhood na? Our daddy has always told us about the deed of brotherhood with you na? And how you are cheating him and taking all the provisions from the barn na?

KAMALO: Not brotherhood but bondagehood! That's what my papa says. We signed a deed of bondagehood. So he and all that belong to him belong to me. That's what my papa says.

SAWA: And what do you say na, uncle? Your papa is saying something which is not just na? What do you say na? And how can your papa say that of my daddy na? Unless he is not really your papa na? Because your real papa will not like his nephew to suffer like my daddy is suffering na? Unless your papa is not really your papa na?

KAMALO: Bush girl, is it because I say you are nice looking that you think you can talk to me just anyhow? My papa is really my papa and his hawk's eye will always spot a resource wherever it is hidden. You were brought here not to task my head but to balm my body. That is the only way to humiliate you for disrespecting authority and your stubborn father for daring to think that we are brothers. That's what my papa says. And so shall it be. Have you ever slept on a bed made of gold and sheets of silk? Come along now, and I will give you the pleasure. *(He grabs her arm and tries to pull her along; but because she resists, he lifts her from her feet and carries her off. She is protesting and screaming from the depth of her soul).*

Blackout

Fourth Movement

Kamala's home. Stage properties consist of three old cane-chairs with a low cane-table occupying central position. Ngong, Kamala's son, in old shorts and jumper, is pacing about nervously. His physical bearing is one of dejection and anxiety.

NGONG: Where could she have been taken to? From the footprints in the wet ground they were two. Redone says he saw nothing although what he really means is that because he was asleep from too much drink he could only have seen nothing. If father comes back now, what account will I give? That I cannot take charge of things when he is away? She is partly to blame, anyway. If she had come with me... But she said it was too hot and she could not walk that long distance and still be able to do effective work. See what has happened. I hope no harm comes to her. Apparently, there was no struggle. Otherwise she would have cried out or shouted or something. If father comes now what will I tell him? But even he is part of the problem. 'We signed a gentleman's agreement. We signed a brotherhood bond' he keeps saying. What's the use of an agreement when the other party is so insensitive to any sense of justice or morality? Answer me, good people; is there any sense in an agreement which is so obviously disregarded and even violated by one of the parties? Is it possible for a cockroach to hold dialogue with a fowl? A pig has never been known to consider the hunger in another's stomach. 'Give him time. He will understand sooner than later that solidarity is the foundation stone of unity, progress and prosperity for all' he chimes back when I confront him with Kamalo's open disregard for him. Of recent things have gone badly; so badly that father came back very angry and, for the first time, talked about his own father. I had never known we had a grandfather who was still alive and kicking. He was going to find out from grandfather what kind of deed he had signed with Kamalo. Six days ago. If he arrives now... What will I tell him has happened to Sawa? *(Sings a sad song about his misfortune).*

Sawa, dear sister, where have you gone?
Your face, like the moon in cloudless night sky
Has it caught the attention of an ogre
Keen on inflicting suffering on your poor brother
And further grieving father's bleeding heart?

Sawa, dear sister, come back to me
Before father's bleeding heart explodes
'Gainst poor brother's irresponsibility
For ogre is only a sucking loathsome louse
That must change for good of all or fall deep.
(His sad song is interrupted by who comes in completely distressed and in agony).

SAWA: How can this happen to me na? Brother! Ngong, how can this happen to me na? How can uncle do this to me na? I am dead na? I am dead. Brother Ngong, I am dead na? What will daddy say na? Daddy will surely kill me na? Brother Ngong, I am dead; I am dead na?

NGONG: What happened, Sawa? Where have you been? Why will father kill you? What did uncle do to you? Speak Sawa. Say something.

SAWA: *(Breaking down completely).* Uncle has killed me na? That man is a beast na? That man is the devil, even seven devils in one na? That man has killed me, Ngong. That devil has finished me na?

NGONG: Sawa, calm down. Collect yourself Calm down. Calm down. Yes, just calm down. Good! Now, listen to me carefully and answer the questions as I ask them. Do you hear me?

SAWA: *(Grunts and nods her head).*

NGONG: You're coming from where?

SAWA: From uncle's house na?

NGONG: How did you go there? Who showed you the way?

SAWA: Some two people came and took me na? 'Your uncle Kamalo wants to see you immediately. And our mission is to take you to him,' they said na? So I went with them na?

NGONG: Without telling me? Why did you not wait to tell me? You don't know that the careless bush-fowl ends up in the cooking pot?

SAWA: You were away na? And they said uncle is not the type of man to be kept waiting na? And they also said that we had to pass by the shops and buy some clothes for me na? And shoes too. I was looking too wretched in my old clothes na? That's what they said na?

NGONG: That's why you came back weeping. Is it only today that uncle knows we need clothes and others basics? And why only when father is away? Why didn't you tell Redone?

SAWA: He was sleeping na? You know him na? He was sleeping from too much drinking na?

NGONG: So they took you to the shop and then to uncle Kamalo?

SAWA: *(Breaking into tears and utter distress again).* He is a devil na? To have done what he did to me na? He is not uncle na? He even said that he and daddy are not really brothers na? Daddy's brother could never do that to his brother's daughter na? And he said he wanted to teach daddy a lesson na? And humiliate me na?

NGONG: What did he do to you Sawa? Don't tell me that the brute...

SAWA: *(In frenzy of agony from remembering the fact of having been raped by Kamalo).*

That man is Satan na? With that his giant size na? And the power of a horse na? He just carried me to his bed na. Pull off my wrapper na and ... and ... and... *(She breaks down completely).*

NGONG: It's not true, Sawa. Tell me that it is a mere figment of your imagination. You never even saw uncle. After all, you don't even know him. We have never seen him. Only heard about him from father. Sawa, it's not true what you are saying. Tell me it's not true. Unless, unless he is a real monster without any feelings; any morality, any ... any... Oh God! What's happening to the world? What will father say? What will father do? This will surely drive him mad, mad, mad, maaaad! *(Ngong and Sawa cling to each other in grief, seeking comfort. Then Sawa begins to sing a dirge and Ngong joins in).*

Solo: Oh Ngew wun no du wabai!

Chorus: Oh Ngew, Oh Ngew wun no du wabai, Oh Ngew!
Solo: Oh father where are you now?
Solo: Oh mother where are you gone?
Solo: Is this the fate for your progeny?
Solo: Is this what you call brotherhood?
Solo: That some sweat and others eat and sleep?
Solo: And inflict torture as if on slaves?
Solo: Oh Ngew wun no du wabai!
Chorus: Oh Ngew, oh Ngew wun no du wabai, oh Ngew!

(While the dirge is still going on Kamala comes in, stops short, listening to the lament of his children).

KAMALA: My children, stop lamenting. I am still here. And while I am alive we will continue to struggle for justice. Kamalo cannot get away with this ... this... fraud and immorality. The other day he told me that might is right. You know what I told him? We will prevail through the force of argument; not the argument of force. I see he has removed Redone and put two others there. They tell me that from today I am not allowed to leave this farm. I will no longer have access to the barn nor be able to see Kamalo. So, you see, we have to prepare our minds for the great task ahead of us. Lamenting will solve nothing. It is time for us to put our heads together in order to face the faceless enemy. Yes, he has become faceless from the moment he refuses to see me. We are now faced with a faceless monster. Get up. Let us go inside and put our heads together.

Blackout

Fifth Movement

Kamala's home as in Fourth Movement. Stage properties consist of three old cane-chairs with a low cane-table occupying central position. Kamala and Ngong on stage. Kamala is sitting while Ngong is pacing about pensively.

NGONG: Father, how do we proceed? How are we to solve the problem? Is it possible to cure the baboon of his red buttock?

KAMALA: Very good question. How do you cure the baboon of his red buttock without killing him? But there is still a better question: what is the problem?

NGONG: The sun shines in the day and the moon at night, father. We both know what the problem is.

KAMALA: Both? Where do you place Sawa? She too has her say. Unless the sun has already set for her.

NGONG: Her sun is just rising, father. The chick scratches about for food by watching mother-hen.

KAMALA: I see you have been invoking the spirits of our fathers. If I follow your saying you should be talking about cock, not mother-hen.

NGONG: Ask her opinion and see whether she will not start crying again, father. Women are always too emotional. And that is not good for thinking.

KAMALA: How do you know that crying is not good for thinking? Don't you know that when people cry or laugh or get angry or generally express their emotions they relieve themselves of tension and so become relaxed and can think better? *(raising voice)* Sawa, please, come out here and join us in thinking.

SAWA: *(joining them)* Daddy, you're there to take care of us na? See na, just for the short time of your going, see what happened to me na? You know what is good for us na? When I think of it, I will only just be crying na? Just be crying. *(She begins to sob)*.

NGONG: Father, I said it. A toad is not a frog even though they look alike. *(Kamala begins to sob too. Before long, Sawa is wailing, followed by Kamala.)* Father ... father... what is going on? What has happened to you, father? Tell me, father, or I will cry too. *(Father nods head and Ngong burst into wailing. A short while later, Kamala smiles through his sobs and soon is laughing heartily until he rolls on the ground. Ngong is the first to join in the laughter followed by Sawa. They laugh very loud and most heartily).* Father, when did you become so playful? One minute you're wailing like a woman and the next one you are laughing your heart to the skies.

VOICE I: *(Off. Ngong, Sawa and Kamala freeze).* You can laugh as loud as you can, useless nothing things.

VOICE 2: Kamalo says you must prepare some folk dances for the amusement of his papa who will be visiting his son's estates in the very near future. A good variety that takes account of our great cultural diversity.

VOICE I: Kamalo himself will be coming in the next few days to see what you have prepared. No argumentations. No questions. This is an order.

VOICE 2: So you better get to work instead of opening your stinking fangs that you are laughing. All the play-play you were making with that drunkerman is finished. No play-play with *us. (They sing Song of sadism).*

We rape your daughter
We seize your goods
We turn you into slaves
To toil for the pleasure of Kamalo
To sweat for the 'musement of his papa.

BOTH VOICES: With us there is no Bible, no Church, no God. No play-play with us. *(Sawa bursts into wailing while Kamala smiles broadly, trying not to laugh).*

NGONG: Father, the palaver is more serious than we thought and you are smiling? In this game of cockroaches in a gathering of fowls? What is the secret of your strength, father?

KAMALA: Ever since my father told me that he wasn't really my father...

NGONG: Your father not really your father?

KAMALA: And that Kamalo's papa is not really his papa, but that we are real brothers... I have come to realise that the world is full of evil and intrigue resulting in iniquity for ordinary people. And have learnt to look at life from a different perspective. Now I seek to understand why things are the way they are. So the palaver, as you put it, is not that serious as I see it. So long as we can identify it and look it straight in the face, that is already the beginning of the solution.

SAWA: But daddy, how can that be possible na? Your father is not your father, uncle's papa is not his papa and you are brothers. How can that be na? He even told me that you are not his brother na? 'He is not really my brother, that's what my papa says'. He kept saying many times na? Until he carried me by force and... and... *(She begins to sob again)*.

NGONG: Sawa, stop it! You want us to start... to start... to start... *(He too is sobbing. Kamala does not join)*.

KAMALA: We can't do the same exercise over and over. Give me your hands. Let's form a circle and play some other games.
SAWA: I don't want to play, daddy. You don't know what that man did to me na? I don't want to play anything na?

NGONG: Father, we came out here to think, not to play. We have problems, father. KAMALA: If we don't play we cannot think. And, don't forget that Kamalo has ordered us to prepare folk dances for his entertainment and the amusement of his papa. And... the threats from our new companions. You heard them, didn't you? So let's get into a nice little circle and start preparing the folk dances.

SAWA: How can three people form a circle na, daddy? We are not many na?

NGONG: I have an idea. Let's ask our new companions to join us. After all, they are Kamalo's people and should be the first to dance for his entertainment. Sawa, why don't you call them. You know them better.

KAMALA: Very good idea, son. Sawa just raise your voice and ask them to join us. SAWA: *(hesitantly)* You ... you ... you people should come na? And join us in the folk dances na? Come and join us in dancing na?

VOICE I: You think we are children or slaves to be dancing?

VOICE 2: Our duty is to keep you under farm arrest. You cannot leave until Kamalo comes.

VOICE I: And no visitors. No movement! No visitors! These are our orders.

VOICE 2: No communication with us unless we talk to you. Next time we will make all of you stand gazing at the sun for six hours.

BOTH VOICES: So get back to work now!

SAWA: Those people are devils too na? How can they make us to be gazing at the sun for six hours na? Unless they also have a problem na? They don't even know that they have a problem too na? Kamalo is using them na? And they don't know na?

NGONG: Sawa, very well said. Father, I withdraw my saying about toad and frog resembling. They belong to the same family.

KAMALA: Wisdom is beginning to come. Sawa, what do we do about the small circle now that our companions have refused to join?

SAWA: *(nodding in the direction of spectators)* Let's ask for volunteers among them na? They are only sitting there smiling at us and doing nothing na? Let's go and get some of them to join us na? *(Sawa, Ngong and Kamala go into spectators and return with as many volunteers as they can find. However, the stage should not be over-crowded. Actors and spectators form a circle and perform a popular dance such as the Njang, Bensikin, Ndong, Bagalum, etc. Then they engage in simple relaxation exercises for controlled breathing and the body).*

KAMALA: *(addressing spectators)* Good people, this is only the beginning. But a very promising one. We will be practising here every day until Kamalo comes to see what we have prepared for his entertainment and the amusement of his papa. Will you, please, kindly join us every day for the practice sessions? As you can see, dancing and playing are very good for the heart and the soul; for the body and the mind. Just go back and take your seats while we work out how to proceed with the rest of the elements which will be included in the folk dances because dancing is talking with the body, the heart and the soul. And the spectators must listen with their bodies, their hearts and their souls. Take your seats, good people, and we will continue to work together.

(Kamala, Ngong and Sawa position themselves on stage in such a way that there is hardly any divide between actors and spectators).

NGONG: I feel like a kite sailing high up in the blue, sunny sky. I have never known that dancing is very good medicine.

SAWA: All the heaviness in my head is finished na? My body is very light and I am feeling very happy na? Daddy, we will be dancing every day na? Even after uncle Kamalo's folk dances na? I am sure he just wanted to punish us na?

KAMALA: I have a suggestion: can we stop for a short while and just relax?

SAWA: We are ready for action na? If we stop now my happiness will reduce na?

NGONG: Why do you want us to stop, father? Why do you want to remove the pot from the fire when it is not yet ready?

KAMALA: The dancing shook up my stomach. As we used to say in primary school, I want to go and obey nature's call. Just a short break. But when we come back each person will say the problem that is worrying them most.

SAWA: Only one? I have many na? I can even give five na?

NGONG: You think that we will spend the whole day only listening to your problems? I suggest that we take three. Sawa, you can say the three most important of your problems na?

SAWA: Ngong, I don't like it. I don't like it na? Daddy, you see how Ngong is always provoking me and making me angry na?

NGONG: I am sorry, Sawa. I was only joking na? Let us agree on three problems instead of five and make progress.

KAMALA: Sawa, he was only joking. He has apologized. If we have all agreed on three problems, we will present them in order of importance: from the most to the least important. If I don't rush, I will disgrace myself before you children. *(He rushes off)*

Blackout

Sixth Movement

Same as in previous movement Sawa and Ngong are playing some theatre games before Kamala's entrance upon which the three practice some Njang steps followed by a breathing exercise. Then they position themselves in such a way that there is hardly any divide between actors and spectators.

KAMALA: Can I present my problems or where do we start?

SAWA: Daddy, let me start na? My own problems are just too many na?

NGONG: You can start, Sawa. After that I will give mine. And father will be last cocoyam. But remember that you are giving only three, the most important three of your very many problems. Not so, father?

KAMALA: That's what we agreed. Each of us will present three of their most pressing problems from the most to the least important. That was our collective decision. Sawa, over to you.

SAWA: My three problems are: uncle Kamalo, no mother and poverty na? Those are my three problems na?

NGONG: You are really wonderful, Sawa. How did you come to think of no mother? We have grown up without a mother all our lives. I am sure that one will even surprise father; not so, father?

KAMALA: Let us present the problems first. We will discuss them later. But let us do the presentations. Ngong, your turn.

NGONG: I wish I could put lack of mother somewhere?

SAWA: Ngong, just say your problems na? Don't put my own inside your own na? Just say your own problems na?

NGONG: Poverty, too much work, no future. Those are my three problems.

SAWA: Why are you copying na? I also said poverty na? You're copying na? *(appealing to spectators)* Ngong is copying me na?

KAMALA: Are we not talking about our problems in this community, in this estate, Sawa? Therefore, it is possible for many people to say the same problem because it is common to all of us. It is my turn. My own problems are: my identity, lack of discussion with

Kamalo and bad management resulting in poverty. So, you see, poverty is common to all of us.

SAWA: And even Kamalo na? Kamalo is the one causing all our problems na?

NGONG: The discussion has already started? If so, there is a burning question which father must answer, our lack of a mother.

SAWA: Yes, daddy, tell us why we don't have a mother na? If I had a mother that man would not have done what he did to me in your absence because mama would have been here to take care of us na? NGONG: Father, what happened to our mother? Why don't you have a wife?

SAWA: Daddy, tell us na?

KAMALA: I wish I could avoid talking about it. It pains my heart so very much. What your mother did.

SAWA: But daddy, you said that when we talk about our problems we are already solving them na? And we need to know our identity too na? Uncle Kamalo is not really your brother and your father is not really your father. You are who na? And who are we, your children, without a mother na?

NGONG: Tell us, father, who we are. A toad may resemble a frog but toad is toad and frog is frog. Who are you, father? And who are we? Beginning with our mother. We didn't fall from the sky like rain, did we?

KAMALA: You didn't fall from the sky, my children. You do have a mother...

NGONG/SAWA: Where is she? Why is she not here with us? Why did she abandon us? Why did you send her away? Answer us na, father?

KAMALA: I did not send her away. I loved her very much especially after she had given me two lovely kids. Shortly after Sawa was born, (turning to Sawa) you were scarcely eight months old, she got up one fine morning and told me that I was a fool to have signed a deed of brotherhood with Kamalo. She accused me of being blind because I could not see the fraud, cheating and immorality popping out of Kamalo's eyes. I tried to reason with her in vain. She went away to another man leaving me with two kids. Ngong was just three years old and you eight months.

SAWA: She was right na, daddy? Mummy was right na?

NGONG: To abandon us and run away to another man? She was right, Sawa?

SAWA: I am talking about uncle na? He is a very bad man na? And daddy did not see na?

KAMALA: Sawa, in those days we had different barns. I took care of my affairs and he took care of his. There was really nothing to worry about. Until he persuaded me into this single barn thing. But that was long after your mother had gone. I suppose her beauty went into her head and my naivety disappointed her. So she left.

NGONG: Where is she, father? Where are they? She and her man.

KAMALA: They are living on another estate far, far away. She went to a man, you will be shocked to hear, who already had three wives. The last thing I heard about her was that she had had ten children for him. It is difficult to understand why a woman will abandon a man and two kids and marry a polygamist. I don't understand the logic. Just because of the deed I signed with Kamalo. I don't understand women's erratic logic. *(To spectators) Do you* understand it, good people?

SAWA: But it is simple na, daddy? The quest for happiness na? See how unhappy all of us are here na? She was looking for happiness na?

KAMALA: But we were happy, Sawa. In those days we were happy. The one barn thing only came long after she had left. There was no reason really why she left at the time abandoning an eight months old little girl. She should have worried about you kids, even if she didn't care about me. But she is happy where she is. She has her own farm and does whatever she likes with her harvest. And her man supplements her income ever so often. She is happy over there and we are sad here. Just because of Kamalo. And then he does this terrible... horrible... thing to my Sawa. A man I trusted as my brother betrays me in this most horrific and despicable act. It is more heinous than... than the forgery in the deed of brotherhood. Kamalo, how can you do this to me? Kamalo, how could you do this to my daughter? Kamalo, how could you do this to your own daughter, your niece? And now, because of the horror of the act, because of the despicable and hideous nature of your act, you don't want to see me? *(Sawa and Ngong are already sobbing).*

NGONG: Stop it father, please stop. You are killing us, father. Please, stop! *(Highly emotional silent pause).*

KAMALA: Sawa, Ngong, my dear children. I love you deeply, kids. Kamalo is our problem because he wastes away our resources making us poor. His papa is our problem because he has enslaved Kamalo who in turn has enslaved us. Can a slave ever know anything but poverty? We are our problem because we are doing nothing, absolutely nothing to regain our liberty and dignity which Kamalo and his papa have taken away from us. That is the problem as I see it. I do not know how you see it. But that is the way I see it. Good people, that is our problem. The way I see it. Or am I wrong? Am I wrong, Sawa? Ngong? My children, tell me, tell us, tell all these good people what you think our problem is. If it is not Kamalo and his papa. *(Sawa begins to sing the dirge and is soon joined by Ngong, Kamala and the spectators).*

> Chorus: Oh Ngew! Oh Ngew wun no du wabai, Oh Ngew!
> Solo: Oh father where are you now?
> Solo: Oh mother where are you gone?
> Solo: Is this the fate for your progeny?
> Solo: Is this what you call brotherhood?
> Solo: That some sweat and others eat and sleep?
> Solo: And inflict torture as if on slaves?
> Solo: Oh Ngew wun no du wabai!
> Chorus: Oh Ngew, oh Ngew wun no du wabai, oh Ngew!

SAWA: But you also say that we are our problem na, daddy? Because we don't even know who we are na? You have told us about our mummy na? But what about our grand-mummy and grand-daddy na? That is the only way to know our identity na? Who we are and how we are family with uncle Kamalo na? Who are we na? Where did we come from before all these problems fell on us na, daddy? It is important for us to know our family story na?

NGONG: Father, Sawa is right. Your father says he is not really your father. He also says Kamalo's papa is not really his papa. Kamalo himself says you are not really his brother. How do we get the wind to show us the fowl's anus? Father, how do we know where and when the rain started beating us? Where and when the harmattan came on us suddenly?

KAMALA: My father, who now says he is really not my father, says that Kamalo knows our family story. But Kamalo has refused to see me or even talk with me. Even when I could meet him in his comfortable palace, it was like talking with a mad man or a fool. 'I conceive, you execute. That's what my papa says' was all I heard from him. We have to go into the whole community and ask the elders of the clan about our story. We have to look in history books and diaries kept by people who are known for telling the truth; especially priests, philosophers, travellers and even soothsayers. My mother is still alive; but only Kamalo knows where she is being held.

NGONG: Why? Is she a prisoner? Why is Kamalo hiding her from us?

SAWA: He is ashamed of his own mother na? I can never be ashamed of my mother na? She even left us and ran away na? But I cannot be ashamed of her na? *(Looking at cyclorama or portrait of old woman)* Even in her old age our grandmother looks beautiful na?

NGONG: And rich. Beautiful and rich, Sawa. That portrait tells me that we have to find our family story. Our past must have been truly glorious and happy.

KAMALA: You're right, son. Even today our estate is fertile and rich. There is really no reason for our wretched condition other than mismanagement, misplaced priorities and the looting done by Kamalo's papa.

SAWA: How shall we do na? To know our family story na?

KAMALA: I cannot be of much help because I am under farm arrest. I may not leave this place and I am not allowed any visitors. Both of you have to get the necessary information. Don't forget that we have not really started practising the folk dances for Kamalo and his papa.

NGONG: Our family story is more important.

SAWA: We can even refuse to dance for them na?

KAMALA: We will dance for them. As slaves, that is our duty. To entertain our masters and owners. But it is also an occasion for us to dialogue with Kamalo through song and dance. Both of you shall now go out into the community and find out our family story. Our history. I will be doing some ploughing in the field.

Blackout

Seventh Movement

Same setting as in previous movement with Ngong leading, the three come in dancing to the tune of Sima Pe oh! Sima Pe Yoo yovo! Yo yoyo! Yo yovo! They change to three other songs and dance steps. The impression should be given that they have already been practising the folk dances off and this is a continuation. Spectators are invited to join in at the end of which there is applause while spectators return to their seats.

SAWA: It is not good to be in the dark na? Now like this I am very happy na? All the people like Kamalo who pretend that they have power, it is just because they know certain things na? Which other people don't know na?

NGONG: Knowledge is power! Father, of all the things that you have ever done for us, this one is the best. Going out to look for the story of our family has been the best school that we have gone to. (to spectators) Good people the best inheritance that you can give your children is education, information. A person who is informed, who is aware of his surroundings, who is educated, can never become the slave of another man or woman. I am now ready, we are ready to dance for Kamalo and his papa not because we are their slaves but because knowledge of who we are has liberated us and given us dignity, pride and a sense of purpose in life. Father, we will dance for Kamalo with all our hearts, souls and minds. I have never been so proud of these rags that have been the symbol of our enslavement after what I have learnt about our family.

KAMALA: My dear children, good people, now I know that the easiest way to make someone your slave is to deny that person knowledge. To deny that person an identity. To deny that person the story of his roots, his origins. In short the best way to make someone your slave is to take away that person's identity and give them yours. That is what Kamalo tried to do to me and my children. At last, he has been found out. Let us learn this new song:

Chorus: In one family, in one family, in one family
We can change the whole world.

Solo: Dear children, my children, in one family
We can change the whole world.
Solo: Dear Sawa, dear son Ngong, in one family
We can change the whole world.

Chorus: In one family, in one family, in one family
We can change the whole world.

SAWA: That is a very nice song na, daddy?

NGONG: Very meaningful too. Kintashe nu mungai! Unity is strength. United we stand, divided we fall. That should be the motto of this family: Kintashe nu. mungai! It's only a proposal I am making. What do you say, father?

SAWA: Kintashe nu mungai! Unity is strength. Wonderful motto na?

KAMALA: Adopted?

SAWA/NGONG: Adopted. ALL: Kintashe nu mungai! Unity is strength. Adopted.

SAWA: This is how things should be na? Ngong proposes, we discuss and agree na? That's how things should always be na? Instead of somebody's papa saying na?

NGONG: When we discuss and agree...

KAMALA: It means that we all conceive and execute. Not, as Kamalo says, 'I conceive, you execute. Period.' It means that we know what we want and how to get it.

SAWA: It means that we know our problem and how to solve it na?

NGONG: We have already identified our problem- Kamalo and his papa.

SAWA: All the other problems come from that one na?

KAMALA: So the very first of our problems is Kamalo and, by extension, his papa. How do we solve it? Because Kamalo is our problem because his papa is his problem and he doesn't know that his papa is his problem. That is why I asked both of you to go out and find your family story. Because if you don't know where you are coming from, you will never know where you are going to. Or you will always take the wrong direction. So what did you find about your story? Our family story?

SAWA: Grand-mummy is a goddess na? The people say that one day she emerged from the smoking volcano of Mount Kamada. That's why they call her Kamada na? She can never die because of her extreme beauty and wealth na?

NGONG: And the people offer sacrifices every now and then to Kamanda, the Mountain Goddess. Because of her great beauty and wealth many foreign traders passing through the estate always sought to seduce her in order to capture her love and more especially, her wealth.

SAWA: She could not get a man from her clan na, because she was worshipped as a goddess na?

NGONG: Unfortunately for her, all the traders passing through the clan and her estate were albinos and she had a terrible dislike for the colour of their skins and the way they squinted their eyes and were always sneezing.

SAWA: The first trader was called Baakingoom na?

KAMALA: Baakingoom? The one who says he is not really my father? SAWA: Yes na? The second was called Yaman na?

KAMALA: Yaman? Who is that one now? Are you sure you don't mean Fiekafhim, Kamalo's papa?

NGONG: That is the third one. Kamalo's papa is the third trader.

SAWA: You cannot know everything na, daddy? That is why you sent us to look for the family story na? Nobody can know everything na?

KAMALA: You are right, Sawa. Even a newly born baby is knowledgeable in its own way. That is why we must tap all the human resources available to us in order to increase our knowledge of ourselves and our surroundings.

NGONG: So there are three traders struggling over grand-mother's attention: Baakingoom, Yaman and Fiekafhim.

SAWA: All of them albinos na? And grand-mummy doesn't like them na?

KAMALA: And no man from this clan can marry her because they worship her as a goddess?

NGONG: Some of her people even encourage her to choose among the three suitors although from the beginning there are really only two: Baakingoom and Yaman. Fiekafhim only comes in after the elimination of Yaman.

SAWA: When the people encourage her like that na, she prefers Baakingoorn na?

NGONG: So she secretly sends a message to Baakingoom asking him to come to her at night.

SAWA: And the person instead goes to Yaman na? He does not know the difference between an albino and an albino na?

NGONG: But grand-mother knows. And when Yaman shows up she wants to know what he wants in her house at that time of night. Yaman is a powerfully built man and very strong too.

SAWA: He rapes grand-mummy na? Just like what Kamalo... *(she breaks down)*.

KAMALA: It's all right, my daughter. You will be fine. Let us not spoil that beautiful story now. We will give it to Kamalo just the way you are telling it. May be he will see reason and mend his evil ways.

NGONG: Grand-mother is so traumatized by the horrible deed that she loses her mind. Meanwhile a quarrel develops among the traders- Baakingoom, Yaman and a new arrival, Fiekafhim. Baakingoom and Fiekafhim ally against Yaman and eliminate him. And since grand-mother is already half-mad she doesn't care whoever sleeps with her. And both Baakingoom and Fiekafhim indulge themselves without any scruples.

SAWA: She becomes pregnant na? And Baakingoom and Fiekafhim claim responsibility for the pregnancy na?

NGONG: Grand-mother, Kamanda delivers twins, both of them boys.

KAMALA: Kamala and Kamalo?

SAWA: Kamalo and Kamala na? There is even a fight na? Until the elders of the clan intervened to stop the fighting between Baakingoom and Fiekafhim na?

NGONG: One of the twins is bigger than the other. But they bear no resemblance to either Baakingoom or Fiekafhim.

SAWA: So Baakingoom takes the smaller boy and Fiekafhim claims the bigger boy and his mother Kamanda na?

KAMALA: So the brothers are really brothers.

NGONG: It is the fathers who are not really fathers. That is what the elders of the clan say because neither you nor your brother resemble either Baakingoom or Fiekafhim except in stature.

KAMALA: Who is our real father, then? Which man brought us into this world? What do the elders say?

SAWA: They are thinking that because of grand-mummy's madness she might have slept with Wakadu na?

NGONG: Wakadu the mad musician and great dancer of the clan. He played very good music and danced very well. But he was mad. Even before grand-mother lost her head she used to enjoy listening to Wakadu's music and watch him dance. And would give him many presents after each performance.

KAMALA: So we are the offspring of two mad people? The one because of his music and the other because of what Yaman did to her?

SAWA: That's life na, daddy? We cannot choose our parents na? Or decide where and when to be born na? The only thing is to know who we are and how to make the best of life na? That's the only way na?

NGONG: Listen, Sawa. Someone is saying something.

VOICE: *(off)* Kamalo is coming in two days to see what you have prepared for his entertainment and the amusement of his papa. You all know what will happen if he is not happy with your performance. Six hours standing and facing the sun. So be warned. No play play with us.

SAWA: Let him even come now. We are ready na? Let him even come now if he wants na?

KAMALA: Are you sure, Sawa?

SAWA: Yes na, daddy? We will begin with *Sima Pe*, change to *Ofung*, then *Njang* and *Ndong* na?

NGONG: And then we will perform the family story. I agree with Sawa. He can even come now if he wants.

KAMALA: But we have not rehearsed that family story. Who will play what? Where do we begin the story even? There are still many questions to be answered. And don't forget that we can only keep his attention if the story is interesting. And if it makes him angry he will make us stand facing the sun for six hours. You heard him.

SAWA: Let me say it again na, daddy? We begin with the traditional dances na? Then we play the family story na? And then we can even ask him to say whether he likes the story or not na? That's all na?

KAMALA: Where does our story begin? Where does it end? What is the middle? The story must have a beginning, a middle and an end. What do we put inside and what to we leave out? How many characters does the story have? From what I can see, there are already quite a good number of characters: grandma, Kamanda, and at least her three lovers- Baakingoom, Yaman and Fiekafhim. There are only three of us! If you see what I mean.

NGONG: *(looking into audience)* We can ask them to volunteer. They joined in the dancing and even danced better than myself. *(to audience)* You will surely join us, won't you?

SAWA: I think we can even ask Kamalo na? He is part of the family na? Since I am the only woman here, I will play grand-mummy na?

KAMALA: Thank you, Sawa. That is a very concrete and practical suggestion. Who will play Baakingoom? And Yaman? We can leave out Fiekafhim. His influence is already too much even in his absence. He does not need to appear on stage; and the message will still carry.

SAWA: Daddy can play Baakingoom na? And Ngong will play Yaman na?

NGONG: To make it relevant to the folk dances, I suggest that we should also have a storyteller. So that it will sound like a folktale. In the modem world they call it narrator who will also be impresario or MC, Master of Ceremony. I am sure that we need one, to make the show impressive and spectacular. Sawa, you can do that na?

SAWA: Daddy, you see how Ngong has started provoking me again na? I don't like it na?

KAMALA: Why do you think that you are the only one who should speak like that na? Anyone can speak like that na? It's even good na? That we all want to speak like Sawa na? *(They all burst out laughing)*.

SAWA: Daddy, you can really be funny na? Very funny na?

KAMALA: Yes, na? To maintain my sanity I have to crack jokes and be funny na? You will play story-teller na? And impresario and MC na? Okay shall be begin? You go backstage and come in again. Kamalo and his papa are already sitting there with these spectators.

NGONG: What about costumes? She must look as beautiful and as rich as grand-mother.

SAWA: But this is only a rehearsal na, Ngong? It is not yet the real thing na?

KAMALA: You are right, Sawa. Ngong, this is only a trial, an improvisation, before we even come to the rehearsal. Let's go! Sawa, backstage! Count down from five to zero.. Five, four three, two one, zero! Action! *(Sawa comes on stage applauded by Ngong, Kamala and the rest of the spectators)*.

SAWA: Thank you for the hand-clapping na?

NGONG: Stop, Sawa. You are no longer Sawa. You are MC, impresario and narrator. You must capture the attention of the spectators. You will not succeed if you continue to say na, na, na all the time.

SAWA: Then you go and do it na? I will not play it again na?

KAMALA: Sawa, you can do it. And you will do it. Ngong is right. You are no longer Sawa. Now you are MC, impresario and narrator. Later on you will be grand-mother, Kamanda. So just think positive, concentrate, improvise and move. Sawa, backstage. Count down. Five, four, three, two, one zero. Action! *(Sawa comes on stage to general applause)*.

SAWA: Your Excellency Kamalo, the only one who conceives, Your Excellency Kamalo's papa, distinguished ladies and gentlemen, welcome to this afternoon of great entertainment. I can promise you that by the time you leave these wonderful grounds, you will all be bubbling with happiness and joy. You will also be taking back to your palaces and comfortable homes some food for thought for our show is not only entertaining, it is also teaching. Giving us all something to think about as we return to our homes. *(When she stops speaking there is applause).*

NGONG: Sawa, you are go-o-o-o-d! Father, could you have done better? I am absolutely proud of you, Sawa. You are a genius, a phenomenon even!

KAMALA: That was some spectacle, Sawa. I think we are ready for our guests, Kamalo and his papa.

SAWA: Daddy, that song you taught us about one family na? We must put it inside the play na? And we must sing Kamalo's name too na? So I am suggesting that we learn it again na? *(Kamala leads in the singing as they all sing).*

> Chorus: In one family, in one family, in one family
> We can change the whole world.
>
> Solo: Dear children, my children, in one family
> We can change the whole world.
>
> Solo: Dear Sawa, dear son Ngong, in one family
> We can change the whole world.
>
> Solo: Kamalo, dear brother, in one family
> We shall change the whole world.
>
> Chorus: In one family, in one family, in one family
> We can change the whole world.

Blackout

Eighth Movement

Same setting as in previous movement. Preceded by two bodyguards in plain-clothes, Kamalo comes from backstage, moves to DSC, looks about him with a lot of authority and then takes a seat reserved for him in the front row. He signals his bodyguards to withdraw. Sawa, costumed like the grand-mother's portrait in the cyclorama comes in with a flourish from backstage in the role of MC and impresario, moves to DSC and then addresses the spectators.

MC/IMPRESARIO: Your Excellency Uncle Kamalo, the one who conceives, it is a great pleasure for us of this small community of father, a son and daughter, to welcome Your Excellency to sample the great variety of folk dances which we have enjoyed preparing over the last few days for the up-coming visit of our most distinguished visitors, their Excellencies Uncle Kamalo, the one who conceives and his papa, Fiekafhim. Let me hasten to point out, Your Excellency Uncle Kamalo, that folk dances belong to the community of all the peoples of Kamanda, this great estate our grand-mother, Kamanda, bequeathed to us before taking her deserved place in the pantheon of Gods and Goddesses of Kamanda. Folk- dancing is therefore a community experience and is, consequently, participatory. The entire community participates in the singing and dancing. We will plead the indulgence of Your Excellency Uncle Kamalo to kindly do us the great favour of active participation, even if it is just the nodding of the head. Again, the participatory nature of our show gives Your Excellency Uncle Kamalo the pleasure of interfering at any point to correct or amend or explicate a point that we might have missed out bearing in mind that Your Excellency Uncle Kamalo is the one who conceives and we execute. The name of our show, Your Excellency Uncle Kamalo, is Family Saga. Your Excellency Uncle Kamalo, we find ourselves on this estate because we are one not by choice but by the will of the Gods and Goddesses of Kamanda. Uncle Kamalo, welcome to this spectacular performance of the folklore, the family story, the family saga of Kamanda! *(Kamalo applauds enthusiastically as Sawa joins Ngong and Kamala, who have had a change of costumes, backstage for the start of the performance. They enter to the tune of the song,* In one family. *This is followed by a performance of* Ofung). *Then Sawa as Story-teller).*

STORY-TELLER: Once upon a recent time, in the land of Kamanda, the people woke up from their peaceful sleep with a jolt because of loud rumbling coming from the direction of Mount Kamanda. They rushed from their houses and watched in awe as fire balls and smoke rose from the tip of the mountain. As they watched the molten lava flowing slowly down the side of the mountain, they soon discerned a human figure, a female human figure in sparkling golden wax wrappers and rich jewels glittering all over her. As the apparition strode confidently and authoritatively towards the people they all fell on their knees and, raising their arms in supplication, implored Kamanda, Goddess Kamanda, to shelter them from the wrath of their ancestors. Never before, had the people ever set eyes on a woman of such exceptional beauty and wealth. Never before, had their forebears shown such concern for them by sending a goddess in the form of this exceptional woman of beauty and wealth as witness of their love and concern for the well-being of the living. *(Now playing the role of Kamanda).*

    KAMANDA: Arise! people of Kamanda, arise!
    I come as a sign of love from the hereafter.
    I come as signal of the wealth of this land
    The ancestors bequeathed to you and those after you.
    I come as warning for vampires and vultures shall descend
    Descend on this land, sucking your blood and eating your flesh
    Through your own flesh, your own loins, your very offspring.
    I come as sign of love and as post of warning
    The wealth they bequeath to you shall come to nought,
    Shall come to nought, unless you stand as one family;
    Unless you hold each other's hand in bond of brotherhood,
    Unless you uphold the mores of the land and shun greed;
    Unless you hold your heads high in the pride of your cultural heritage;

Unless ... unless ... unless... you love each other as the forebears love you.

Your ways will drive the ancestors mad when you drive me mad

And there shall be dissent and hatred and envy and above all, greed.

Greed shall drive you to lose all and become slaves of others

Who shall be your false fathers because of the beauty and wealth I bring.

STORY-TELLER: The people swore by Kamanda and all their gods and goddesses that they would never lose faith in the eyes of their ancestors. And immediately proceeded to offer sacrifices to their ancestors through the Goddess of Mount Kamanda. Kamanda lived for a long time. Never changing, never growing old, always looking younger. And the people believed in her as a veritable Goddess sent by their ancestors. And the land prospered and the people prospered; and the fame, wealth and generosity of Kamada reached other lands.

BAAKINGOOM: *(played by Kamala using appropriate make-up, mime and props)* I was a common trader, hawking trinkets and mirrors and books and cheap alcohol. I heard of the fame and wealth of Kamanda and came to see if I could scrape a bit of that untold wealth for myself. When I reached here, when I got to this land, I was amazed at the wealth that was just wasting away. I was even more amazed at the untold beauty of Lady Kamanda whom the people worshipped as a goddess letting her beauty waste with no man to love her and fondle her. I was amazed by this eternal beauty that was wasting away. And didn't I try? I tried very hard. But always she turned her face away in disgust. Utter disgust. Did I stink? I wondered aloud to myself.

YAMAN: *(played by Ngong using appropriate make-up, mime and props)* I was a common trader, hawking trinklets and mirrors and books and cheap alcohol. I heard of the fame and wealth of Kamanda and came to see if I could scrape a bit of that untold wealth for myself. When I reached here, when I got to this land, I was amazed at the wealth that was just wasting away. I was even more amazed at the untold beauty of Lady Kamanda whom the people worshipped as a goddess letting her beauty waste with no man to love her and fondle her. I was amazed by this eternal beauty that was wasting away. And didn't I try? I tried very hard. But always she turned her face away in disgust. Utter disgust. Did I stink? I wondered aloud to myself. See, I am tall and big and strongly built. I will protect you from all enemies. Again she turned her face away in disgust.

KAMALO: *(moving up to Ngong)* There you lie, son. Uncle Kamalo is the one who is fat and big and strongly built. I will protect her from all enemies. I will protect you from all enemies *(Ngong steps aside)*.

STORY-TELLER: Kamanda had lived among the people for so long that she did not remember how long. Perhaps the ways of humans were beginning to tell on her? What motivated the elders to approach her with the suggestion that she could not continue to look away from her two albino suitors? But was she really beginning to develop some human weaknesses? When she sent for Baakingoom was it not because she wanted to give him some bars of gold and elephant tusks and ask him to leave her people alone? Was she going to make the same proposal to Yaman? Unfortunately, the messenger took her message to Yaman, not Baakingoom.

YAMAN: *(now played by Kamalo with no make-up, etc.)* My Lady Queen, I am privileged to respond to your summons.

KAMANDA: Who summoned you? What do you want here at this time of night?

YAMAN: I am honoured to respond to my Lady Queen's summons.

KAMANDA: Get out of my sight. It is not you I summoned. Get out of my sight. *(aside)* I am choking with his stench. Please, get out of my sight.

YAMAN: What makes him better than I am? I will protect you from him. I promise.

KAMANDA: *(choking)* Please, get out of my sight.

YAMAN: Do you know how long I have waited for this moment? This is my moment of truth. I will not let it slip from my fingers. I will not let you slip from me ever. I will ravish you. Might is right. I am strong. You are weak. I take the upper hand. I will have you now! *(He lifts her, protesting vehemently)*.

SAWA: Not again na, uncle Kamalo! You will not do that again to your own brother's daughter na, uncle Kamalo. *(Kamalo freezes with Sawa in his arms)*.

STORY-TELLER: *(now played by Ngong)* Baakingoom heard of Yaman's rape of Kamanda and it drove him mad especially as the message had been meant for him. Yaman went about boasting that he was Kamanda's man and that he had demonstrated his manhood more than Baakingoom. Baakingoom was so mad at Yaman that he conspired with Fiekafhim, another newly arrived trader, to eliminate, to kill Yaman. When Baakingoom rushed to Kamanda with news of Yaman's elimination, the grand, beautiful lady only laughed wistfully and asked: Are you not him? And Baakingoom realised that Kamanda had lost her mind. So he and Fiekafhim took advantage of Kamanda's madness to plunder her and her people of their beauty and wealth. Then the people noticed that Kamanda was pregnant. Baakingoom and Fiekafhim noticed that Kamanda was pregnant and each was hot, very hot, making claims to the authorship of the pregnancy. Lady Kamanda did not care because she had lost her mind. When the pregnancy came to term, Kamanda gave birth to a set of twins, both of them boys. Kamanda named them Kamalo, meaning the big one, and Kamala, the small one. But the twins resembled neither Baakingoom nor Fiekafhim and rumours began to spread in the clan that they resembled Wakadu, the mad village singer and great dancer who used to entertain Kamanda, for she loved listening to his voice and watching him dance. But because both Baakingoom and Fiekafhim wanted a firm grip on Kamanda's beauty and wealth, Baakingoom took Kamala while Fiekafhim seized not only Kamalo but also Kamanda whom he has locked away so as to better exploit Kamalo and the wealth of his people, especially his brother Kamala and his two children, Ngong and Sawa.

KAMALO: *(unfreezing and gently placing Sawa on her feet)*
Nothing can be hidden from the face of the sun!
History can never be changed or forgotten.
The truth, at last, has come out!

Cursed be the day I saw the light
To have been so evil to my own brother
To have committed these abominations
Against my own niece, my own daughter
The offspring of my dear twin brother.
Goddess Kamanda, why did you permit
This evil to stride the world?
What sacrifice, to what Gods shall pacify
This horridly, damnable abomination
That has visited the peace-loving people of Kamanda?
My daughter, Sawa, I do not ask for forgiveness
For such abominations are not, and can never, be forgiven.
Sawa, my daughter, I ask you to condemn me to the cruellest death.

(kneeling before Sawa)
I await the pronouncement from your lips, my daughter.

SAWA: *(Taking his hand and lifting him to his feet)* It was not your fault na? It is that your papa who was fooling you na? Now that you are truly sorry, I am sure that the elders of the community can find a solution na? Or we can even sit together and discuss what to do na? There is no problem without a solution na. We can sit in a circle and discuss what to do na?

NGONG: Uncle Kamalo, it is enough that you have realised that you were in error and that you are very sorry for your terrible acts against your own brother and us your children. There is no illness without a cure. The mere fact that you have finally consented to mingle with us is the beginning of the cure.

KAMALO: My nephew Ngong, Ngong my son, What I deserve is the most horrifying death imaginable. Sawa, my daughter, if you have forgiven me, call me uncle Kamalo.

SAWA: I have forgiven you na, Uncle Kamalo. Uncle Kamalo, I forgive you na?

KAMALO: Thank you my daughter, Sawa.
I thank you deeply.
My brother, Kamala, I am not worthy to be called your brother.

I wronged you most ignominiously by using my brute force on you.
Now I agree with you that the force of argument is better
Than the argument of force.
I am only an ignoble vampire who should be uprooted and burnt
In the deepest furnace, deeper than the furnace of Mount Kamanda.
But we will need to rescue our mother from the jail of Fiekafhim
Who misled me into thinking about my pleasures and greed
At the expense of my family, my community and even my health.
Henceforth, we must join hands and minds and hearts and the resources
Of this estate for our own good, our own prosperity.
(Taking off his three piece suit).
This suit, the first symbol of my enslavement, shall never
Touch my body again.
Brother Kamala, give me one of your jumpers.
I feel so free and relieved without those clothes of enslavement.
From today, Brother Kamala, you will conceive and I will execute.

KAMALA: No, Brother Kamalo. We cannot replace one evil with another. Henceforth, all our decisions and actions shall be participatory. We shall all conceive and execute, each according to his ability. But first, we shall cleanse you from the incest which you committed inadvertently. All that is required is a spotless, white he-goat, a piece of rope, a club, a mat, seven cowries and some palm-wine. Having made peace with our forebears, we shall then sit in a circle and, as you have suggested, strategize to release our mother from the claws of Fiekafhim. The good people here present will surely help us out with some suggestions.

KAMALO: Brother Kamala, is it possible for me to be released from that baseness? No sacrifice is big enough so long as Sawa will forgive me.

SAWA: I have already forgiven you na, uncle. We have all forgiven you na? We are very happy that we have become one family again na, Uncle Kamalo?

KAMALO: I now know that I have behaved worse than an animal towards my brother and my own children. The ancestors and our dear mother, the Goddess Kamanda, forgive my baseness. Brother tune the song about one family. From today it will be our rallying call, our anthem in the land of Kamanda.

(Curtain call to the tune of In one family *after which actors mix with spectators and strategize on how to rescue Kamanda from Fiekafhim's hold).*

The End

Part III

Lake God

Dramatis Personae
(in order of appearance)

SHEY BO-NYO:	Narrator, diviner and priest of the Lake God.
FATHER LEO:	Parish priest of the village and patron of the Fon.
FON:	Educated chief of the village and fanatic Christian.
TWO GUARDS:	Doggo and Kinchin, they double as bodyguards and errand-boys of the Fon.
NKASAI:	
NKFUSAI:	
KIMBONG:	
KIMA'A:	
YENSI:	Leaders of the women's cult, Fibuen.
DEWA:	Fulani cattle grazier.
SHEY TANTO:	Leader of the Kwifon, the men's secret cult and most important authority in the people's lives.
LAGHAM:	A palm-wine tapper.
MA KUSHAM:	An old woman who administers the oath of the Fibuen.
FISIY:	
FORGWEI:	
MAIMO:	Village men and friends of Lagham.
ANGELA:	Fon's wife and headmistress of the village school.
MBWIN:	
MUJEI:	
BOLUNG:	
KIBOW:	
WONG:	
BOKUW:	Leading members of Kwifon.

MASKED FIGURE: Errand boy of the Kwifon.
WOMAN:
GIRL:
BOY:
MAN: Survivors of the disaster.

Prologue

From backstage a mourning song, Mangvun, is heard. It rises gradually to the rhythm of the Ngem or double-gong bell. Then a lone person makes his entrance on stage, performing unsteady funerary steps and chanting the mourning song. He makes a round across the playing area and finally stops around centre stage with one last stroke on his Ngem. He looks around uneasily and wipes a tear or two from his eyes. Then he addresses the audience.

NARRATOR

So it is true what the elders said?
But what elders, which elders?
Here I am standing...
A lone reed in a swelling river
Harassed, buffeted from left to right
And from right to left without respite.
Here I stand... and open my mouth.
Yet no words come out.
What my eyes still see is beyond
Any words man can utter.
And you all sit there gazing at me
And saying in your bellies
Poor fellow,
He is the only survivor of a village
Of a thousand.
Wonder how a scrawny fellow like him
Was spared when every
Man, woman and child,
Fowls, dogs and cats,
Cattle, goats and pigs,
Wild animals in the bush including
Rats and flies;
I said flies. Do you hear me?
Yes, flies. Even flies.
Every living creature,

The Lake God of death swept them all
Into his kingdom in swift, silent whirlwind.
And you all sit there gazing at me mad.
It is true what our ancestors said.
When death strikes, it is your kinsman
That mourns with you. It is he
Who wipes the tears from your eyes
And brings comfort to your heart.
Yet after the holocaust
There is no kinsman to mourn with me;
No kinsman to wipe my tears and comfort me.
I mourn the dead and mourn my death
For what is life when bereft of company?

He takes up the mourning song again and does a turn around the stage, stopping abruptly when an idea dawns on him.

What foolishness is this?
I know you will never forgive me.
But my brothers and sisters;
My dear brothers and my dear sisters,
Forgive the foolish and idle words
Of a man stricken by sorrow.
Forgive the madness of one overtaken by old age.
Forgive an idiot mad man overcome by calamity.
Only yesterday I was a man!
A husband with five wives and a compound
Bustling with life and ringing
With laughter and song.
Only yesterday, I was just one person in a
Teeming village of several hundred people.
Today, I am the weather-beaten owl
Scampering into dark grove at the approach of
Dawn, fearful of the terrible silence
Descended over the land.
I thought a foolish thought and said a mad word.

You are my kinsmen for you heard my wailing
And came to wipe the tears and bring
Comfort to an agonized heart.
But there is just one small problem.
I have heard some foolish talk about toxic gas.
Beware of words that are likely to arouse again
The anger of an already vengeful god.
Beware! I say, for my god is a god of terror!
A god of terror! A god of terror!
A god of terror! T E R R O R ! ! !

A whirlwind rises and overwhelms the whole auditorium. Blackout. Darkness and silence reign supreme. The lights are turned on slowly, simulating dawn. All over the playing area are bodies of humans and animals lying still. It is a macabre and terrifying scene. After a while, one of the forms stirs uneasily and with great difficulty. It is a woman about thirty years old. She rises slowly and lurches and falls on another figure which remains frozen. She pulls herself together and examines the form, prodding it and turning it over. It is obviously lifeless. On all fours, she drags herself around the playing area stopping to examine the other forms for any signs of life. She is horror-stricken and terrified. After crawling, struggling and staggering about for a while, she discovers life in another form, a little girl about four years old. She tries to lift the girl but is obviously too weak to do so. The girl cringes upon seeing the still forms lying all over. She clings to the woman and makes as if to scream, but there is no sound. The woman, realising her new responsibility, pacifies and comforts the child as much as she can. Then both of them continue to explore the devastated land, the girl holding tight to the woman. A little while later, they find signs of life in another form, a boy, a little bigger and older than the girl. He is looking equally dazed. He behaves almost in the same manner as the girl when she was first discovered except that, thinking of himself as a man, he gives the impression that he can take care of himself to a certain extent. The three explore around a bit more and then they exit. Blackout.

Fragments

Fon's palace. Action opens in the reception courtyard where all business is done - receiving visitors and holding village councils. His throne is on a dais up centre stage. His two guards, tough-looking thugs, are standing on either side of the throne. The rest of the characters will place themselves either to left or right of downstage as occasion demands. Stage decoration should reflect the Fon's bias for Western civilization at the expense of traditional culture. Even his costume reflects his obsession with Western culture. He is receiving a missionary, Father Leo, when their conversation is interrupted by a loud voice off. It is narrator, Shey Bo-Nyo.

VOICE
Terror! God of terror! Terror God! Terror! I say God of Terror! Beware Fon! Fon beware the God of terror!

FATHER LEO
It is Shey of the gods again.

FON
That mad man again? *to guards* Stop him!

Before guards can move Shey Bo-Nyo makes his entrance, clutching the Ngem. The guards bar his way.

SHEY BO-NYO
Keep your hands off me, you scoundrels. I will see the Fon. He must listen to me. The white man has brought trouble to the land. He has killed our gods and the Fon is impotent.

DOGGO
Shurrup! You dis crissman.

KINCHIN
You wan see Fon for weti?

SHEY BO-NYO
I must warn the Fon. I say lay off your hands! Sons of bitches and prostitutes! It is an abomination for the Fon to surround himself with thugs and sons of whores and people who will kill us and destroy the land.

FON
Why is he always accusing me?

FATHER LEO
Typical behaviour of the mad. They always have an obsession. Something they cling to. Something they repeat all the time. I wouldn't pay any attention. What trouble have I brought to this village? The church has brought new life and progress to this village. And yet he says the white man will kill people and destroy the land. Sheer madness.

DOGGO
We go show you say we be akwara woman dem pickin. Tekam!

There is a deafening scream as they half-drag, half-carry him out.

FON
Those idiots will kill the old man. All bulk and no brains.

FATHER LEO
That seems to be the only language that will pacify him. In civilized society he would be chained in a home for the mentally disturbed.

FON
We will never catch-up with Europe, Father. We will never catch-up. Thank God you came. Praise be to Jesus who sent out his disciples to convert the heathen.

FATHER LEO
I have converted most of the pagans in this village except the mad Shey. He is always talking about sacrificing to his lake god.

FON
He will never be converted, Father. He is the priest of the lake god just as you are the priest of the Almighty God in heaven.

FATHER LEO

How dare you, Fon! How dare you make such a comparison! In spite of all my efforts? In spite of all that I have done for you? You even dare to make reference to idols in my presence?

FON

Sorry, Father. I am very sorry, Father. Very, very sorry, Father. It was a slip of the tongue.

FATHER LEO

My dear Fon, you must choose between Satan and God. Why do you allow such evil thoughts to bother you? It must be Lucifer. Where is my vial of holy water? *He searches his pockets and brings out vial which he sprinkles on the Fon.* I bless you in the name of the Father and of the Son and of the Holy Spirit.

FON

Amen!

FATHER LEO

May the Virgin Mary, mother of God, pray for you.

FON

Amen!

FATHER LEO

Let us kneel and say the 'Our Father'.
Both kneel and chorus it.

FATHER LEO

May the Almighty Father look with compassion upon his servant, Fon Joseph, and give him the strength to stand up against Lucifer and his evil gang!

FON

Amen!

FATHER LEO

Let us rise. I am now going back to the mission. I am having lunch with some two men who arrived last night.

FON

They are just visiting or what?

FATHER LEO

I don't know exactly. They arrived at about seven last night and set out very early this morning for the lake. I sent my steward-boy to show them the way. They say they are returning to the capital immediately after lunch.

FON

What could they be looking for in the lake?

FATHER LEO

I will find out during lunch. But you know we, Europeans, are always hungry for knowledge and more knowledge.

FON

Are they from Europe?

FATHER LEO

Yes. Europe and America. There is more progress coming to this village if they find what they want.

FON

I would have liked to have them for tea this evening. But then you say they are leaving this afternoon?

FATHER LEO

Yes. I talked to them about you. Apparently, they have heard about your progressive rule and respect for the civilized world.

FON

Well, Father, let me not detain you too much. Please, give them my best wishes. And God bless you.

Father Leo exits. The Fon sits in his throne and is soon attracted by singing in the distance. As the sound becomes more and more audible, he recognises the song of the Fibuen, the women's secret cult, which has not been heard in the village ever since his enthronement.

FON

What could be the meaning of this? The Fibuen in the kingdom of an enlightened Christian monarch? There must be...

Doggo rushes in almost out of breath and prostrates before the Fon.

DOGGO

They are coming, Mbe! They are coming!

Kinchin also crashes in and in the manner of Doggo.

KINCHIN

Mbe! The women! A whole crowd of them!

FON

Rise at once! Have you never seen a crowd of women? How many times have I told you that such honour is given to God, and to God alone? The first commandment of God- 'Thou shalt have and honour none other than the Lord God who is Almighty'. Now, tell me what that eerie chanting is all about.

The guards look at each other, then at the Fon, and at each other again as the chanting gets louder.

FON

Well! Have your tongues suddenly been plucked out by the devil? Speak!

DOGGO
What my eyes have seen, my mouth cannot speak, Mbe!

FON
I say, speak!

KINCHIN
Mbe! I... I... am lost for words.

FON
Will you speak, you good for nothing slaves!

GUARDS
The women are carrying a body, Mbe!

FON
Body? What body? Whose body?

GUARDS
Don't know, Mbe!

DOGGO
They will desecrate the palace, Mbe! The Fon does not see a corpse and live.

FON
What? Bar the entrance at once! Stop them!

Fon exits. As the leading women appear on stage, the guards advance in a most threatening manner.

GUARDS
Stop! Stop! What do you want?

CHORUS
The Fon! We want the Fon! We will speak with our Fon!

DOGGO
You will speak with your Fon?

CHORUS
Yes!

KINCHIN
You mean, you want to desecrate the palace!

CHORUS
The gods forbid! The ancestors be our witnesses, no!

GUARDS
The body!

DOGGO
What about the body?

The women laugh heartily.

FIRST WOMAN
You mean Dewa?

SECOND WOMAN
He is not dead. He is alive.

KINCHIN
God forbid! It is Dewa? Bring him forward, quickly.

The women move forward.

DOGGO
Not everybody! This place is not large enough for all of you.

Four women advance bearing a bamboo stretcher on which there is a man with hands and legs bound.

KINCHIN
It is really Dewa! God forbid! God forbid!

DOGGO
I must inform the Fon at once. *Exits.*

KINCHIN
You women will bring trouble. What is Dewa's crime?

FIRST WOMAN
You know Dewa's crime. There is not a single person in this land who doesn't know what crimes people like Dewa commit.

DOGGO
The Fon will receive you, but not everybody. He commands that you elect a maximum of five leaders and he will listen to your grievances.

CHORUS
Yes! We have our leaders! Where is Nkasai? Nkfusai? Kimbong? Kimaa? Yensi?

DOGGO
That's enough! That makes five. Where are they? Yes, advance. Come forward.

The five women lean forward, their hands on their knees in deference to the throne. Doggo exits and returns almost immediately.

DOGGO

His Royal Highness, the Fon!

The women prostrate and ululate as the Fon enters.

FON

Enough! Get up! On your feet, I say!

Confused by the terrifying voice of the Fon, the women finally fall back on the original posture, their hands on their knees.

FON

How many times must I tell you that this is a Christian kingdom? How often must I drive it into your heads that the heathen era of idol worship is history? How many times must I decree that the age of savagery and jungle law is over and done with in this land? How many? How many? How many? *to guards* Release that man at once! Undo those shackles of my disgrace right now.

Guards release Dewa who gets up uncomfortably and looks at the women with a mixture of fear and contempt.

FON

What is his crime?

He looks at the women one after the other but none of them responds.

FON

What names were you given at birth?

NKASAI

Nkasai.

NKFUSAI

Nkfusai.

KIMBONG

Kimbong.

KIMAA

Kimaa

YENSI

Yensi. They call me Yensi.

FON

Yensi, tell me, what crime did this man commit that you bound him hand and foot?

YENSI

This is not the first time that the women have brought Dewa and other cattle rearers before the Fon.

CHORUS

It is not!

FON

But, why Dewa today?

NKFUSAI

All the women who have farms in Ngangba will starve this year. Dewa's cattle have ruined all the corn. The Fon knows that harvest is very near.

KIMBONG

And when we went to his *kiban* to demand an explanation, he laughed in our face and told us to take him to the highest court in the land.

KIMAA

He called the Fon by name!

CHORUS

Ai-ye-ye-ye-ye!

NKASAI
And said the cattle were not his but those of the Fon.

CHORUS
Ai-ye-ye-ye-ye! Fishang!

YENSI
And asked if we had seen his people buying food from kombi ever since the Fon started selling land to them.

CHORUS
Ai-ye-ye-ye-ye! Fishang! No!

KIMBONG
He challenged our men to make fences around our farms or the cattle rearers take no responsibility for their laziness and poverty.

NKFUSAI
And when we said he would be hearing from Kwifon, he spat in our face and said the Fon had... the Kwifon.

CHORUS
Ai-ye-ye-ye-ye! Fishang! Fishang!

KIMAA
So we put our heads together and said, 'If Dewa says the Fon has... the Kwifon, the Fibuen which has been asleep all these years must come to our rescue.'

The horn of the Fibuen is heard and the women ululate.

CHORUS
Here we are before the lion, king of the land. Here we are before the lion.

YENSI
Whose thirst must be assuaged first!

CHORUS
Here we are before the lion!

KIMAA
Whose hunger must be satisfied!

CHORUS
Here we are before the leopard!

NKFUSAI
Who pounces on his own kind just to prove he is a leopard!

CHORUS
Here we are before the elephant!

KIMBONG
That will trample on the shrubs in the forest while pretending to pull down the baobab!

CHORUS
Here we...

FON
Enough! Are you accusing me? Your Fon? Did you expect me, a Christian Fon, to sit back and watch a handful of senile fanatics perpetuating the barbaric and heathen custom of human sacrifice?

CHORUS
Ai-ye-ye-ye-ye! Fishang! No!

FON
(to Dewa) You bin talk all da foolish talk?

DEWA
Kai! me no talkam no noting, Mbe. Allah! Me no talkam no noting.

FON
Na weti happen?

DEWA
Cow dong go drinki water fo Ngangba sai wey na kontri fo Bororo.

FON
Fo sika sey me tell you fo go shiddon dere da wan mean sey na wuna kontri?

DEWA
No bi na gomna don talk sey na place fo cow?

FON
Which gomna, you bloody fool? You look the palaver wey you don bringam fo my head?

DEWA
Allah! Me no bringam no trobou fo Mbe.

FON
You go pay all da chop wey you cow don choppam.

DEWA
No bi na ma nyun, Mbe! Na you nyun don choppam corn.

FON
Shurrup you mup, bloody fool! *(to guards)* If he opens his mouth again...!

CHORUS

The lion is great! The lion is king!

FON

You go pay all da chop.

DEWA

If na so Mbe don talkam.

FON

(to women) How much compensation do you want for the crops?

CHORUS

Nothing.

FON

What do you mean? Nothing? You don't want money for your crops?

CHORUS

No!

FON

Why not?

CHORUS

The Queen will explain.

FON

Oh! You have already talked to Angela?

CHORUS

She is not Queen! Harvest is near. The Fon will lead the people in sacrifice to the Lake God and consummate our love and kinship by sharing the royal bed with the Queen. And we shall have more children and a good harvest.

FON

Enough! I have told you, I am a Christian king. The Church of Christ forbids the taking of a second woman. And I forbid the offering of sacrifices to heathen gods.

YENSI

The Church of Christ does not forbid the selling of land to nomads. But then, who are women in the land?

FON

Woman! Are you accusing me, your Fon?

YENSI

All that we demand is for Dewa and his kind to leave this land. We have borne the suffering long enough.

CHORUS

Yeah!

FON

But that is impossible. Where would they go?

KIMBONG

Where did they come from?

FON

But they are people of this country. Some of your men own cattle. Will they too go?

YENSI

If they must stay, their cattle will go!

CHORUS

Yeah!

FON

You mean I... No. I cannot do that. The law forbids; and progress here is tied with cattle.

YENSI

Is that the answer we shall carry to the women?

FON

Yes, I am afraid. What they demand is not done. I have asked Dewa to pay you people compensation of two thousand francs each. How many women have farms there?

YENSI

Ten.

FON

Good. That makes twenty thousand francs. I have spoken. He is ready to pay you now. *(to Dewa)* No bi you gettam twenty tosand fo dere?

DEWA

Yes, Mbe. Me gettam. Allah de! Me tink sey me go sellam leke five cow befo me pay da chop. Allah de!

FON

You go muf two cow fo you nyun puttam for me nyun. Woman cow wey get leke three year so dat small tam dem get belle. You don hear fine, fine?

DEWA

Me don hear, Mbe. Kai, wusai Allah don go?

FON

(to women) What do you say?

NKASAI
The cattle and their owners must go!

The horn of the Fibuen is heard and the women ululate and take up the song. Exeunt.

FON
Give me de money. I go lef back pay dem. (*Dewa hands over the money*). You fit go now. Pass fo dis sai. (*to one of the guards*) You go with him as far as the stream. (*to other guard*) And you make sure no one gets in here, you understand?

KINCHIN
Even Father Leo?

FON
Except Father Leo, idiot!

Blackout.

Shey Bo-Nyo's retreat in the grove by the lake. The only significant prop is a sacrificial pot placed prominently and decorated with **nkeng***, shrub of the gods. There is also a bamboo stool. When action begins, Shey Bo-Nyo is lying flat on his back on an old mat which is also his bed. He gets up with some difficulty and walks slowly and with difficulty across to the pot. He dips his hand into it and brings out horns of various sizes which apparently contain some medication. By a process of taking each one to his nose he finally picks one. He then returns to the mat and proceeds to massage his body with its contents.*

SHEY BO-NYO
That is better! Good! Really good!
I wonder why I didn't think of this earlier.
Concoction of the gods... instant relief!
I must really be growing old. Or losing my head
Because of what I see coming to this land.
Those scoundrels could have killed me.

Thugs and sons of unknown fathers!
And the Fon sat there watching them, unperturbed.
This land has really gone to the dogs.
I wonder why I even bother myself
And get brutalized by brutes, like today.
Faith! Hope! Faith and hope.
Faith in our gods and hope that the Fon
Might yet be held by the hand and led back
Unto the right road.
He is only a child, after all.
Over-enthusiastic about the magic of the
White man's cleverness and the things
Father Leo has brought to the land.
Father Leo! *mock laughter*
I remember how he used to sneak in and out
Of the land in the days of the late Fon
Trying to convert the women and children
To his god. He did succeed though!
That is why we have a Fon
Who fails the tradition of the gods!
Father Leo was a young man, fresh from
The white man's country. He was so shy.
As shy as...

VOICE

(off) Is Shey there?

SHEY BO-NYO

Yes. Come inside. My house is your house.
Shey Tanto enters. He is about the same age as the diviner but he looks stronger.

TANTO

So my guess was right!

SHEY BO-NYO

Did you pass through my homestead? Sit down. I am quite comfortable here on the mat.

TANTO

No. With all the troubles in the land, I knew you would be here.

SHEY BO-NYO

I only just came. I tried to see the Fon and his thugs nearly killed me. Don't you see this horn? I have been massaging myself.

TANTO

What happened?

SHEY BO-NYO

They beat me up severely. The Fon called me mad and asked them to take me out. He did not want to listen to me.

TANTO

Was the Fibuen there at the time?

SHEY BO-NYO

No. I heard the Fibuen as I was struggling up the slope on my way here. I was aching from pain and licking my body like a dog.

TANTO

The things that are happening in this land are pregnant.

SHEY BO-NYO

Let me be. Was it really the Fibuen? Sometimes I think my mind is full of hallucinations. That is probably why they call me mad.

TANTO

When I first heard it, I thought it was my mind playing old tricks. Then the noise and the singing disappeared towards Ngangba; and I said to myself, where could the Fibuen be going to in that direction?

SHEY BO-NYO

But I heard it in the direction of the palace!

TANTO

Let me finish. Sometime afterwards, when the sun was high in the sky, I heard the noise and singing returning to the homesteads from Ngangba. I called for my first wife to find out if it was really the Fibuen. One of the children said she had gone to Ngangba with all the other women. It was only then it dawned on me that I had not seen any of them since sunrise.

SHEY BO-NYO

Why did they go to Ngangba?

TANTO

That is the real story. You know Dewa?

SHEY BO-NYO

The Fulani man?

TANTO

The Fulani man whose cattle have been destroying crops in the land. This time the women tied him with ropes on bamboos and carried him to the palace.

SHEY BO-NYO

The gods are still alive! Is that what happened?

TANTO

But the Fon released the man after the women refused to take two thousand francs as compensation.

SHEY BO-NYO

Two thousand francs? That man must be mad. Where is he now?

TANTO

Who? The Fon?

SHEY TANTO
Dewa, of course.

TANTO
He went back to his *kiban*.

SHEY BO-NYO
And the women, what did they do?

TANTO
Nothing. But I hear they say Dewa and all cattle owners must leave the land. Do you know that half of Dewa's cattle belong to the Fon?

SHEY BO-NYO
But that is how he came to the throne; bribing king-makers with money and meat. You did not know?

TANTO
No! And the women now know. I hear they told him a number of things.

SHEY BO-NYO
That man is either going to destroy himself or the whole land. Why is he so unlike his late father?

TANTO
It is this Christian thing brought by Father Leo.

SHEY BO-NYO
It may surprise you that I laugh. But just before you came I was saying to myself how in the days of the late Fon this Father Leo was as shy as a dog that had stolen its master's food. You know, its tail between the hind legs and ears drooping. A real *ngong*. Today, Father leo strolls into the palace and goes right into the Fon's inner chamber!

TANTO

What is to be done? Are we going to allow the women to take over in this land? After eight years of silence the Fibuen was heard today.

SHEY BO-NYO

You people say the Kwifon is in detention. So what can be done?

TANTO

But is that not true? Has the Fon apologized or even attempted reconciliation with Kwifon? What Kwifon did was for the good of the land. And the lake god returned with fertilizing waters. Did we not have a good harvest that year?

SHEY BO-NYO

But the Fon said human sacrifice was barbaric and heathen. He did not realise that it was an emergency solution because of his own negligence of the annual lake sacrifice. He called the police and they took Kwifon into detention. The land has really gone to the dogs.

TANTO

Look, Shey, why don't you cast your cowries? In the light of what has happened today.

SHEY BO-NYO

You mean the action by the women?

TANTO

Yes. Let us see what the future holds.

SHEY BO-NYO

(getting up to fetch the cowries from the pot) Where is kola? My cowries don't speak with an empty mouth. You know that.

TANTO

If I lack anything, it cannot be kola. Here, take!

Shey Bo-Nyo breaks the kola and adds one lobe to his seven cowries which he proceeds to throw on the floor several times after sharing the rest of the kola with Tanto. After a series of throws, he shakes his head sadly.

TANTO
What... what is the matter?

SHEY BO-NYO
Worse things are yet to come. Did you notice that all the cowries have been falling on their bellies?

TANTO
Yes! I noticed that.

SHEY BO-NYO
How many times did I throw?

TANTO
I don't know. Four... five times?

SHEY BO-NYO
Yes. Five times. With the same results. If the Fon does not offer the sacrifice to the lake god as his fathers before him always did, we can get ready for the worst.

TANTO
The Kwifon must do something. Even at the risk of being arrested again. We cannot allow an irresponsible man to destroy the land.

SHEY BO-NYO
How will the Kwifon act? The Fon is unrepentant over the detention of Kwifon.

TANTO
This is an emergency, and there are still men in the land. Kwifon will forget the crimes of the Fon in order to save the land. I will get

the seven pillars of Kwifon and they will put their heads together. They will meet here since they can no longer gain access to their sanctuary in the palace.

SHEY BO-NYO

This place is still sacred even though the boys always come to disturb the rats, cattle of the gods. The grove belongs to the land.

TANTO

You will be hearing from me any time.
Exits.

SHEY BO-NYO

There are still men in the land. It might still be saved.

Blackout.

A moonlit night. There is a crowd of women in the village square. After the abortive encounter with the Fon, and because of the fever of the Fibuen, they display a spirit of defiance that would shock their men folk. Something like mob action in which the women have no inhibitions. When action begins, there is the sound of the now familiar horn of Fibuen followed by an exhilarating ululation. Then the women perform dance steps to such lyrical songs as 'Kwessim kwe bo lang e Banya'. When they have worked themselves to fever pitch the horn sounds again and, again, they ululate.

YENSI

(performing the Kinsheng) E-chong E-chong E-chong E-chong o o o!

CHORUS

Ho ya ho ya ho ya!

YENSI

I lack the words with which to express my joy. The happiness that is in my heart cannot be shown on my face. The happenings of today have shown that in spite of what some people say, the ways of the land are alive. We must be one person to succeed in our present undertaking. We must be one woman. Some here have only recently been given into marriage. Their bellies are hot. There are others who cannot control their emotions of love and sympathy. There are still others who will easily succumb to threats and the fear of being beaten. You all know where we have built the sanctuary of the Fibuen. We have taken it away from that place which I don't want to call by name. The sanctuary is the refuge for those without a heart. Go there if you cannot look your man in the face and tell him to go and eat shit.

CHORUS

(laughter) He he he! Haaa! Wus!

NKASAI

Listen, Yensi, this thing is not as easy as you want to make it look. There are women here who, as soon as we disperse, will start disclosing everything as if their mouths are leaking.

KIMBONG

You speak the truth, Nkasai. Where is Ma Kusham? We must all take the oath of sealed lips.

YENSI

Ma Kusham? Ma Kusham? I beg you to come forward and conduct the rite.

An old woman carrying a clay pot in both hands moves forward and places the pot on the floor.

MA KUSHAM

Are such things still performed in the land of Christians? These are pagan things. Things of Satan.

YENSI

Ma, don't Christians have crops that are destroyed by the cattle? When the harvest is poor do the Christians not starve with the rest? When there is drought in the land, does the rain fall on the farms of Christians? Hunger has no friends and no enemies. Go ahead with business.

MA KUSHAM

Thank you, my daughter. These are things of the land. Things of our gods and our ancestors which the white man has fooled us to abandon. Things of the white man have brought suffering to the land.

She dips her hand into the pot and takes out broom-sticks of equal length which she proceeds to distribute to all the women.

MA KUSHAM

These broom-sticks have been cooked in the most potent medicines and herbs in the land. However, the most important ingredient as far as our oath is concerned comes from the sacred pot of the lake god which Shey Bo-Nyo guards jealously. The link is simple. There is no Queen in the palace and the Fon has refused to lead the people in sacrifice to the god of fertility. Now, listen. Hold the stick in your right hand between thumb and finger like this. Cross your lips vertically with the stick like this. Break it in the middle and throw both ends behind you while repeating the following: If my mouth discloses what my ears have heard in this gathering, may my tongue swell and fill up my mouth with dumbness.

The rite is performed in strict silence after which Ma Kusham sprinkles the women with the liquid from the pot.

YENSI

We are now going to disperse and go back to our homes. And if your man should ask you what is going on, ask him if women ever know what is happening in this land of men. May our enterprise succeed. E-chong e-chong e-chong e-chong oo!

CHORUS

Hoo ya ho ya ho ya!

Blackout.

DEAD - END

Mime sequence to the sometimes slow, sometimes brisk rhythm of the Njang. A man complains of hunger to his wife. For three days, she has not given him food. Does she want him to die? Does she want to kill him? The woman replies that he should continue to sit around with other men, drinking palm-wine, while she is fighting with cattle rearers and their cattle in the farm. The cattle have destroyed all the crops and there is no way she can place a bowl of foo-foo in front of him. After begging, coaxing and threatening, the man decides to beat up the woman. But she escapes while he pursues her.

As they exit, another woman comes in and sits. Her husband shows his face and beckons at her. He wants them to go to bed. It is bed time. She ignores him. He repeats the movements while advancing towards the woman. She turns her back on him indicating that she is sick and so cannot share the same bed with him. After coaxing and threatening to no avail he exits, a defeated man. The woman jumps up, does a victory dance, and exits.

Another woman appears. She is pursued by a man who is also being pursued by three other women, his wives. The man discovers with shock that the four women will attack him if he tries to beat up any one of them. After failing to browbeat the women into submission, he tries to win them over one by one, in an attempt to reinstitute their old division and rivalry for his love. But they all reject him. In desperation, he exits and soon returns with a matchet, spear and calabash. He is going to his palm bush to tap wine. The women do a vigorous dance in celebration of the victory over the husband they share. Exeunt.

Afternoon. A clearing in Lagham's raffia bush where he usually entertains those who choose to visit him in the palm bush. Four men are drinking palm-wine and telling jokes. The calabash is almost empty now.

LAGHAM

(lifting the calabash) Where is my mother! How can three people finish a whole calabash of wine? Has palm-wine become food?

FISIY

You tappers are really unpredictable. What was your reason for placing a calabash before us if you didn't want us to drink? Even if you brought out two like this one, we would still be thirsty. You forget that Forgwei is here?

LAGHAM

I wanted you to drink; but not to empty a whole calabash. The way people like Forgwei drink, I wonder if your stomachs ever have room for your women's foo-foo.

FORGWEI

If I tell you that I have not eaten for four days now will you believe? That is the truth. I know it is a shameful thing to admit; but it is four days since I last ate foo-foo.

The others are stunned by what Forgwei has said, each of them having had the same experience.

FORGWEI

Don't look at me like that. I didn't ask anyone to pity me.

MAIMO

It is not a question of pitying you, Forgwei. It just happens that my own wife has not given me food in the last four days.

FISIY

My case is a lot more serious, then. Since the day cattle destroyed farms in Ngangba, Yensi has not placed a dish of foo-foo in front of me.

LAGHAM

There is something going on in this land that will deliver an indescribable monster.

FORGWEI

You too, Lagham? You mean the women have decided to starve us, their men?

LAGHAM

How can a man use his wealth to buy trouble for himself? This morning I called Mom, that mother rat whom I recently bought with my money, and asked her to make sure my dish of foo-foo was ready when I return from the bush. You know what she told me? (*mimicking female voice*) There is no time. I am going to Ngangba to make sure cattle don't destroy the rest of the crops. What effrontery! I was going to whip her thoroughly. But you know what happened? The other women, all my wives, three of them, bought with my wealth... They came and stood between us and said in loud voices that Mom was right.

MAIMO

You didn't beat all of them?

FISIY

There is something definitely wrong in the land.

LAGHAM

You know me. I am used to punishing any of my wives when they disobey me. But what I saw today...

FORGWEI

I said before that the women are determined to starve their husbands.

FISIY

Ever since the day the Fibuen was heard again in this land after so long a time, I knew there was trouble coming.

MAIMO
You mean the day they tied up Dewa with ropes and carried him to the palace?

LAGHAM
Yes. The day the Fon asked them to accept two thousand francs for all the crops in Ngangba.

FORGWEI
Was it two thousand or twenty? I heard that the Fon asked Dewa to pay twenty and the women turned their back.

FISIY
Does it really matter how much money it was? The women did not want money at all.

MAIMO
Then why did they tie Dewa with ropes? Why did they carry him to the Fon?

LAGHAM
They want all the cattle out of the land. They also seem to know that part of Dewa's herd belongs to the Fon.

FISIY
And the Fon does not want the cattle to leave because that is the source of his wealth.

LAGHAM
Exactly. The Fon says the cattle cannot leave.

FORGWEI
Where do we come in? What is our own crime that we starve?

MAIMO

Can't you see? The women want to get justice by starving us. Unable to withstand hunger, we will put pressure on the Fon.

LAGHAM

If it were only hunger of the stomach, a man can browse here and there like cattle. For almost a week now, I have lived on palm-wine and roasted cocoyams or plantains. That is not food, but it is something. But it looks like they are also making use of the other weapon, hunger of the loins.

FORGWEI

No! That is not possible. Just not possible! I will kill someone.

FISIY

Lagham, sometimes you can really imagine abominations.

LAGHAM

Fisiy, why don't you consider what I have said? Has any of you called his wife to your bed in the last week? Ever since the Fibuen was heard?

FORGWEI

My first wife is nursing a baby. The other has the periodic sickness.

LAGHAM

For one week?

FORGWEI

I called her about three nights ago and she complained of periodic sickness. Since then I have returned home too drunk to bother about sleeping with a woman on the same bed. What can a man even do with a woman when there is hunger in the stomach?

MAIMO

Lagham might have a point. This last night, I was gripped by desire. My friend kept nodding and nodding like a lizard. So I called my son, Chinfon, and asked him to call his mother. You know what message she sent back? She said if I had anything to tell her, I should come over to her house because she was too tired from chasing cattle out of the farm.

FISIY

Did you go?

MAIMO

Could I even walk without betraying myself?

FORGWEI

So, what did you do?

MAIMO

I went to bed with all my troubles. When she sends back that kind of message, there is nothing to do.

FORGWEI

She may just have been tired.

LAGHAM

No, my friend. Haven't you noticed that the idea of cattle destroying crops is always mentioned? When your wife complained of periodic sickness the other night, did she not say something else?

FORGWEI

Let me see. I think she mumbled something about Ngangba. Since she had already mentioned her periodic sickness, I did not pay any attention.

LAGHAM

You see? It is a well-orchestrated plot. When you ask them what they have been discussing in the Fibuen, do they say anything? There are even rumours that Ma Kusham administered the oath of sealed lips.

FORGWEI

You mean the women could really go that far?

LAGHAM

Were you not here when I told the story about what happened to me this morning? I forget that when you start drinking wine, your ears develop wax.

FORGWEI

Was that story as serious as women swearing oaths? You and I have allowed our wives too much freedom.

MAIMO

No, Forgwei. It is not a simple question of being stubborn or obstinate. Two days ago, I asked Kimbong about food. All day long, I had not eaten anything. She said there was no soup. The following morning, I went to inspect my traps at Kingongoo. Luckily I found a small hare in one of them. So I went home happily, looking forward to a good meal that evening. When the moment arrived, Chinfon brought a calabash of water and a dish full of meat. I washed my hands quickly, expecting the bowl of foo-foo to arrive any moment. Nothing came. I tasted the soup for salt and pepper. It was a really delicious sauce and I felt as if there were a thousand famished dogs in my stomach. I called out angrily for Chinfon and asked him where the foo-foo was. Do you know what I heard? Laughter! A lot of it. And my wife was laughing loudest. I waited a little while and still there was no foo-foo. So I went over to find out what was going on. 'Where is the foo-foo?' I asked. Kimbong laughed again and said cattle had destroyed everything. Before I knew what I was doing, I had given her a sound slap in the face. The house went dead. Then I realised what I had done. Never beat your wife in front of the children. That is what I have always told myself. But hunger betrayed me. My wife wiped the tears from her face, looked straight into mine and said in a cold voice that if I really wanted to eat foo-foo, I should go to Ngangba and make the cattle leave the land instead of beating up a defenceless woman who has been fighting all her life to feed her husband and the children. After that I could not even eat the delicious hare. I thought I could make up for our dispute last night, but I have already told you what her answer was.

FISIY

That is a heavy story. It shows that the women are determined.

FORGWEI

What is to be done?

LAGHAM

Good question. What can we do to expel the cattle people and their cattle; especially as our Fon and our own people are also cattle owners? It is clear that until the cattle leave the land, no adult male is going to eat properly or sleep with a woman.

FORGWEI

Who gave such powers to the women?

MAIMO

You mean, who gave us such a greedy and reckless Fon?

FISIY

We cannot really blame the women. The Fon is the one who is breaking the laws and destroying the land in the name of this new religion brought by Father Leo.

FORGWEI

But Father Leo has done a lot of good for us. The school for our children, the health centre where we all go in time of sickness, a good water supply and a motor road. Without Father Leo, our women and children might still be going about naked. Today, we have a Fon who can speak and gomna will listen. Would this have been possible without Father Leo?

LAGHAM

I do not question the wonderful things Father Leo has brought to this land. But I blame the Fon for allowing himself to be misled by Father Leo. Was it not the late Fon who allowed Father Leo to start the school? But he continued to rule the land in the way that it had always been ruled. He continued to lead the people in the yearly sacrifice to the lake god. He always listened to Kwifon and never allowed the cattle rearers to settle in the land. Is there Kwifon in this land today? The Fon has reported Kwifon to gomna and Kwifon is in detention.

FORGWEI

We agree that the Fon is to blame for what is happening in the land. Being the illiterate that I am, I could not submit myself to the power of Father Leo the way our Fon has. But my question still stands. What is to be done?

MAIMO

Do you want us to lead a delegation to the Fon?

FISIY

Have you not heard how Shey Bo-Nyo was almost beaten to death the other day?

LAGHAM

Where is my mother! So, you think those castrated slaves can touch any of us? Let them dare! There are still men in this land, you know?

FORGWEI
Are we going to see the Fon, then?

FISIY
Maimo, what do you think?

MAIMO
That question should go to Lagham. He is the eldest among us.

FORGWEI
Well?

LAGHAM
Instead of going to see the Fon who might refuse to receive us, I suggest we go and talk with Shey Tanto. He is the most influential of the Kwifon. This is an emergency and the Kwifon must do something. I will be surprised if they are not already taking action.

MAIMO
Shall we go? I don't think I can stay another two days without eating foo-foo or feeling the warm smell of my wife.

FORGWEI
Let me empty my cup.

FISIY
Look at the man who was shouting about what should be done.

FORGWEI
What do you mean? I am ready. Let us go.

Exeunt.

Black out.

Morning in church. Doctrine class for women. When action begins Father Leo comes on stage and addresses his congregation of women- the spectators.

FATHER LEO

Let us pray, In the name... of the Father and of the Son and of the Holy Spirit. Amen.

He fixes his eyes on the spectators, choosing the women among them.

My dear sisters and daughters. Many of you in this church this morning are young enough to be my daughters; but the Lord God on high chose that I should be his unworthy servant.

Dear sisters and daughters in Christ, I want to talk to you this morning about the recent events of the last few days in this village. The Fon, your Fon, has told me that there is a group of five rebellious women in this village who are leading the rest of you astray. They are pulling you away from the steep and narrow road that leads to everlasting life and taking you along the big motor road that leads directly to hell, where Satan reigns supreme, and where you will burn in everlasting fire. Yensi, Kimaa and the other devils; yes, they must be called by the name they deserve. Yensi, Kimaa and the other devils are taking you on a fast and easy ride on the big motor road to Lucifer's kingdom. *(pointing out women in the audience)* You were in the Fibuen, not so? And you too. And even you, sister Maria. You are not ashamed that you went to soil the Virgin Mother's name in Satan's play? You all were in the Fibuen, participating in Satan's play and eating of his food and swearing oaths. All for what, my children? Mere corn? Common corn? Have you forgotten so soon what the Lord Jesus said? 'Therefore, I tell you, do not worry about life, what you will eat or drink; or about your body, what you will wear. Look at the birds of the air; they do not sow or reap or store away in barns, and yet your heavenly Father feeds them. Are you not much more valuable than they?'

Have you forgotten so soon the words of the Holy Scriptures? ' Man does not live on bread alone, but on every word that comes from the mouth of God.' Have you forgotten that Christ spoke these words to Satan himself in the wilderness when he was facing temptation? Get thee behind me, Satan! Satan is taking advantage of your weak bodies to install his kingdom in this God-fearing village. Have you stopped to count the blessings which the Lord has showered on you of this village? Have you stopped to ask yourselves how we have been able to perform these wonders? Of course not. But let me tell you now that when I receive a little money from my country, I give it to your Fon who invests it in the purchase of cattle. That is how we have been able to move mountains. If the cattle leave, we will not be able to continue to give you the services which you now have. A school for your children, a health centre for the young and old, sparkling pipe-borne water and a big motor road. Above all, God has blessed this village with an educated Christian Fon who is held in high esteem by the government of this country. And instead of offering prayers of thanks to God, you will starve the very Fon to death by refusing to sell food to Angela, his wife, and the headmistress of your school? If she also refused to teach what will become of your children? You don't want your children to be as great as your Fon? Or even greater? Are you women not ashamed that the wife of your beloved Fon should go to a Fulani man to get food with which to feed your great leader?

Get thee behind me, Satan! You even refuse to feed your own husbands. Remember what the Holy Book says, 'For this reason a man will leave his father and mother and be united to his wife, and they will become one in flesh.' How can you be one in flesh when you refuse your husbands food? How can you be one in flesh when you refuse to sleep with your husbands? You Christian women have a duty to obey your husbands and to satisfy the hunger in their stomachs and in their lower parts. The polygamous pagans have no right to such privileges, however. They are being punished for their greed and lust.

Get thee behind me, Satan! My dear sisters and daughters, when you leave this church now, I enjoin you to go home and obey your husbands or suffer the pangs of everlasting fire.

May the Holy Spirit descend upon you and remain with you for ever and ever. In the name... of the Father and of the Son and of the Holy Spirit. Amen.

Blackout.

Late afternoon. Well-furnished and comfortable living room of the Fon where only the most intimate guests like Father Leo are received. While Angela is making tea, the Fon is reading the Bible. She laughs mockingly which catches the Fon's attention.

FON
What's going on, Angela?

ANGELA
Nothing, Mbe.

FON
Now, that smacks of mischief. You know you may only address me that way in public.

ANGELA
Are you not Fon here? Why, then, should I only acknowledge the fact in public?

FON
I see you're gearing up for a quarrel.

ANGELA
Quarrel? Who is Angela to cross words with His Highness the Fon?

FON
I am reading.

ANGELA
His Highness Fon Joseph. Na wa oh! Paramount Fon Joseph. Lion, King of the land. His Highness the Fon. Leopard and Elephant!

FON
Are you provoking me?

ANGELA
The Paramount Fon Joseph. Standard Bearer of Christendom and Defender of the Faith. Na wa oh!

FON
You really want to quarrel, not so?

ANGELA
Are these not the numerous titles Father Leo and your subjects have given you? And yet the divine ruler is powerless before a pack of illiterate, native women who insult his wife in public. 'She is not queen!' they croaked in their toady voices. And what did the lion of the land do, if I may ask?

FON
What did you expect me to do? Those women could have burnt down the whole palace.

ANGELA
Which is more powerful? That gang of murderers which you disbanded, or a handful of naked village women who cannot even step into my kitchen?

FON
Angie, calm yourself. Have you forgotten Christ's teaching about humility? Have you forgotten that being my wife, you must also bear the cross that I am carrying on my shoulders?

ANGELA
But they said I am not queen! They want you to marry one of their kind and make heirs to the throne. I have told you to go ahead and marry as many as you want. When my parents told me, ' Don't marry a graffi man, especially the son of a chief ' I refused to listen.

FON

Angie, na weti don happen?

ANGELA

I know you want children. I know you want to marry another woman, their queen. And which graffi man ever had only one wife? But for Father Leo, you would have married their queen long ago.

FON

That's not true, Angie! If no graffi man ever had only one wife, then I am the first and history will bear me witness. When I was enthroned eight years ago there were more than twelve queens in the palace; brides who had been brought to my late father, the Fon, when they were still mere babies. I used to think they were my step-sisters until they began to complain in loud voices that a non-queen was monopolising the royal bed. What did I do, Angela? Didn't I send them packing to their families or wherever they came from? As for the other women, I consider them all as my mothers, although custom decrees that the widows must also be inherited. The whole village rose up in rebellion, declaring that such a thing could never happen in the land. I stood firm, with you by my side. Didn't we win? I am a Christian king. I do not want a second wife even if in the eyes of the ignorant you are not queen. We will have children by God's grace.

ANGELA

I have given up hope. Do you realise it is already ten years? Ten years since we got married.

FON

Angie, so long as there is life, there is hope. I have faith and I keep asking. I keep knocking at the door. I keep seeking. How long did Abraham and Sarah wait? By God's grace we will have children. Can you imagine the progress this village has made ever since I became Fon? Before then, there was only a village school which did not even have a good enrolment. How many pupils do you have in the school now?

ANGELA

Let me see... three hundred and ninety-two.

FON

You see? Almost four hundred children. I am not going to be like my late father, marrying a queen because of their heathen sacrifice.

ANGELA

Your people do not want an enlightened ruler. In fact, they do not want you at all. Otherwise, how can you explain the present troubles? They even refuse to sell me food, knowing very well that I am their Fon's wife and the teacher of their children.

There is a knock at the door and Father Leo enters.

FATHER LEO

God bless this house.

ANGELA

Oh! Good evening, Father.

FON

Welcome, Father. Angie was just about to serve tea.

FATHER LEO

Is that so? You know I love tea and honey.

ANGELA

Sit down, Father. I will get you a cup.

FATHER LEO

Did the Fon have a busy day? With all the troubles in the village?

FON
We were talking about them just before you came in. Angie was asking what I was going to do about the revolt of the women.

FATHER LEO
I wouldn't call it revolt. Just some uncoordinated action by a handful of undisciplined village women. I talked to the Christian women this morning in their doctrine class. It's all over. They promised not to disobey their husbands any more.

He looks patronisingly at the Fon.

FON
Father, sometimes I ask myself whether without you I would still be on this throne.

FATHER LEO
Uneasy lies the head...

ANGELA
...that wears the crown.

FATHER LEO
You have heard that adage a thousand times, Fon. True leaders are forged by problems; not by an easy and luxurious life in office. The young countries of this continent need young men of mettle like you. They need people of great courage and insight who can take unpopular but right decisions for the general good. Your benevolent rule and the progress you have brought to this village is a shining example to be emulated by any leader worthy of the name.

ANGELA
Oh! What flattering words, Father!

FON
But Father, I owe everything to you. You brought me up.

FATHER LEO

Your late father was a hard-core traditionalist. At first, he wouldn't let me start the school. It was not until he went to the Divisional Office and saw another Fon riding his own car that he agreed to give me one of his own sons to bring up in the way of the Church. That was you. From the very first day, I saw courage and determination. I saw a true leader so long as he was given the right training. The rest of the story: primary school, secondary school, Grade II, Grade I, and here you are; almost the best educated Fon in the whole region. I hear the other one is a member of parliament. You will get to parliament too. You are already climbing the ladder to parliament after all. Branch president of the party here and vice-president at the section level. We are on our way to parliament!

FON

But the women want to spoil my chances, Father. If the cattle rearers are forced to leave, my chances will be lost. development in the village will stop and government might even revoke my first class chieftaincy.

FATHER LEO

There is absolutely nothing these village women can do. If we could succeed in neutralising the Kwifon, that terrible secret cult, what more of a handful of ignorant village women? I warned them that without cattle, there would be no development.

FON

That is exactly my fear. These ignorant village women are using strange weapons which no one has ever heard about.

ANGELA

And they don't want me, Father. They say I am not queen.

FATHER LEO

For every new disease there is a cure. Most of the women in the village are good Christians. They have seen the good things that the Church has brought. Even their men are more concerned about drinking palm-wine than eating foo-foo. They want their sons to have the kind of education their Fon has had. They see the happy change that education can bring into their lives. Many of them even own cattle; and are interested in making money and drinking beer which, before, they could never afford to buy. There is just no way the women can succeed. I talked to them this morning. They are terribly frightened by the thought of burning in hell fire.

FON

Father?

FATHER LEO

Yes?

FON

I ... don't know ... how to put this. But ... I have been having some terrible dreams. I have been seeing my late father... and he is always blaming me for the trouble in the village.

FATHER LEO

Are you superstitious?

FON

No. Not really. A good Christian shouldn't.

FATHER LEO

Good. Now let me tell you something. Your father never wanted you to become Fon. He thought I had too much influence over you. But the people wanted a progressive Fon. They wanted their village to catch-up with the forward march of progress. Are you feeling a little tired or sick?

FON

Yes. I feel a slight temperature in the evenings.

FATHER LEO
Malaria. Have you been to the health centre?

ANGELA
No, Father. He hasn't.

FATHER LEO
I will send Sister Frances to have a look at you in the morning. But I think I have some coquina at home. I will take one of the guards with me and send you whatever I can find. When you take the tablets, drink a cup of tea and go to bed. You should feel better by morning. I better get going. Good night.

FON
God bless you, Father.

ANGELA
Father, good night and God bless you.

Father Leo exits.

Blackout.

Early morning. The sacred grove by the lake. The seven most important members of Kwifon, known as the seven pillars, are present. They are dressed in the formal garbs of Kwifon: a hand-woven, tinted large cloth worn on a broad leather belt around the waist and almost overflowing to the ground. Their heads are adorned by colourful hand-woven cotton caps, or by the **nkeng**, *shrub of the gods. Each of them has in his right hand the staff of office, a tall bamboo pole painted black and white. There is also a masked figure who is carrying a calabash of palm-wine decorated with* **nkeng** *and a cock. The mood is serious and sombre.*

SHEY TANTO
Invoking the spirits of the land and pouring libation.
Hiiiii Wong! Hiiii Bo-Nyo! Hiiii Kwifon!
Here present are the seven pillars of Kwifon!
Here present are the seven corners of the land.
We cannot give food and drink to illustrious ancestors.
We cannot even gain access to the sanctuary of Kwifon.
Hiiii Wong! Hiiii Bo-Nyo! Hiiii Kwifon!
Here present are the seven pillars of Kwifon!
Here present are the seven corners of the land.
We cannot grease the sacred pot of the land.
It is now six years since we last saw the pot,
Because Kwifon has been exiled from the land.
Hiiii Wong! Hiiii Bo-Nyo! Hiiii Kwifon!
We are met in this sacred grove of the lake god
Because the land is no longer the land
You illustrious ancestors handed over to us.
Kwifon is in exile; and the women of this land
Are waging war against their men-folk
Because the Fon, our Fon, the Fon you gave us;
The Fon we thought you gave us, has sold the land.
The Fon has banished Kwifon and given the land
To strangers and rearers of cattle.
And now the women starve their men!
Hiiii Wong! Hiiii Bo-Nyo! Hiiii Kwifon!
Here is drink for you gods!
Here is drink for you ancestors!
Give us patience,
Give us peace of mind, Show us the right path
That we may bring peace again
To this land which you gave us.

CHORUS
Ya'a!
Tanto drinks from the horn which he now passes to the rest of the members.

MBWIN

Where is Shey Bo-Nyo?
Let him bring his cowries.

The masked figure exits and soon returns with Shey Bo-Nyo who is clutching his ngem and looking very nervous.

TANTO

Shey Bo-Nyo, cast your sacred cowries
And read the stars to the seven pillars.
Tell the seven corners of the land
What the gods have in store for us.

SHEY BO-NYO

No need to cast the cowries,
No use to read the stars.
The waters of the lake boil!

CHORUS

What?

SHEY BO-NYO

The waters of the lake boil!

MUNJEI

Since when this boiling?

BOLUNG

What meaning, this boiling?

SHEY BO-NYO

The god's anger boils over.
Today is day four.

BOLUNG

Cast your cowries, Shey!

There might be salvation yet.

WONG

Yes! Let the cowries speak!

KIBOW

The cowries!

BOLUNG

Speak!

Shey Bo-Nyo throws the cowries. The seven pillars converge and then turn their backs and drop their heads. Shey Bo-nyo picks up his cowries and exits mournfully.

TANTO

We cannot give up.
Turn, Kwifon! Turn!

MBWIN

We cannot despair!
Kwifon always resolves issues.
There is a way out.

CHORUS

Sure?

MBWIN

Which is more serious?
The lake boiling or the lake disappearing?

KIBOW

I see.
The lake disappeared six years ago.
Kwifon went to the Fon and demanded
That he perform the sacrifice of the lake
Like his fathers before him had always done.

Once every year, they led the people in sacrifice.
The Fon, dressed in enthronement robes
And surrounded by the seven pillars of Kwifon
Would descend into the depths of the lake,
A cock in his right hand, a hen in the left.
Having given food and drink to the lake god
He emerged from the waters as dry as he descended.
Kwifon then gave the signal for the feasting.
That night the Fon slept with the Queen
A consummation of the deep faith and love
Between the people and the lake god;
God of benevolence and god of fertility.
Six years ago when the lake left the land
Taking along the fertilizing waters
And the Fon refused to lead in sacrifice,
Did Kwifon not seek and find a solution?

WONG

For that solution Kwifon was banished
From the land it had saved.

TANTO

This is an emergency.
The land must be saved again.
Kwifon must leave anger aside.
We must leave history for the moment
And return to history at this moment.

KIBOW

Two years after Kwifon saved the land,
Two years after the Fon banished Kwifon,
The lake god was again hungry for sacrifice.
This time the lake generated land-slides which
Brought down whole hills, destroying houses and farms.
But because no lives were lost, and because
Kwifon was smarting from the treachery of the Fon,

No one took any notice.

There is noise of thunder. The seven pillars look at each other in fear.

TANTO
Let us move.
We go straight to the Fon.
He must lead the people in sacrifice.
Hiiii Wong! Hiiii Bo-Nyo! Hiiii Kwifon!

Blackout.

Afternoon. The Fon's reception court-yard. The Fon is sitting on the throne. The seven pillars of Kwifon, still in their ceremonial dress stand facing him.

FON
(clearing his throat) Well, what is the matter? What do you people want again?

TANTO
There is trouble in the land.
The cattle are destroying farms.
The women are starving their husbands.
The Fon must do something.

FON
What do you expect me to do? The land is there for both cattle and crops. I have designated farmlands and separated them from grazing lands. If you allow your women to encroach on grazing land, the cattle rearers cannot take responsibility for anything. As for the starvation, you don't expect the Fon to run your homes for you. If you allow your women to starve you, that is entirely your responsibility. If there is nothing else, you may now leave. Father Leo will not be happy to find you here.

BOLUNG
This is an emergency.
Have you seen any of us here
Ever since your betrayal of Kwifon?

FON
I have no use for Kwifon. And if you want to start trouble again, you know what happened last time.

MUNJEI
Personal safety is not our concern
But rather the salvation of the people and the land.

MBWIN
Your own safety is our concern too.

WONG
Your own life!

FON
I will call the police! I will send for the gendarmes! This time, all of you will be shot in public. By firing squad.

TANTO
If we take you away, no one will ever know.

FON
No! Father Leo will know! Father Leo will know! Police! Help! Help!

KIBOW
Stop wasting your breath, Fon.
No one in this land wants you
Apart from your cattle.

FON

Help! Help! Guards! Where are those castrated idiots?

TANTO

Calm yourself, Fon.
You are still Fon, you know?
Lion! King of the forest!
Leopard of the open savannahs!
Mbe! Mbe! Lion!
King of the forest!
When the seven pillars of Kwifon
Appear in broad day even the squirrel
Hides its face in the ground.

FON

You dare? You dare?

TANTO

They are all cowering behind bolted doors.
Children, women and men. Even men!
Have you heard any noise in the land since morning?

FON

Leave me alone! What do you want?

TANTO

Calm yourself.
You might be saved yet.
You must lead the people in sacrifice
To the lake god. Failing which...

FON

Yes? Failing which?

MBWIN

Nothing! Nothing, Mbe!

TANTO

The lake god is angry.
The waters have been boiling for four days.
The lake god must be pacified through sacrifice.

FON

I see. You mean there is movement in the water?

TANTO

No! Boiling! The water is boiling.

FON

Did you put your hand inside?

TANTO

No. Shey Bo-Nyo told us.
And we heard noise of thunder
Coming from the depths of the lake.

FON

Common thunder. It is the rainy season, after all. And I wouldn't believe anything a mad man said. No way.

TANTO

Shey Bo-Nyo is not mad!

FON

He is. Even Father Leo has noticed.

MUNJEI

We don't want Father Leo in this business.
What matters now is for you to lead
The people in sacrifice to the lake god.

FON
Me? A Christian king? An enlightened monarch? I do not worship idols. I worship none other than God Almighty.

TANTO
You will destroy the land?

FON
The Lord Jesus has already saved the land. I will ask Father Leo to offer a special mass of thanksgiving for all the things God has showered on us.

WONG
The Fon is mad! He is beyond salvation.

TANTO
Look, Mbe! Tomorrow is market day.
Set the day for the sacrifice and
Kwifon will carry the message to the
Seven corners of the land.

FON
I do not participate in heathen sacrifice; and I do not allow idol worship in a Christian land.

KIBOW
Is that your answer?

FON
That is my answer. But let me warn you people: if you try anything I will send for the police. Can I have some peace now?

TANTO
You will never have peace
Because you have denied your people peace.
Your ancestors will never allow you respite

Because you have ruined the land.
You are destroying the people.
But Kwifon is alive yet.
The land might still be saved,
And the people too.
Hiiii Wong! Hiiii No-Nyo! Hiiii Kwifon!

Exeunt.

Next day, evening. The Fon's living room. Angela is making a cup of tea but suddenly becomes nervous and overturns the cup.

FON
Can't you be more careful?

ANGELA
I don't know. I am very nervous. Ever since the events of yesterday. I cannot even sleep. You know I didn't sleep at all last night.

FON
Me too. I am really feeling tired. And I am still having those terrible dreams. Last night, for instance, I dreamt that I was with Father Leo in a dungeon. He kept telling me not to worry. Then, suddenly, he was no longer there. I was all alone; in that dark dungeon. I was so frightened I started shouting and groping about in the terrible darkness. A little while later, I saw a tiny light flickering in the distance. As I stumbled towards the light, I soon saw the shadow of the late Fon, my father. Then the light disappeared and I woke with a start.

ANGELA
That is when I shook you, because you were making a terrible noise. What will you do now?

FON

May be we should ask Father Leo to bless the house. You think they will try anything?

ANGELA

Who?

FON

The Kwifon people.

ANGELA

I don't know. But I have a terrible feeling something is going to happen.

FON

What?

ANGELA

I don't know. But something very serious is going to happen.

FON

You know, Angie? Sometimes I am not sure if I am married to a Christian woman.

ANGELA

I beg, lef me da white man palaver. You ought to listen to your people sometimes.

FON

You mean like offering the sacrifice to the lake god?

ANGELA

Yes. It will satisfy them, at least.

FON

Sometimes I wonder at your naivety, Angela. These people are not interested in the lake god. They are just jealous that we own cattle. They will do anything to become rich too.

ANGELA

I don't think so. This thing is more serious than you think. Take this talk about the boiling lake. Have you tried to find out?

FON

They didn't see the lake boiling. Just rumours being spread by Shey Bo-Nyo.

ANGELA

But have you tried to find out?

FON

No. Why should I bother? This is the rainy season and the lake is likely to overflow its banks.

ANGELA

Why don't you send one of the guards there tomorrow. Sometimes I wish I were Fon.

FON

You can never be Fon. You're a woman.

ANGELA

And not even queen, being a woman!

There is a terrible scream off. Then absolute silence.

FON

What's that?

ANGELA

One of the guards.

                    FON

What happened?

                    ANGELA

I don't know.

The Fon advances stealthily towards exit. Angela tries to stop him.

                    ANGELA

Don't go!

                    FON

(calling) Doggo? Doggo? Are you there?

                    ANGELA

Try the other.

                    FON

Kinchin? Kinchin? Where are the bas...?

Another terrible scream.

                    ANGELA

What's it?

                    FON

I don't know.

                    ANGELA

I am afraid.

                    FON

Me too.

There is derisive laughter off.

ANGELA

Who is it?

FON

I don't know. Who is there? Who is out there?

More derisive laughter.

VOICE

Yosew Kimbong? Yosew Kimbong?

ANGELA

They are calling you by name!

VOICE

Yosew Kimbong? Kwifon is waiting for you. Come out at once!

ANGELA

(clinging to him) No! Don't go! They will kill you.

VOICE

He cannot escape, woman. Kwifon does not want to shed more blood than necessary. Yosew Kimbong, come out at once!

ANGELA

No! Go away! Go away! Go...

She is suddenly mesmerised and in a dreamlike manner, the Fon moves with uncertain steps towards exit. A short while after the departure of the Fon, Angela recovers. Finding that her husband has been taken away, she throws a shawl over her head and, as she exits, there are rumblings of thunder.

Blackout.

Same evening. Father Leo's study. He is reading. Suddenly there is urgent knocking at the door.

FATHER LEO

(getting up and going to open the door) Who could that be? Someone dying again?

When he opens the door Angela almost collapses into his arms.

ANGELA

Help, Father! Help! They have taken him! They have taken my husband.

FATHER LEO

Who? Who, Angela?

ANGELA

I don't know, Father. But they have taken him!

FATHER LEO

The Fon?

ANGELA

Yes. They have taken the Fon. They called him by name. They will kill him, Father.

FATHER LEO

Who? Who took him?

ANGELA

I don't know. But they said it was Kwifon. They will kill him!

FATHER LEO

Did you see any one?

ANGELA

No. But they took him away! I tried to stop him, but I don't know what happened. I suddenly went asleep.

FATHER LEO

How?

ANGELA

I don't know, Father. Help! They will kill him! They will kill my husband!

FATHER LEO

Where were the guards? What did they do?

ANGELA

I don't know. But we heard screams before they asked him to come out. I screamed too and held him. Then I don't know what happened. I became unconscious. And when I recovered he was gone.

FATHER LEO

This is serious. How did you get here?

ANGELA

I walked.

FATHER LEO

Alone?

ANGELA

The whole village is quiet. I only heard some strange noises coming from the direction of the lake. They are going to sacrifice my husband to the lake!

FATHER LEO

Are you sure they went towards the lake?

ANGELA
I am sure, Father. They will kill him.

FATHER LEO
The police! We must get the police. We must go and get the police right away. I'll get the keys of the land rover.

As Father Leo exits, there is a loud bang. A few minutes later, Father Leo is heard coughing wildly. Angela begins to cough too and suddenly crumbles to the floor.

Blackout.

Passage

A destitute landscape characterized by an anthill from which a little smoke is emanating. There is the sound of wind in the background; otherwise silence reigns. Woman, Girl and Boy of the Prologue re-enter in continuation of their exploration. A man also enters from opposite direction.

WOMAN
So there are still men in the land?
Or is this one come back from the hereafter?
Children, do you see what I am seeing?

BOY/GIRL
Yes. It is a man.

BOY
A man.

GIRL
Man.

WOMAN
Man! Are you really man?
Are there men left in this land?
Is there man left?

MAN
I am a man. Yes, I am a man.
Not a ghost come back to haunt the land;
A land stricken overnight by desolation.
So there are still women and children?
Did the evil spirit that swept through the land
Leave a lone tree and two shrubs in the wake
Of its passage?

WOMAN

Who are you, stranger?
Or are you one of the land?
The voice is not strange to me?

MAN

You don't know me anymore?
Did death spare body and muddle mind?

BOY

It is the father of Tata.
Where is he, father?
We agreed to go hunting rats today.

MAN

Did you, son?

BOY

Yes. We agreed to go to the grove.

MAN

Which grove?

BOY

The one by the lake.
That's where we always go for rats.

MAN

Don't your mothers cook foo-foo
And green vegetables that you
Must go to the grove to hunt rats?

GIRL

Where is my mother?
Where is my mother?
Where is...?

                              WOMAN
Ssssshi! Quiet, child.
Don't disturb the dead.
They are asleep.

                               GIRL
My mother. I want my mother.

                               BOY
Don't you hear that they are all dead?

                              WOMAN
Keep quiet, Boy!
Fale? Is that your name?

                               BOY
Yes, of course. That's my name.

                              WOMAN
Good. Fale, this is your little sister.
Look after her.

                               GIRL
He is not my brother.
He is always fighting with my brother
Because of rats.
Where is my brother?

                              WOMAN
Dead.

                               GIRL
And my father?
                               MAN
Dead.

                BOY

But how can every one die in one night?

                WOMAN

Rats.

                BOY

Are you joking, mother?

                MAN

She is right, son.
The rats you boys hunted in
The grove by the lake.

                BOY

But I don't understand that.
Hunting rats, everybody dead.
I don't see the link.

                MAN

Hunting rats in the grove by the lake!

                BOY

But no one ever told us.
No one ever stopped us.
No one ever forbade us.

                MAN

Are you sure, son?

                BOY

Of course, I am sure.
No one...

WOMAN
Quiet, son.

MAN
Do you know Shey Bo-Nyo?

BOY
Of course I know him.
Everybody knows the mad Shey
Who lives in the bush.
Whoever listened to a mad man?

MAN
So, someone did forbid you from
Hunting rats in the grove.
And Shey Bo-Nyo was never mad;
He is not mad.

BOY
A man leaves his wives and children
And is living alone in the bush,
Running after boys with a spear,
Because they are hunting rats
And you say he isn't mad?

WOMAN
Son, Shey Bo-Nyo never abandoned his family.
He only went to the grove from time to time
To make sacrifices to the lake god.
But he always returned to his family.
I wonder what has become of them.

MAN
I wonder.
But we cannot blame this calamity
On the boys alone.
Hunting rats in the grove was nothing

Compared to the transgressions of we, the adults.
And when Shey Bo-Nyo spoke of the terrible
Things to come as consequences of our deeds,
We all laughed at him and called him mad.

WOMAN

The new religion of the only son of God.
The new civilisation of only money and book
The barbarism and heathenism of our tradition.

MAN

The Fon, father and guardian of all the land,
Offspring of a long line of illustrious ancestors,
The fountain-head of tradition
And shelter of all the land.
The Fon made alliance with strangers
And called Shey Bo-Nyo mad.
He turned a deaf ear to Kwifon,
Supreme and most feared authority in the land.
And now this.

WOMAN

He sold the land to strangers
And made alliance with rearers of cattle
Which destroyed crops causing famine
And suffering the people had never known.
He rejected tradition and denied
The women a good yield even though
They clamoured for a queen and the lake sacrifice
And now this.

MAN

What do we do?

WOMAN

Bury the dead.

MAN

Woman! Are you mad?
Bury which dead?
One man bury a thousand dead?
I don't even have the strength
To scratch a single hole for my wife;
Not to talk of the children.

BOY

So Tata is dead?
We had agreed to go hunting rats!

MAN

Son, death does not respect contracts.
Everyone in this land is dead.
You are the only survivors.

WOMAN

We are the only survivors.

MAN

No. You. I came in this morning.

WOMAN/BOY

From where?

WOMAN

You didn't sleep in the land?
Didn't we meet at the market yesterday?
Although it all looks like ages ago?

MAN

Yes. We met at the market.
But... after our ... talk...
I travelled to Ewawa.

WOMAN

But that's far!
Almost half-a-day's journey.

MAN

For a man, it takes less than half-a-day.
I had to honour an invitation.

WOMAN

From a man. From a man, of course.

MAN

No.

WOMAN

From a woman, then?

MAN

Yes.

WOMAN

I was right, then.
That talk in the market-place
Came from your mouth only.

MAN

No. From the heart.
From the depths of my heart.

WOMAN

Stop it!
What am I doing?
What are we doing?
There are corpses heaped all over the land
And here we are chattering away like
Idiot, unfeeling wild beasts that will feed on their kind.

MAN
You speak the truth.

WOMAN
Will you help me bury my husband?
At least, you won't refuse him that honour.

BOY
How can we bury so many people?

MAN
You are right, son.
We have to go and ask for help.
There are people in Ewawa.

GIRL
Look! Mother, look!
There is someone coming.

BOY
It's a man!

WOMAN
Yes. It's a man.

MAN
Coming from the lake!
BOY
Hei! It's the mad man, Shey Bo-Nyo.

MAN
Yes indeed!
It is the old man, Shey Bo-Nyo.

GIRL
He is going to fall, mother!

WOMAN

He has fallen; he needs help.

Man and Boy exeunt and soon re-enter supporting Shey Bo-Nyo on either side. He is holding tight to his Ngem and in his right hand is the staff of Kwifon, the bamboo pole painted black and white.

SHEY BO-NYO

You leave me alone!
Leave me alone, I say!

MAN

Don't worry, old one. You will be fine.

SHEY BO-NYO

Yes, I am fine. But leave me alone.
I can look after myself.

BOY

Let me hold your Ngem, old one.

SHEY BO-NYO

What insolence! Who are you to touch the gong of the gods?

WOMAN

He just wants to be helpful, old one.

SHEY BO-NYO

I know he wants to be helpful;
But the gods need no one's help.
They demand allegiance and sacrifice
Failing which they unleash death.

MAN

Old one, are there... any... survivors

In the homesteads up there by the lake?

SHEY BO-NYO

What survivors?
Not one that I know of.
Last night, I did battle with the gods.
All night long, I was in the grove
As I have been these past five days
When the waters of the lake began to
Boil over with the wrath of the gods.
When the messenger of death finally emerged
From the depths of the dark waters
With strict instructions to sow desolation,
I was there on my knees pleading for mercy.
Give them one last chance, I cried.
Listen, Kwifon is on the way with sacrifice.
But in his impatience and terrible wrath,
He knocked me out of his way.
When I recovered, it was already morning.
As I staggered downhill towards the homesteads,
My first encounter was with the sacrificial train:
The seven pillars of Kwifon, the Fon in their midst,
Their faces buried in the earth for terror, in awe.
I was greeted by the eternal silence of death.
Without thinking, I snatched this pole and stumbled on.
In my homestead, I forced the doors open;
But everyone was dead: five wives
And all my children dead.
I screamed and cursed the god
That would not even spare
The family of his servant priest.
My god is an unfeeling and vengeful god.

MAN

Old one, the god might hear you.

SHEY BO-NYO
What else can he do that is worse?
My miserable life is not worth his anger.

WOMAN
Forgive the forwardness of a poor woman, old one,
But did you look around in the other homesteads?

SHEY BO-NYO
Woman! Don't you understand simple language?
I am not speaking in parables.
Every living thing up there is dead;
Including rats and flies. Even flies!
I wonder how you survived.

MAN
The woman and the two children,
It is they who survived.
I came in this morning
And had to force open the doors.
Everyone was lying comfortably in bed;
But they were all so cold, so very cold.
They were all taken as they slept.
I leapt out of the house and screamed,
I raised an alarm for help.
But I only heard the echo of my voice
Mocking and laughing at me.
Neither cock-crow nor the barking of dogs
That are so common-place in every land.
Nor did I hear the singing of birds
And the fowls scratching around for food.
Then I went from homestead to homestead
Encountering nothing but corpses;
Some in the yard and others
Along the village footpaths,
Until I got here and found these three.

Old one, your god has done us.

SHEY BO-NYO

Our god has done us, young man, not my god.
Does it really matter now?
Where did you come from this morning?

MAN

From Ewawa, old one.
This thing did not go beyond this land.

SHEY BO-NYO

It couldn't have.
They have different gods in Ewawa.
We shall seek refuge there.
Perhaps they will help us bury our dead.
They are good people and will be glad
To give us food and shelter.

MAN

Old one, shall you lead the way?
Boy, you take your sister's hand.
Daughter, you give your other hand
To your mother and I will keep the rear.
Now, are we ready?
Old one, do you remember the Mangvun?

SHEY BO-NYO

Who is the elder among you?

MAN

Forgive my foolish words, old one.
Shall we go now?

SHEY BO-NYO

Wait a little; I am encumbered.

(to Boy) Son, since you wanted to be helpful,
Here, hold the staff of Kwifon and guard it well.

MAN
Lead the way, old one, and we shall follow you.

Exeunt to the rhythm of the Ngem and the mourning song of Mangvun.

The End

Part IV

Betrothal without Libation

Dramatis Personae

Fointam Ngong:	Final year student in Higher Institute of Education.
Elisa Eyong:	Final year student in High school.
Itoh Eyong:	Teacher in High School, father of Elisa Eyong.
Mrs Eyong:	Teacher in High School, mother of Elisa Eyong.
Sama Ngam:	Final year student in Higher Institute of Education, friend of Fointam Ngong.
Paulina:	Proprietress of a Native Liquor Bar.
Bobe Ngong:	Fointam Ngong's father.
Nandoh Bih:	Fointam Ngong's mother and Bobe Ngong's first wife.
Bobe Chia:	Friend of Bobe Ngong.
Waingeh:	Half-brother to Fointam Ngong.
Eyong Fointam:	Son of Fointam Ngong and Elisa Eyong.
Tita:	One of Paulina's clients.
John:	House boy to the Eyongs and Fointams.
Simbong:	Park tout.
Four Park Collectors.	
Five women:	Some of Bobe Ngong's fifteen wives. Also many children and women.

Act One

Scene I

Evening. Home of Mr and Mrs Itoh Eyong, highly educated couple teaching in local high school. Mr Eyong is sitting in a chair reading a newspaper or magazine. Noise of cooking from kitchen offstage and Mrs Eyong's voice is heard now and again issuing orders to the boy. Then she rushes into the sitting room and stops short, scandalised to find her husband doing nothing.

Mrs Eyong: Darling?
Mr Eyong: Yes?
Mrs Eyong: Do you know what time it is?
Mr Eyong: My watch says it is seven o'clock. Thanks for reminding me. I should have the news again from the BBC.

He gets out of the chair and is moving over to the side-board to tune the radio.

Mrs Eyong: No, darling. I am not talking about the news.
Mr Eyong: What now Evenge ? Is anything the matter? What are you looking at me so reproachfully for?
Mrs Eyong: Darling, Fointam is coming home for supper.
Mr Eyong: I know. But shouldn't Elissa's fiancé come? You could have asked your daughter to tell him.........
Mrs Eyong: What?
Mr Eyong: That you no longer want him for supper. I don't see what you are looking so unenthusiastic for.
Mrs Eyong: Darling, that is not the point. He will be here in thirty minutes or less; and you are just sitting about doing nothing.
Mr Eyong: But what do you want me to be doing, Evenge?
Mrs Eyong: Look at the table, darling. It is not yet set for supper. And I am too busy in the kitchen to start doing that now.

Mr Eyong:	Where is John? He can make the table, can't he?
Mrs Eyong:	He is roasting the chicken. I didn't want to make a chicken stew. John is roasting it the way the Bikoms do. After that all you need to do is add oil and salt and pepper. The water for the corn-fufu is already boiling and I have to start making it. That is why I don't have the time to make the table.
Mr Eyong:	And where is Elissa? Why can't she help set the table?
Mrs Eyong:	Darling, I have already told you her fiancé is coming to supper. I have sent her to her room to make up her hair and dress up.
Mr Eyong:	Is it the wedding already? Why must she make her hair and dress up specially? After all these several years that they have been together does she still need to entice him with her looks?
Mrs Eyong:	But, darling, don't you mind the way I look sometimes? A man always wants his woman to look smart.
Mr Eyong:	Of course, she can look smart without all the fuss. If he were coming to take her out I wouldn't quarrel. Now you want me to make the table ready for supper just because you want her to make her hair. Alright, go and see to the fufu.
Mrs Eyong:	Oh! Thank you, darling. You are always so very understanding.
Mr Eyong:	Fortunately for me there is only one other daughter to give away in marriage. I hope that when my three boys come of age the fathers of their fiancées will also set the table for them.
Mrs Eyong:	Yes, darling. You don't know what pride a mother feels when her daughter finds a good husband.
Mr Eyong:	I bet your father never did the things I am now doing when I was courting you. He was only interested in how many bottles of gin and whisky I brought.

Mrs Eyong: But, darling, you are different. You are not a die-hard traditionalist like my father. The water must be boiling over already.

Exits

Mr Eyong brings out a table cloth from the side-board and begins to make the table. Then Elissa comes in. She is dressed smartly and has a beautiful hairdo. She is shocked to see her father making the table.

Elissa: What are you doing, Father?
Mr Eyong: Getting the table ready for supper, daughter. Mummy says Fointam will soon be here and things are hardly set. And you were doing your hair, and John is looking after the chicken. So I was the only loafer and her vigilant eyes caught me.
Elissa: I am here now, Father. You go and sit down. I will do it.
Mr Eyong: No, daughter. I will stay right here and help you.
Elissa: Alright, father. Just as you wish.

There is knocking at the door.

Mr Eyong: That must be him. Keep to time very strictly. I will open the door for him.

Fointam Ngong enters. He is carrying a parcel.

Mr Eyong: Hello! young man. Come right in.
Fointam: Good evening, sir. I hope I am not late.
Mr Eyong: You are even early. You can see for yourself that Elissa is still making the table. Make yourself comfortable. And let me relieve you of your parcel.

Curtain

Fointam: Thank you sir. It's just a little drink for you.

Mr Eyong: That's very kind of you, Fointam. Elissa, tell your mother that Fointam is already here.

Elissa: Yes, father.

Exits

Mr Eyong: While waiting for the women to straighten out things in the kitchen the men better be whetting their throats. Beer as usual I guess. Or would you rather have something hot?

Fointam: No thanks. I'll have beer as usual.

Mr Eyong: Elissa, Elissa?

Elissa: Yes, father.

Mr Eyong: Why don't you bring us something to drink? Make it beer for both of us.

She exits to fetch the drinks.

Mr Eyong: Now, Fointam, let's have a little man-to-man talk before the women come in. Are you sure you want to marry Elissa? What I mean is, are both of you conscious of what you are doing?

Fointam: Yes, sir. I think we know what we are doing; and I am sure I want to marry her. I have known her for years, Sir. We have known each other for seven years!

Mr Eyong: Yes, seven years is a long time. I hadn't thought about that. However, it is you that I am doubting. What do your parents say? I guess you have already told them?

Fointam: I wrote a letter to my father last week telling him about Elissa. And I was going to ask your permission to go down to my village with her; so that my people can see her.

Mr Eyong: She is perfectly free to go with you. How soon do you intend to go?

Fointam: I was thinking of the weekend. We'll leave on Saturday and come back on Sunday.

Mr Eyong: That will be fine. I only hope that your father has not been making other plans for you. I know what I am talking about. Because when I was courting Elissa's mother I got hell from her father. He swore that he wouldn't let his daughter marry a Nyangi. With my father it wasn't really a problem because my mother is Bakossi. I wonder if your people will take it kindly.

Fointam: There is no doubt that they will put up some resistance. But my father has a lot of confidence in me. He trusts my judgement. He won't hold out for too long.

Mr Eyong: Well, the sooner you people get married the better. I am tired of seeing a full-grown woman around the house.

Fointam: Yes, sir. As soon as we go to my village we should be able to fix a date for the wedding.

Mr Eyong: What's she do with the drinks? Elissa? What about the beer?

Elissa comes in carrying a tray with dishes on it. She is closely followed by her mother who is also carrying a tray with more dishes on it.

Elissa: Mother says we better eat first.

Mrs Eyong: That's true, darling. Good evening, Fointam. I was held up in the kitchen.

Fointam: Good evening, Ma. I was going to come and help you in the kitchen.

Mr Eyong: Help her in the kitchen? So you're going to spoil Elissa, helping her in the kitchen? We will soon make these women ride us.

Mrs Eyong: No, darling. It is just a question of being reasonable. Let's go to the table before the food gets cold. Elissa you can now bring them the beer.

Mr Eyong: By the way, Elissa, Fointam says you are going to see his parents over the week-end. So you better begin to prepare yourself for the journey.

Mrs Eyong: That's good news, darling. The day is drawing near, at last. There is nothing as annoying as a home being run by two women. The sooner she leaves this house the better for me. I better get a drink for myself too. There is something to celebrate.

Scene 2

Next day, afternoon. Fointam Ngong's room. He is sitting at the table, scribbling away. When curtain rises he has just finished writing and is now reading over a number of pages. Several books on the table; some open, others closed. There is a knock at the door.

Fointam: Come in, dear.

Elissa: How did you know it was me?

Fointam: My blood told me. I always know when you 're coming. How are your people?

Elissa: They are doing fine. You don't know how excited mother is. After you left last night she was singing and dancing until father got bored and went to bed.

Fointam: Your mother is a very jovial person. But your father is a quiet type. Almost withdrawn, like yourself.

Elissa: Are you different? Why didn't you get up to welcome me when I came in if you are not as withdrawn as myself?

Fointam: It is just a remark, my dear. Nothing to quarrel about. You are the loveliest woman in the whole wide world. And you know you are the only apple of my eye.

Elissa: Thanks for the flattery. What have you been doing? What is this? An essay?

Fointam: Yeah. It is an essay for Mr Ndi, the history teacher. Since we won't be here during the week-end I thought I should do it now. It is due on Monday.
Elissa: I hope your people know we are coming?
Fointam: Yes. I wrote to my old man last week.
Elissa: Has he written back?
Fointam: The letter did not need a reply. I was merely informing him about our visit.
Elissa: Don't you think he will object to you marrying a Nyangi?
Fointam: I don't think so. Come to think of it you are not a Nyangi. At least you are not what people think the Nyangis are. And your father tells me his mother is Bakossi.
Elissa: Yes, his mother is Bakossi. And my mother is Bakweri. And you are Bikom. And our children, when they grow up, that is if we ever have them, might get married to Metta or Bamilike or Douala people. What a family!
Fointam: It may seem strange but I like it that way. If everyone in this country did like your grandfather, and us, this would soon become a tribeless nation. And we will have gone a long way in solving some of the numerous problems that are plaguing this country.
Elissa: Anyway I am not interested in solutions to your political problems. All I want is to marry you; because I love you as a person, for what you are.
Fointam: We are saying the same thing, my dear. If I didn't love you as a person I would not be wanting to marry you. I am only saying that such marriages can help solve some of the nation's problems.
Elissa: How early are we leaving on Saturday?
Fointam: Fairly early because we will make a stop-over in Mankon and buy a few gifts for the folks. You better be ready by seven.
Elissa: What about the house you were building? Is it already finished.
Fointam: Come on, dear, I told you it was already completed and even furnished. I slept in it during the last Christmas

	vacation. There is nothing to worry about really.
Elissa:	I am not worrying, Fointam. I am just being inquisitive.
Fointam:	Well...
Elissa:	How far is it to Njinikom? That's where the vehicle leaves us; not so?
Fointam:	Yes, dear. It is some fifty kilometres; and it takes something like two hours now that the weather is still dry. In the rainy season it takes several hours.
Elissa:	The road must be as hilly as all the roads around Bamenda.
Fointam:	You just wait and see. Sections of the road are terribly steep. But you will see for yourself.
Elissa:	Your mother will be happy to have a daughter-in-law?
Fointam	Definitely. She has been pestering me about taking a wife and beginning to make children. She will be happy.
Elissa:	And when we return from there?
Fointam:	We will be able to fix a date for the marriage. Imagine courting a woman for seven years! If things don't move fast she will soon grow mouldy.
Elissa:	It's your fault, isn't it? Always I want to make sure. I don't want to rush anything. I hope you have made sure now?
Fointam:	Yes, dear. You are the onliest woman in my life. After Elissa I see nothing but a vacuum, a void.
Elissa:	And after Fointam what does Elissa see?
Fointam:	A void my dear. Unless you have found some smart-looking guy this morning.
Elissa:	I will be going back to my books. It will be a double victory for me if I win a husband and also pass my exams.
Fointam:	Yes, dear. You better go back to your books. I have my own books to turn to. If I don't pass my exams I won't have the money to keep you happy and bring up the kids.

Curtain

Scene 3

Mid-morning. Paulina's Native Liquor Bar. Fointam Ngong and his friend, Sama Ngam, are some of Paulina's clientele.

Tita: Pass me two bottles for here.
Paulina: Two bottro?
Tita: Yes, two. And bringam quick. This sun fit kill man.
Fointam: Sama do you want another bottle?
Sama: Sure, Fointam, sure. The wine is first class. When I taste this kind of wine I never want to stop drinking.
Fointam: Paulina?
Paulina: Sah?
Fointam: Four bottles-eh?
Paulina: Yes sah.

Fointam Ngong clears his throat as an indication that he has something serious to say.

Fointam: Sama son of Nain.
Sama: I am here, Fointam son of Bih.
Fointam: I have made up my mind to marry Elissa.
Sama: Have you? That is good news.
Fointam: Yes, after all these years of friendship I think we should marry and settle down to making children. In June she will be writing the G.C.E. Advanced level and you and I should also be graduating. I don't see what we are waiting for.
Sama: I have been wondering too what you people are waiting for. Even if she wants to go to University nothing stops her from doing so as a married woman.
Fointam: And there is no problem about my posting. All I need to do is just to indicate to my friend in the Ministry where I should like to work.

Sama: That's one lucky thing with us. If you have a friend or relative who is well-placed you always have things your own way. The other day it was announced over the radio that Ngobe, you remember him don't you?

Fointam: Sure, I do. He was always the last person in his class.

Sama: That's right. That's him. It was announced that he had been given another appointment. He is now the head of some school in the East. And that is now his fourth appointment in two years! You better take advantage while your friend is still there.

Fointam: From here I go straight to the capital. I want Elissa to get a degree fast. I can even get registered in the university too; and get myself a good degree.

Sama: What do Elissa's parents say?

Fointam: No problem whatsoever. I was there the other night for supper and her mother had a big surprise for me. Will you believe that I ate roast chicken and corn-fufu?

Sama: You are telling me!

Fointam: Roast chicken and corn-fufu! Just the way our people prepare it back home.

Sama: You make my mouth water. I have not eaten roast chicken for a long time.

Fointam: And yesterday Elissa told me how very excited her mother is about the match.

Sama: So they too have been wondering what you people have been waiting for?

Fointam: You've said it. But you know how it is with our people. I have never wanted to rush anything; more so marrying a girl whose tribe is said to be notorious in certain respects. But now my mind is made up and we are going down to Njinikom next Saturday to see my parents.

Sama: Her parents have given their blessing then?

Fointam: Yes. They have. Only her father was a bit hesitant; not because he doesn't like the idea; but he was rather

	worrying about the reaction of my parents. He says he is already used to these types of marriages since his own mother is Bakossi and, of course, as you know, his wife is Bakweri.
Sama:	I guess you have told the old folks about the visit?
Fointam:	Yes. I sent Bobe a letter about ten days ago telling him about her and the visit. Why don't we go together so that you can give me moral support and see the folks too? Each time I am down there everyone keeps asking me how is Sama? Why doesn't he come to see us anymore?
Sama:	I should love to come with you and Elissa. It is true that their tribe is notorious in certain aspects. You only need to go to where they live in Mankon at dusk and you will understand. But with this new revelation about her origins I now understand why she is such an exemplary girl. You know I always thought she was Bikom? She looks exactly like a Kom girl. The only thing which betrays her is her backside. She doesn't have enough of it. Give her a bit more backside and she will pass anywhere for a Bikom. Does Bobe know that she is not Bikom?
Fointam:	No. I didn't think it necessary to talk about her origins. Isn't it enough that she is an exemplary girl? He doesn't imagine that I am fool enough to marry a girl whose character is doubtful?
Sama:	There you are right. Character above everything else. There aren't two Elissas in this school. When you put her side by side with all the other girls in this place there's none to approach her. Fointam you're a lucky fellow. But I have never really understood why our people insist on marrying only Kom girls. If I found a girl today who barely approaches Elissa I would marry her; whether she is Banso or Bali or Yaounde.
Fointam:	You think Bobe will object to the marriage just because Elissa is not Bikom?

Sama: What would you do if he did? Forget about her?

Fointam: You think that after studying this girl for seven years I will give her up just because my old man wants me to marry a Kom girl? Never. It will be Elissa and no one else.

Sama: Fointam, if I know our people well, you better get ready for a show-down with Bobe. As for the women they can grumble. But their opinion does not really count for much. However, we will really have to convince Bobe that Elissa is the only girl to settle for. And don't expect that things will be all easy and cosy this first time.

Fointam: But why should he object? Doesn't he have any trust in me? Doesn't he trust my judgement of what is good for me and the family, for that matter? Then how can he say that I am already a man if he won't let me take my own initiative in a matter that affects me directly? Sama I am losing my patience.

Sama: You don't need to, Fointam. I can trust your judgement because I know the facts of the situation; and furthermore, because I am as educated as you are. But your old man and mine and the rest of them are still buried in the past. They live in a world where everything that is foreign to the clan is not only suspect but outright unacceptable. The only good thing is that which comes from the tribe. And in the matter of taking a wife there is no question of initiative with our people. They always expect you to go with their choice because they believe their judgement is the best. It will take them a long time to accept that man is basically the same whether he be Bikom or Metta or I don't know what tribe.

Fointam: With this type of tribal sentiments do you think that we will ever succeed in building a strong and united nation? If every tribe were to fence itself in, the concept of the nation would flounder in no time. I

	think it is our most urgent duty to prove these die-hard traditionalists mistaken in their judgement.
Sama:	It is surely incumbent upon us to do that. But we need many more liberal-minded people. It is going to take time, a long time, a very long time.

Curtain.

Scene 4

Early morning, Saturday. Fointam Ngong, Elissa and Sama Ngam are shopping in a market in Mankon. The time is about eight o'clock.

Salesman:	Good morning, Madam. You want something?
Elissa:	How much for this wrapper?
Salesman:	You want de wrapper? Na very good material. Imported. No be Cicam-oh. Dat na real wax print. Straight from Holland country. Only six thousand for six yards.
Elissa:	Say Fointam, won't this be good for your mother? It looks so beautiful; only it is rather expensive.
Fointam:	How much is it, dear?
Salesman:	Madam, de wrapper no dear at all. You no fit get wax print for de whole Mankon market for dat price. Na morning time market I di makam with wuna. Six thousand na very good price.
Fointam:	If you think it's good you can take it for her. I think I should also buy a blanket for the old man. He has been complaining too much about the cold. You know what he calls a blanket?
Sama:	A log of wood, I bet. My old man too calls it a log of wood.
Elissa:	Why do they call it that? Because it gives off warmth?

Salesman:	Na so madam. De blanket na really firewood. And na only four thousand, Oga.
Fointam:	You too all your own cargo na only. Wrapper na only six thousand; and now blanket na only four thousand.
Salesman:	Oga sah, na good price I di give wuna. Na really better price. And I go still move something since wuna di buy plenty things.
Sama:	Fointam, I am sure you also need to buy some soap and sweets for the women and children. Going to the village is real trouble. You have to think about everybody or risk witchcraft.
Fointam:	There you're right, Sama. Mr Shopman, I want fifteen savons; the one for one hundred and twenty-five francs. And a packet of bonbons.
Salesman:	Yes, Oga sah.
Elissa:	What are you buying so many savons for what? Isn't fifteen too much?
Fointam:	Not at all, my dear. There's just one for each of my old man's fifteen wives. To come from a large family is real trouble; especially when everyone looks up only to you.
Sama:	We better hurry or we won't be able to catch the first vehicle.
Fointam:	What are we hurrying for? After all, we are going to sleep there and come up tomorrow. Unless some evil spirit throws dust into our eyes. But I don't think there is anything to worry about. The women will all be waiting at home. Today is the country Sunday you know?
Elissa:	The day on which the women don't go their farms?
Sama:	Exactly, Elissa. But how did you know Fointam?
Fointam:	I have the eight days of the week all fixed up in my head. Mr Shopman na how much we di pay?
Salesman:	De total amount na twelve thousand and twenty-five francs, Oga. But I don move wuna five hundred. So

	na eleven thousand five hundred and twenty-five francs only.
Fointam:	You again with your only. Here you are. No be the money correct?
Salesman:	Yes, Oga. You no go buy dat hat for madam? Dust dey for road plenty and madam go spoil yi hair. De hat no dear, Oga. Na only seven hundred.
Fointam:	Elissa, do you want the hat?
Elissa:	No. I have a headscarf in my bag. I will use it against the dust.
Salesman:	But, oga, the hat nice plenty. Just buyam for madam. She go wearam for Sunday go service.
Fointam:	Not today, Mr Shopman. Some other time. Sama, Elissa, let's be going. It is getting late.
Salesman:	Good-bye, Madam. Good-bye, Oga sahs. Please call again.

Exeunt.

Curtain.

Scene 5

Same morning. The motor park in Mankon. There are several park collectors announcing divers destinations at the top of their voices. At the approach of likely passengers there is a rush as each park collector tries to win the passengers for his vehicle. This usually results in a scuffle between the park collectors and sometimes, an incensed passenger can strike out at his assailants. It is this kind of situation that welcomes Fointam Ngong, Elissa, and Sama Ngam. As much as possible the park collectors should be shouting at the same time; and this goes on in the background throughout the scene.

First Park Collector:	Bafoussam, Bafoussam, Bafoussam, Bafoussam, Nsamba Douala. Foussam, Douala, Foussam, one man for Foussam, one man. Un personne, un personne. One man for B'foussam.
Second Collector:	Banso, Banso, Banso-Ndu -Nkambe! Banso here. Only one man for Banso here. Ndu here. Nkambe here. Banso - Nkambe, one man only, one man only, one man for here!
Third Collector:	Bali, Bali, Bali-Guzang, Bali, Bali, Bali-Guzang here. Direct to Bali - Guzang, one man to Bali Guzang.
Fourth Collector:	Njinikom, Njinikom, Njinikom,. Kom line here. Kom line here. Three man for Kom line. Kom line...... Hei, Simbong, lef da people.
Simbong:	I leffam say na you one get motor? *(to Fointam)* Are you going home with Nawain? *(to Elissa)* Nawain come this way and sit in front.
Fointam:	She does not understand Bikom.
Simbong:	Doesn't she? You mean she grow out of Kom or what? Even then, some parents must be terribly careless. Not to teach their children our language.
Fointam:	She isn't Bikom at all.
Simbong:	Is that true? And she is your wife? Stop deceiving me. You book people are very daring. Anyhow, Madam, come sidong for front here.
Fourth Collector:	Simbong, no fool dat people with country-talk. You don take truck pusher fullup motor den you begin talk say motor don near for fullup? Oga, wuna lookam say na people wey dem di wakka dis? Wusai dem cargo? De motor never even get one passenger self.
Simbong:	But no be na so you too be begin? You want say I do how?

Fointam:	You say na how many place lef?
Fourth Collector:	Three, Oga. Hei! All passengers up. Driver, oya! Steam de engine. Motor don fullup.
Fointam:	Wusai we go sidong?
Fourth Collector:	Wuna enter for middle here. Dat front seat some Bororo man and him woman dem don pay seven, seven hundred.
Sama:	How much we go pay?
Fourth Collector:	Na one-two for wuna tree since wuna no get cargo.
Sama:	Isn't this lucky for us, Fointam? Sometimes one spends hours on end in this place. But now we'll be off in a short while, ha-ha.
Fourth Collector:	Driver, oya. Steam de engine and give chance for oder motor.

Curtain.

Act Two

Scene I

Fundashing. Early morning, Saturday. Bobe Ngong is sitting in his house warming himself by the fire. He is smoking a pipe. He mumbles to himself for several moments; then decides to seek the counsel of his first wife, Nandoh Bih.

Bobe Ngong: Bih-oh? Oh Bih? Bih-oh!
When Nandoh Bih comes in she remains stooping until Bobe asks her to sit.
Bobe Ngong: Isn't that a seat?
Nandoh Bih: How would I have known that you wanted me to sit down?
Bobe Ngong: You know, of course, that your son is coming today?
Nandoh Bih: You told me so the other day.
Bobe Ngong: He said in the book that he will be coming with a woman. I guess it is the woman he wants to marry. Otherwise what should he be bringing a woman to this compound for?
Nandoh Bih: Do you know the woman? I mean has he ever discussed the affair with you?
Bobe Ngong: Which me? Sometimes you talk as if there is wine in your head.
Nandoh Bih: I was just asking; because when you men discuss your things you never tell us. We know we are there to carry out instructions and obey orders.
Bobe Ngong: Whatever the case I am only hoping that she is a girl from these parts. Kom is very large and there are very many girls going to school and college; it is impossible to know many of them; even those from around Fundashing.

Nandoh Bih: I don't believe that he can bring a woman from outside. But if it happens, what will we do?

Bobe Ngong: I don't really understand what happens to you that sometimes you speak nonsense. I cannot hear of him bringing a woman from outside.

Nandoh Bih : This their new kind of thing they call book will come with something. How can a child suddenly inform his own father that he is coming with a woman ? We have always known that it is the family which looks for the woman; from a good family that is well-known to us. That is why I have been thinking all the time about your bosom friend's daughter.

Bobe Ngong: Don't say it again. I have been wondering all this morning what I am going to tell Bobe Waindim. To disappoint a friend just because of the madness of this boy.

Nandoh Bih: When they start going around and meet some loose girl they can't think straight anymore? Their heads become twisted and they lose their senses. All the same, I know Fointam is reasonable. I don't think he can do anything so foolish.

Bobe Ngong: I hope there is something for them to eat when they come ? I will ask Waingeh to go and get a calabash of wine from Sama of Waindoh.

Nandoh Bih: There is only a little fowl like this which is not even up to anything. Do I have a fowl again anywhere ? There are fifteen women in this compound; but each time there is need for a fowl, you see only me.

Bobe Ngong: But you are the head of the women !

Nandoh Bih: I am the head; but do I own their property. In their eyes I am just an ordinary woman like the rest of them.

Bobe Ngong: Alright, you ask the children to catch that my big cock; the one my *Chong* brought from Bobe Yibain's funeral. But don't kill it until they arrive. I

	don't want some prostitute to come and eat my cock.
Nandoh Bih:	So, what is going to happen ?
Bobe Ngong:	I have now made up my mind to go and consult a soothsayer. I must know the bottom of this thing before he arrives.
Nandoh Bih:	Why didn't you think of it ever since you received the book ?
Bobe Ngong:	I have been thinking about it. But my mind was not made up. How did you expect me to believe that *my* own son will be coming to show *me* his future wife ? It is *I* to tell him 'This is the woman I have bought for you.' I wonder if he will be expecting me to pay the price on her head.
Nandoh Bih:	Perhaps he has already paid; who knows ? But it is good for you to know something about the woman before they come. Which person are you going to see ?
Bobe Ngong:	I am going to Wallang Yisa. He is an expert in matters concerning women. He should be able to tell me the truth of the matter. Who will climb that Kikfunen hill today ?
Nandoh Bih:	You better set out now; before the sun gets hot.
Bobe Ngong:	You're right. Give me my walking stick. It is in that corner. You have informed the other women about the visit ?
Nandoh Bih:	Yes, they all know. In fact, last night, Fuen was saying that we should welcome them with *Njang*.
Bobe Ngong:	Kwifon-enter ! Welcome them with *Njang* when you don't know the kind of woman ? Don't let me hear such nonsense in this compound, if it belongs to me, the off-spring of Vibain.
Nandoh Bih:	Do you think I could accept that type of thing ?
Bobe Ngong:	I am off to Kikfunen. I will be back before long.

Exit. Curtain.

Scene 2

Fundashing. It is about mid-day. Fointam, Elissa and Sama are just arriving.

Elissa:	This hill is really steep. How does one ever get up it?
Fointam:	Don't worry, dear. We're almost there. You can see the kids running towards us.
Elissa:	We-e-eh! They are so excited.
Children:	Teacher has come-eh! Teacher has come! He has come with his wife.
Women:	They have come! They have come!
First Woman:	Teacher, is this her? Welcome, my daughter.
Sama:	*(Aside to Elissa)* They are wishing you welcome.
First Woman:	Teacher, whose daughter is she?
Second Woman:	What is her name, teacher?
Third Woman:	Which village does she come from?
Fourth Woman:	A-a-a-a-a. She is a real daughter of the soil. Did she grow up in these parts?
Fifth Woman:	You say her father is Bobe who?
First Woman:	Tell us quickly. We want to hear.

While this dialogue is going on Elissa is going round embracing the women who, in turn, regard her with a lot of admiration.

Fointam:	Mothers, my mothers. I am happy, *we* are happy to be here today amongst you. You want to know everything about this girl?
Women:	Yes! We want to know everything about her.
Fointam:	I won't keep you waiting. This my friend you see here is Bobe Ngam's son. You all know him very...
First Woman:	We all know him very well. You have started that your thing. It is the girl we are interested in. We want to know her too. Tell us quickly and stop showing us the child we all breast-fed.
Fointam:	Alright, alright. This girl you see here is Bobe

	Eyong's daughter.
Fifth Woman:	So this is Bobe Yong's daughter ? Welcome my daughter.
First Woman:	Which Bobe Yong ?
Fifth Woman:	Bobe Yong of Ashing. I didn't know he already had such a grown up daughter !
Sama:	No. It is not Bobe Yong but Eyong.
Fointam:	That's right, Sama. She is Bobe Eyong's daughter. Her own name is Elissa, Elissa Eyong; and she is reading book in that big school where I was two years ago.
First Woman:	Bobe Eyong, did you say ? The name does not sound Bikom. From which village, pray ?
Fointam:	No, no, no. Bobe Eyong and his wife are big teachers in that big school I have just talked to you about. He is Bayangi in Mamfe. Her mother is Bakweri in the coast where some of our people go to work in the plantations. She does not come from these parts at all.
First Woman:	Haven't you heard now ?
Fifth Woman:	I was hearing my own that she is Bobe Yong's daughter. And I know Bobe Yong of Ashing. But where is this Ma-ma-ma...
Sama:	The name is Mamfe.
Fifth Woman:	Mamfe ?
Elissa:	Fointam, what are they saying about Mamfe ?
Fointam:	Nothing. They only want to know where it is.
Sama:	Mamfe is just after Bamenda. You have all heard of Buea ?
Women:	Yes.
Sama:	Good. When you leave from here and you are going to Buea you pass Bamenda, then Mamfe, then Kumba, before you get to Buea. So Mamfe is quite near Bamenda. And her mother comes from Buea.
Fifth Woman:	Why do they go and carry women from so far off

	when we don't know what to do with girls here? How is she going to speak to us now that we can't speak grammar?
Fointam:	She will learn our language. That is not a problem at all.
First Woman:	'She will learn our language'. When will she learn our language? Let me pass. I am going to cook my soup. What women!
Fifth Woman:	My fire must have gone out already. Let me go and see. What women!
Second Woman:	Let me go and wash my baby. What women!
Third Woman:	I am going to fetch water from the stream. Stay with your women!
Fourth Woman:	I had already predicted that this woman will come from outside. Let me wash my feet and go to the market.
Sama:	Fointam, you see what I told you?
Elissa:	What is happening? Don't they want us? Don't they want *me*?
Fointam:	Keep calm, Elissa. There is nothing to panic about. Waingeh, where is Bobe?
Waingeh:	He went to Kikfunen to see Wallang Yisa, the soothsayer. But there is a calabash of wine next to the shrine behind his house. I have just brought it from Waindoh.
Fointam:	And why did he choose this morning of all mornings to go and consult Wallang Yisa? He knew at least a week ago that we would be here this morning. He could have gone to Kikfunen before today. It doesn't really matter now. Go and bring us the wine. Before long, he will be here. Elissa, Sama, let's go and sit down. I hope the wine is good.

Curtain.

Scene 3

Fundashing. Nandoh Bih's house. All of Bobe Ngong's fifteen wives are present. They are talking quietly in twos and threes. Sama Ngam is also present but no one seems to notice him. Nandoh Bih is wailing away as if there is a death.

Nandoh Bih: How can people be saying that I shouldn't cry? My only support has done this terrible thing; and people say I shouldn't weep? The kite has flown away with my only chick; and people say I should not lament? Oh! Woe is me! The leopard has caught my only goat; and people say I should close my eyes? A thief has seized a basket from my waist; and they say I should not lament? Fijoi, my mother, were you there when this thing happened? Where were you when the river swept me away? Where were you when the lightning struck me down? Where were you when the sun beat down until the rivers were dry? Where were you when the kite came? Where were you when the leopard pounced? Where were you when the thief seized my basket? Fijoi, my mother, where were you when this terrible thing happened to me? How can they strike me down and bury me alive? How can they seize my waist-cloth in the market place and turn me into a mad woman? Fijoi, my mother, how come you let them do this to me? Woe is me! Woe is me! Woe is me! It were better not to have a child at all. It were better to remain as barren as the rocks, than to have children whose heads are controlled by foreigners. Where has it ever been heard that a man was controlled by a woman? Fointam, is it you killing me like this? Is it you covering your withered mother with shame? Is it you giving your head to a strange woman whose family is not even known? Where did you pick her, my son? Where did she lay the trap, my father? Where did she throw the hook, my husband? Oh! Woe is me! Woe is me! Woe is me! And people say I should not cry? How can I not lament? When the kite is sailing off with my only chick? How can I not cry when the thief has seized my waist-cloth? How can I not lament when I have been bitten by a deadly snake? Woe is me! Woe is me! Woe is me! Fijoi, my mother, where are you? Where are you, my mother? How can you let this happen to me? Have I wronged you in any way? I have never failed to make an offering in your name. Mother, mother, mother. How can you do this to your daughter? Oh! Woe is me! Woe is me! Woe is me! I have been to the stream and come back without the calabash. The trader has gone to market and returned with neither wares nor money. I have been drenched by the rain in the middle of the forest and nowhere to take shelter. Oh! Woe is me! Woe is me! Woe is me! Wherever she comes from, please, my sisters, tell her to leave my only support alone. Whether it is Mayangi or Bayangi, let her leave him alone. Tell her to leave him, my only support, alone. Woe is me! Woe is me! Woe is...

Fifth Woman: Ebei! Nandoh. Stop it. It is too much. You will make like this and people will begin to think that there is death. Wherever she comes from, she is a woman all the same.

First Woman: That Nyangi, a woman? You don't know what you are talking about.

Fifth Woman: What is wrong with Nyangis? Aren't they women like us?

First Woman: I'm surprised, I am really surprised you don't know the Nyangis. The Nyangis? The Nyangis ? Those people who turn themselves into all kinds of animals – elephants, monkeys, boars – to destroy

	people's farms? Every Nyangi woman lives in the bush in the form of some animal. And all of them, without exception, go around with frogs in their arses.
Fifth Woman:	You too can tell stories.
First Woman:	Yes! This is no laughing matter. They go around with frogs in their arses. Above all, they are experts in love potions. I am telling you that this Nyangi woman has cooked our son in a medicine-pot. He is lost. (*Nandoh Bih moans even more*). Not to talk of the Bakweri! They say her mother is Bakweri. We are even lucky that he had already built this ramshackle of a thing he calls a house before he met the she-devil. From now on every *anini* of his goes to the Bakweri woman. Don't you all see how he came in today empty-handed ? Has Fointam ever come to see us with empty hands ? This is worse than death for us all. And to think that we have all the while been grooming Bobe Waindim's daughter, that poor innocent girl, who is already in Class Four, for him! We will hear more of it when Bobe comes back. But if Wallang Yisa says 'yes' to this thing, I will sooner die than live.
Sama:	Are marriages to be decided by soothsayers these days ?
First Woman:	You ? You this boy, Nandoh Nain's son. You deceived this poor boy into this thing; and now you come here without any shame to laugh in our face ? You, this wicked boy whom we all love. Is this what you make of our love ?
Sama:	But how can you people be jumping to conclusions without even hearing Fointam's side of the story ? Why don't you give him a chance just to explain ?
First Woman:	Give him a chance to explain, indeed! What is he explaining that we don't already know ? She is Nyangi, isn't she ?

Sama:	That is not the problem.
First Woman:	Perhaps, that is not *your* problem; but it is definitely ours. (*Looking out through the door*) Aha-aa. There comes Bobe. We better go out and hear what news he has brought from Kikfunen.

Exeunt

Curtain.

Scene 4

Fundashing. When the scene opens, Bobe Ngong is leaning heavily on his walking-stick, shaking his head in disappointment. His wives and some of his children, as well as Sama Ngam, are standing behind him.

Bobe Ngong:	Fointam, Fointam-oh?
Fointam:	(*Off*) I have heard Bobe.
Bobe Ngong:	Come out here at once.

Enter Fointam

Bobe Ngong:	So you came as you said in the book you sent to me?
Fointam:	Yes, Pa.
Bobe Ngong:	And the woman, did she come with you? Did you bring her?
Fointam:	Yes. She came with me. I brought her.
Bobe Ngong:	Now, tell me, where does she come from? Who is her father?
Fointam:	Pa, her father is a teacher in that big school which I left two years ago. He comes from Mamfe; and his tribe is Bayangi. Her mother is also a teacher in the same school; but she comes from Buea. She is Bakweri.
Bobe Ngong:	Banyangi in Mamfe and Bakweri in Buea? So it is true what Wallang Yisa told me? Is it true that she has cooked you in a medicine-pot? That Nyangi

woman! So she has taken my only son from me? Is this Fointam, my son, or some evil spirit come to tempt me? Fointam, if you are really my urine, let that woman go back to wherever she comes from now. If you want a woman right now, Bobe Waindim's daughter is ready and will go with you. She is already in Class Four. Class Four, and that is enough book for a good house-wife. She comes from a very good family; and her father and I went down to Takum and Yola several times to sell colanuts and bring back gun-powder. I say she is ready to go with you now. But let that Nyangi woman leave my compound immediately.

Fointam: Pa, you and Wallang Yisa say that Elissa has cooked me in a medicine-pot?

Bobe Ngong: Yes. She has. Even now, her mother, the Bakweri witch, is making fire under the pot.

Fointam: Pa, stop making declarations which you cannot support. Do you know what things I have sacrificed just because I thought I should bring myself up as your worthy son? When I left secondary school I could have gone to Britain to study in the university. I had three chances, three. But I turned all of them down. After High School it was the same story. Do you know that I started looking for this girl when I was in Secondary School? And because of a worthless sorcerer you say she has cooked me in a medicine-pot? I know Bobe Waindim's daughter. She is a mere child and hardly gone to school. But if you think she is already a woman worth marrying, you are still strong enough to take another. I am going to marry Elissa and no other woman.

Bobe Ngong: You are going to marry that woman inside there?

Fointam: Yes. I will marry her and no other woman. And know that if you don't poor wine in the sacred horn and give us to drink, it will be the death of you. I will

	abandon this compound and, when you die, there will be no son to fire the gun and no heir to slaughter the sacrificial goat.

Bobe Ngong: I will rather die than bless such a marriage. If I give you wine in the sacred horn and die tomorrow, the ancestors will sanction me for allowing you to marry a Banyangi prostitute.

Fointam: So that is the way it is ? Elissa a Banyangi prostitute-eh? Very well; keep your blessing. (*Raises his voice*) Elissa, come out with the things. We are going back right now. My people say they don't want us. Sama, let's go.

Sama: No, Fointam, wait a minute. Pa, this is...

Bobe Ngong: Where is Vibain, the father of my father! Bobe Ngam's son? So it is all very true what Wallang Yisa told me! You take my son and throw him into the claws of that Nyangi harlot? And you dare to come to my compound and look me in the face? Get out before my blood trembles. Or your father will pick you from here in pieces. Get out, I say!

Fointam: If you imagine that we came to stay, then you are mistaken. I will marry without your libation. Perhaps you think that without it I will die. Keep your blessing. And if I ever step into this compound again, call me a dog. Good-bye.

Exeunt Fointam, Elissa and Sama. Most of the women are now wailing. Bobe Ngong continues to lean heavily on his walking stick.

Act Three

Scene I

Same Saturday, evening. Home of Mr and Mrs Eyong. Mr Eyong is reading while Mrs Eyong is knitting. She looks up, from her knitting, at her husband several times before speaking.

Mrs Eyong:	What do you think they are doing now ?
	No answer from her husband..
Mrs Eyong:	Darling ? Darling ?
Mr Eyong:	Yes, Evenge ?
Mrs Eyong:	What are you reading that you are so absorbed ?
Mr Eyong:	Nothing really. Just a silly novel.
Mrs Eyong:	I was just wondering what they might be doing now. I mean Elissa and Fointam.
Mr Eyong:	I can't take a guess. But I suppose they must be doing one thing or other.
Mrs Eyong:	I am sure his parents will be quite pleased.
Mr Eyong:	You're telling me! Was your father pleased when I came to see him the first time ? Don't you remember that he threw Mr Eyong out of the house ?
Mrs Eyong:	But, darling, this is different. It is the other way round.
Mr Eyong:	Well, I suppose it *is* different. Only, I am not very certain...

Elissa rushes in and falls on her mother's laps and weeps. She is closely followed by Fointam and Sama.

Mrs Eyong:	Elissa, dear, what is the matter ? What has happened ?
Elissa:	*(Talking in between sobs)* Oh! Mother... its' so terrible...

	they don't want me. Fointam's parents don't want me. What am I going to do?... It's such a shame, mother... not to be wanted... What am I going to do, mother?... His parents don't want me... They don't want me... And they kept saying Nyangi, Nyangi all the time... They were probably saying something like... like... 'she is a Nyangi prostitute'... Oh mother, I can't stand it... Mother, take me to my room. It's... it's such a shame...
Mr Eyong:	Evenge, take her to her room, dear.
Mrs Eyong:	Yes, darling.

Exeunt Mrs Eyong and Elissa.

Fointam:	I... I am very sorry, Sir, for what happened.
Mr Eyong:	Sit down, Fointam. Is this a friend of yours? Let him sit down.
Fointam:	Yes, Sir. This is my friend, Sama Ngam. He was with us in my village.
Mr Eyong:	And so, your folks don't want my Elissa? Didn't I tell you so? I warned you because I knew.
Fointam:	They didn't even give us a chance, Sir. It was all accusation and forgone conclusions. Can you imagine, Sir, that my father went to consult a sorcerer about my marriage? After that no one wanted to listen to what I had to say. When Sama, here, wanted to intervene, my father threatened his life. So I got angry and told them off.
Mr Eyong:	Well, what has happened has happened. But I must tell you very frankly that I don't like the state in which Elissa finds herself now. I hope she gets over it bye and bye.
Fointam:	There is nothing to get over, Sir. The marriage is going right ahead.
Mr Eyong:	Young man, you don't seem to know what you are talking about. The marriage cannot go ahead with

	all your family against it.
Fointam:	But, sir, the law says that anyone who is above twenty-one is at liberty to take his decisions by himself. I am already above twenty-one, and I have decided to marry Elissa.
Mr Eyong:	My dear young man, you don't know what you are talking about. I am not, repeat, *not* giving my daughter to a man whose parents do not want to see her. And to think they might have called *my* daughter a prostitute! I am not going to take nonsense from naked villagers. Calling my daughter a prostitute! It is unbelievable.
Sama:	Please, sir, if I may say something, my friend here has broken off with his family over this affair. In the heat of the crisis today he took a solemn oath that he will marry no one else but Elissa. And if you are swearing that he cannot marry her, what are we going to do? Please, sir, the law says that twenty-one is the age of maturity. The age at which a man decides freely. Fointam is already twenty-five. He wants to marry Elissa, your daughter. Please, sir, I am begging you to give him a chance. Forget about the things that might have been said about her. If they were ever said, it was out of ignorance and prejudice. Please, sir, give them a chance? I know Elissa still wants to marry Fointam in spite of what happened. But if she no longer wants him, it will be a different matter. Let's give them a chance, sir. I am really begging you in my friend's name.
Mr Eyong:	Well, young man, I should like to know what Elissa feels about the whole situation. I will be back in a minute.

Exit Mr Eyong. Fointam and Sama are too stunned to say anything. When Mr Eyong returns, he is followed by Mrs Eyong and Elissa, who is much composed now. They all sit.

Mr Eyong: Evenge ?
Mrs Eyong: Darling ?
Mr Eyong: Fointam and his friend have been telling me that in spite of what happened in his village today he still wants to marry Elissa. But my problem is how do you marry a woman whom your parents don't want ? This Elissa is my first child. I don't want her to have any problems in any man's home. They have been quoting laws about he being over twenty-one. Yes, I know there is such a law. But, now, I want to hear from Elissa herself whether she is interested in marrying Fointam after what happened today.
Mrs Eyong: Incidentally, darling, I have already asked her that question. She has told me that although they were speaking in 'country talk', at no point did she get the impression that Fointam was in support of what his family was doing. In fact she says there was almost an open fight between Fointam and his friend here, on the one hand, and the rest of the family. But she can tell you herself.
Mr Eyong: Elissa ?
Elissa: Father ?
Mr Eyong: What do you say ?
Elissa: I still want to marry him, father.
Mr Eyong: And where do you put his family ?
Elissa: They will come round, father. I am sure they will come round to liking me. The only problem now is that they don't know me yet.
Mr Eyong: Evenge ?
Mrs Eyong: Yes, Darling ?
Mr Eyong: What do you say ? Do you approve ?

Mrs Eyong:	Yes, Darling. I approve. Darling, you seem to be forgetting that they have been dating for seven years! You didn't date me for seven years, darling. I give my approval.
Mr Eyong:	Fointam ?
Fointam:	I am here, sir.
Mr Eyong:	I give my approval. You people can marry as soon as you please. I won't stand in the way of two young people who genuinely love each other just because of silly ideas in the head of a 'graffi' man. If Evenge had listened to her father we would never have married. We don't know what plan God has for us all; and for this country for that matter. The sooner these tribal barriers are dismantled the better for the welfare of this country. Elissa, bring us some drinks. And, Evenge, you bring me my special beer-mug. There is a celebration.

The drinks and glasses are brought, and Mr Eyong's special beer-mug. He pours beer into his special mug, drinks a bit and hands it to his daughter who takes a good sip and then hands the mug to Fointam who also drinks. Then Mr Eyong takes his daughter by the hand and hands her over to Fointam saying.

Mr Eyong:	Elissa Eyong, as the head of this house, and as demanded by tradition, I Itoh Eyong, rightful heir of Agbor Eyong, give you in marriage to Fointam Ngong, and may God grant you children as numerous as the stars in the skies of this country.
All:	*Instinctively* Amen.
Mr Eyong:	While waiting for the marriage contract to be signed, both of you are free to live together. Evenge tells me she is tired of having a rival in the house. My dear, play us a beautiful tune before we settle down for supper.

Curtain.

Scene 2

Eve of Fointam and Elissa's wedding. They are in Fointam's room and have been making last minute arrangements for the marriage the following morning.

Elissa:	Fointam ?
Fointam:	Yes, my dear ?
Elissa:	Who will be your witness tomorrow, now that your parents don't want me ?
Fointam:	That is already settled, my dear. Sama will be my witness. Who will be yours ?
Elissa:	My mother asked Mrs Ndi, wife of the History teacher, and she accepted to be my witness.
Fointam:	That is good. I was afraid you might want to take one of your school friends who don't seem to know their left from their right.
Elissa:	How did you expect me to do that kind of thing ? They are all jealous that I am getting married.
Fointam:	Tell them to behave like you and they will soon find husbands too.
Elissa:	We better go to bed, dear. I am so tired. And tomorrow I have to rise early.
Fointam:	Alright, my dear, we better sleep.

They lie down and the lights go off. When the lights come again, Bobe Ngong and Nandoh Bih are discovered sitting by the fire in Fundashing. The impression must be given that what follows is a dream by Fointam.

Nandoh Bih:	Have you heard that they are marrying today ?
Bobe Ngong:	What is that to me whether they are marrying today, or tomorrow, or the day after ?
Nandoh Bih:	But I hear they have sent you a book. What have you done with it ?

Bobe Ngong:	If they have sent a book, it was to *me*. What is your business in it?
Nandoh Bih:	I don't have any business in it. I just wanted to know what they said in the book.
Bobe Ngong:	They didn't say anything; apart from that they are marrying today.
Nandoh Bih:	And what are you thinking?
Bobe Ngong:	Look, Bih, don't bother me. I am not thinking anything. Your son is getting married against my wish and yours. What do you want me to be thinking?
Nandoh Bih:	I have been wondering whether sometimes you are not too stubborn? You know we did not even give them a chance. Ever since they left I have been feeling queer. The kind of feeling that seems to arise from guilt.
Bobe Ngong:	What chance did you want us to give them after Wallang Yisa had made his pronouncement? He communes with the gods; and who am I to gainsay what the gods say?
Nandoh Bih:	I don't understand. My head is very heavy.
Bobe Ngong:	What don't you understand? Can't you understand that it is an abomination for a son of mine to marry from foreign lands? And now he is marrying without a bride-price? The thing will not succeed. Before long he will be running back to us with his tail between his legs like a dog that has been caught stealing.
Nandoh Bih:	If I know Fointam, he will do no such thing. He seems to be convinced that his choice is the right one. Didn't you hear him say that he started looking for her when he was still in Secondary School? It is a long time back, you know?
Bobe Ngong:	We will see who will be proved wrong in the end: centuries of ancestral wisdom or the madness of this boy. I have nothing to say. Go and bring me a

	bit of tobacco. How I long for a smoke!
Nandoh Bih:	All I am saying is that I have been dreaming some kinds of dreams which I don't understand. Can you imagine that last night I was actually holding her child in my hands ? And it was a child with a long penis like this. (*She indicates with her hand.*)
Bobe Ngong:	Go out of here with that nonsense. You think that prostitute of a woman can ever have a child ? Very soon Fointam will be crawling back here on his knees, begging us to give him Bobe Waindim's daughter. You will see. Go and bring me the tobacco.

As Nandoh Bih exits the lights go off. Then they come on again but much dimmer. Fointam stirs and looks at Elissa. She is sound asleep. He smiles at the thought of the dream and wriggles closer to Elissa. The lights go off.

Curtain.

Scene 3

Mbengwi. Four years later. Elissa and Fointam are now teachers in a secondary school. She is heavily pregnant, and is resting on a chair. Fointam is marking papers.

Elissa:	Fointam ?
Fointam:	Yes, my dear ?
Elissa:	I feel so tired. It will come any moment. I mean the child.
Fointam:	When did the doctor say, it might be coming ?
Elissa:	In a week or so. This time, it will be a girl. No more of your boys. You have won the bet twice now. I was really longing for a boy the first time; and he came. The next time, I wanted a girl; but you won again. Now, I'll have things my own way. This time,

	I am having a girl.
Fointam:	I am sorry, my dear, to have to disappoint you again. You are having a child with a long penis like this (*Indicates with right fist*) in his buttocks. You can wait for your girl next time.
Elissa:	Alright, alright, Mr Prophet. Just the way you like. But after he comes, we must go and see your parents, dear.
Fointam:	That will depend...
Elissa:	On what? Look, Fointam dear, you are exaggerating the whole thing. Your old man has as good as apologised for his past behaviour. You remember the presents he sent us after Sama came ? A basket full of fowls and a huge goat. You ought to forgive him and forget his folly.
Fointam:	We'll see, my dear. Let the child come first. Then we'll see how it affects your health. Then the other things can follow.
Elissa:	Eyong is fast growing into a man; and Sama too is not doing badly. These children are your off-spring as well as his. Why should you deprive him of the pleasure of holding his grandsons ?
Fointam:	I am not depriving him of anything, dear. I just want him to see reason. My old man is the most conservative fool in the whole world. Let him learn his lessons the hard way.
Elissa:	And your mother; what about her ? Why can't you think about her ?
Fointam:	I accept that she is more reasonable than my father. There is a dream I have never forgotten. All of these children were predicted by her. I dreamt the dream on the eve of our wedding and she said in a hot argument with my father, that she had held your child in her arms and that it had a long penis like this. That is where I got the expression from. And that was on the eve of our wedding, four years ago!

	As for my father, he never believed that you would have a child.
Elissa:	That's not true!
Fointam:	At least, that is what he said in the dream. Whether he and my mother actually had that kind of argument or not, I don't know. I am just telling you what I dreamt four years ago, on the eve of our wedding. That is why I am in no hurry for us to go down to Fundashing. But when the times comes, we will go.
Elissa:	Well, I guess you are the best judge in the affair. Oh, how tired I feel! Let me have a glass of water to drink, dear.
Fointam:	Come on. Why can't you get out of that chair and get the water yourself? You're making me scared. You're usually so smart! I have never seen you like this.
Elissa:	Fointam, this pregnancy is unlike the others. I have been feeling terribly weak all this week. Just give some water to drink.
	Fointam brings her water.
Fointam:	Are you feeling better now?
Elissa:	Yes, much better. Now, take me to bed. I can't lie in that room alone in my present state.
Fointam:	What, now, Elissa? You know I have to give back these papers tomorrow. What is wrong with your lying in the room alone for a few minutes?
Elissa:	No, I can't stand it. You can finish your marking tomorrow morning. Let's go to bed. I need *you* to hold my belly before I can go to sleep.
Fointam:	Just the way you wish, my queen. Shall I hold your belly right from here?
Elissa:	Don't be silly. Hold me by my waist. Yes, like that. Now, let's go.

Exeunt. Curtain.

Scene 4

Two years after Scene 3. Home of Fointam and Elissa. Elissa is suckling a baby in the sitting-room. There is a knock at the door as Eyong Fointam, her first son, runs up to her.

Eyong Fointam:	Mama! Mama! There is someone with a big goat and another one with very many fowls in a basket.
Elissa:	Eyong, stop shouting. Don't you know you are disturbing your father? Why can't you talk quietly?
Eyong Fointam:	But, Mama, there are people at the door. Don't you hear the goat? And the fowls making that noise? There's a man and a woman.
Elissa:	Go and call your father while I see who they are.
Male Voice:	*(Off)* No man no dey? Who dey house?
Elissa:	I di come-oh, I di come.
	Enter Bobe Chia and First Woman.
Elissa:	Wuna welcome. Welcome, Ma.
First Woman:	Tenk you, my pickin. How wuna dey? Pickin dem well?
Elissa:	We all we well. Wuna sidong. Wusai John-eh? John-oh? John?
John:	*(Off)* Sah? I mean, Madam?
Elissa:	I beg, come take these things for backside.
	John comes in, takes the things and exits. Enters Fointam.
Fointam:	Aaaaa. Is it you, Bobe Chia? Welcome. Welcome, Bobe. Nawain, welcome. How are the old people? I hope they are well. And the children, of course, I hope everyone is in good health?
Bobe Chia:	Fointam, the whole family is well. The children are well now. But a few weeks ago there was a severe attack of measles in Fundashing and many children fell victim. Fortunately neither your people nor mine were affected.
Fointam:	Did many children die, then?
First Woman:	Don't say it again. Children were just dropping dead

	like premature pear fruits in the heat of the sun. It was terrible.
Fointam:	But you say the compound was not affected?
First Woman:	I don't know what god saved us. We were not affected. But we are not ourselves.
Bobe Chia:	That is true, Fointam. Your people are not themselves. Especially your old man. He is not himself. We have a saying that no matter what a 'juju' does to you, you do not unmask it in public. I have come here today to plead for my friend, your old man and father. He is dying to see the children and both of you too. What did you expect him to do? We are all ignorant people, living in a world of our own. Do we know what happiness means to you young people? Do we know that whether a man is Banyangi or Bamileke or Bali, he belongs to the same Cameroon? My son, you have proved us wrong; and taught us, your elders, that marriage is not tribe but character and love. Forgive us all for our ignorance; and bring the children so that we too can see them.
First Woman:	Na how many them dey, my pickin?
Elissa:	Dem dey na four, Ma. Three boys and one girl. Na the girl this for my hand. Na only four months since dem born-am.
First Woman:	We-eh, my pickin, wuna chus we. We sabi jus now say na we dong fall case. We di hungry for see wuna bad, bad one. No bi na number three tam dis wey Bobe dong send people for here? We-eh, pickin, wuna no fit sorry for yi? Wuna no di sorry for we? We been make na foolish. Six years na long, long time. I beg you my pickin make wuna come show we de pickin dem.
Bobe Chia:	And, Fointam, but for the fact that your father is such a big coward, he should have come already. Even if you tie him up and push into a motor

	vehicle he will still jump out. When he sees a motor he just begins to run off. And when he smells petrol he begins to vomit. He should have come already. Now he is too old to do the distance on foot.
Fointam:	Bobe Chia, I know my old man has an aversion for motor vehicles; so I am not worrying about the fact that he has not come himself. However, I have heard what you have said, and I am no longer angry. I have not seen the family for six years just because of some foolish idea that was buried deep in their heads. I am happy you say you now realise that marriage is not a question of tribe but rather character and love. Above all, we cannot build this nation on tribalism and partisanship. I have forgiven my people. In Elissa's case, it has never been a problem. She forgave them the very first time Bobe sent a message to us. When you go back to Fundashing, tell them that we are coming to see them during the next Christmas vacation.
First Woman:	*Ululates and intones a Njang air. All actors join in the dancing before curtain falls.*

The End

Part V

And Palm-wine will Flow

Dramatis Personae

(In order of appearance)

SHEY NGONG:	Chief priest of Nyombom
NSANGONG:	Friend of Shey Ngong
MESSENGER:	From the Palace
KWENGONG:	One of the wives of Shey Ngong / Earthgodess
TAPPER:	Palm - wine tapper for Shey Ngong / Kibaranko
GWEI:	One of the watch - dogs of the Fon
FON:	Ruler of the of Ewawa Various background voices.
SETTING:	Ewawa, imaginary Fondom in the grassfields.

The sacred grove of Nyombom, characterised by an elaborately decorated pot, **nshang wong,** *in which libation is poured to the gods. Elsewhere in the grove are a number of masks, also elaborately decorated with dark fibre or cloth, thus making them easy to be used as disguises by various characters in the play. Other prominent features of the grove are a gourd and a sacred gong. All action takes place in the same place.*

VOICE

(Off) Shey Ngong, are you not coming to the palace? Where are you going to when all roads are leading to the palace?

SHEY NGONG

Is there anything of import, apart from the merry making? I am going to the grove for some peace.

VIOCE

But Shey, do you or do you not know that Kibanya is receiving the red feather today from the sacred hands of the Fon himself?

SHEY NGONG

So I have heard.

VOICE

And palm-wine will flow as usual. Come with me to the palace, Shey. The Fon will not take your absence kindly.

SHEY NGONG

I am going to the grove. My obligation is to the gods of the land. My duty is to the gods. Not to the Fon and palm-wine.

VOICE

Swallow your words, Shey! The cockroach does not call a fowl to a wrestling match. It is a foolish rat that argues with a cat.

SHEY NGONG

So I am the rat? I am the cockroach? You knave. The gorilla can do nothing to an iroko tree.

VOICE

Eh? You are the iroko tree, are you? I see you want to wrestle with the father and owner of this land of Ewawa.

SHEY NGONG

Eh? Who owns the land? Because he takes what belongs to the land and no one lifts a finger?

VOICE

Swallow your words, Shey. I say swallow your words.

SHEY NGONG

I will not. I am the cockroach. A gorilla can do nothing to the iroko tree.

VOICE

Shey Ngong, you will be hearing from the palace before the sun goes down.

SHEY NGONG

Away you fawnig , stooging dog ! Away to your lord and drown yourselves in palm-wine. What a land!

VOICE

Shey I have already warned. You will be hearing from the palace before the sun goes to sleep.

SHEY NGONG

And palm-wine will flow.

VOICE

You said it. And palm-wine will flow! Palm-wine will flow! You just wait and see. Palm-wine will flow.

SHEY NGONG

What a land! what a people! And to think that people in other lands... What a people! *(Moves over to the sacred pot from which he takes out sacred horn and pours some wine into it from the gourd.)*

Oh! Nyombom!
Creator and guardian of the land,
And you our illustrious forebears,
Grant me strength and wisdom
To weather the surging storm.
The Fon has lost vision.
The noble men and elders of this land
Now listen only to the inner voice
Of greed, and fear of a man who has
Surrounded himself with listeners
And watch-dogs to do his bidding.
Nyombom and you, ancestors,
Grant me strength and wisdom
Grant me patience and love....
(His invocation is interrupted by the rising sound of distant music and loud applause and ululations.)
Kibanya must be receiving his red feather now.
From today he will stand in the market place
and beat his chest and speak in a loud voice.
The land! The land! What a people

NSANGONG
(Off) Shey Can I come? Or shall I wait outside? The load that I am carrying must be put down.

SHEY NGONG
Come inside then. Come. This place is cool and peaceful; especially for one carrying a load. Come.

NSANGONG
The place is really cool-eh? It is a boiling pot out there.

SHEY NGONG
Where are you coming from so agitated like a monkey that has missed the hunter's bullet?

NSANGONG
I am just from the palace and .....

SHEY NGONG
You must have missed the crowning moment. What did go there for?

NSANGONG
Shey, listen to me and stop your rambling. The Fon is mad at you and has sworn....

SHEY NGONG
That I will hear from him before the sun goes to sleep. Not so?

NSANGONG
So you know already? Did the tortoise really beat the hare in the racing match? Where is he?

SHEY NGONG
No. No tortoise has beaten the hare. Only that Kibanya's shadow and one of the Fon's watch-dogs wandered by here.

NSANGONG
Wandered? They came on purpose, Shey. Have you ever seen the owl beating its wings in broad day?

SHEY NGONG
What then is their mission?

NSANGONG
Did you really speak? Shey, answer me. Did you say anything offensive? Speak Shey!

SHEY NGONG
Does it really matter, Nsangong? The cat, no matter how full his stomach is, will never spare the rat.

NSANGONG
But did you really say you are the iroko tree? Shey, speak!

SHEY NGONG
He is not the sun that strides magisterial in the sky. We are not shrubs to be trampled underfoot by the elephant.

NSANGONG
I fear and I tremble for you. Look, Shey, get up. Let us go to the palace. Go and give the monkey his banana or he will never give you peace.

SHEY NGONG
The stream never flows uphill. The leopard and the goat have never been bed-fellows. I am waiting to hear from the palace.
A bugle sounds so close that both of them are unnerved momentarily. A messenger enters with 'monkeng' and walks towards Shey Ngong.

MESSENGER
Greetings from the Fon, Shey Ngong. And all his noble men. The Fon desires your presence forthwith.

SHEY NGONG
Go back to your master and his family of hand-clappers and tell them that the stream flows down-hill.

NSANGONG
Wait a little, Shey. Consider what you say.

SHEY NGONG
You keep your mouth out of this, Nsangong. Tell your master that the leopard and the goat have never eaten from the same dish.

MESENGER
But my lord, the lion of Ewawa means no harm. Rather, he wants to share a cup with his revered chief priest.

NSANGONG
That is the truth, Shey. The Fon means no harm. But how could he? The cat and the dog may quarrel over a piece of meat. But they are still friends.

SHEY NGONG
I am no dog that will hunt for the pleasure of another. The game must be shared. Let everyone have his fair share, I say. But your Fon knows none other than his family and those that come to him with gifts in return for the red feather.

MESSENGER
But, Shey, the Fon has refused you nothing. All that remains is for you to ask.

NSANGONG
Is that not what I said? Shey, give the monkey his banana and take back your place among the council of elders.

MESSENGER
That is all.

SHEY NGONG
Does the wise council ever discuss with the Fon? When the Fon pronounces that this farm-land now belongs to himself or one of his family, does the wise council open its mouth in disapproval? I spit on a body that only gives approval and acclaims every decision taken by one man.

NSANGONG
But, Shey......

MESSENGER
Watch your tongue, Shey. The Fon is the wise one.

SHEY NGONG
Your Fon is the pig who knows only the hunger of its own stomach.

MESSENGER
Enh? What did you say? Swallow your words, Shey!

SHEY NGONG
I say your Fon is a goat....

NSANGONG
Shey, please........

MESSENGER
Is that so?

SHEY NGONG
And I am the stream that flows down-hill.

MESSENGER
So be it.
He sounds the bugle in mock honour to Shey Ngong, greets him in the traditional manner reserved only for people of such status and exits with a flourish.

NSANGONG
Shey, your sun has gone over the hill.

SHEY NGONG
And palm-wine will flow.

NSANGONG
You make light of serious matters, Shey.

SHEY NGONG
I do not make light of anything. But since the Fon is the wise one....

NSANGONG
I will follow him and keep my ears close to the ground.
Exits.

SHEY NGONG
(Resuming his invocation)
        Oh! Nyombom!
        Grant me strength.
        Grant me wisdom.
        Show me the right path
        In this moment of trial.....
(More distant shouts and ululations) Another red feather? Only Kibanya was due to be honoured today. When this land was still the land empty shells like Kibanya would never have had access to the palace. Today, nobles have become slaves and slaves nobles. Just because the late Fon....

NSANGONG
(Rushing in terribly agitated) Shey! Shey! Your wives' farm-lands have been seized and given to Kibanya's wives. A messenger is on the way to deliver the Fon's pronouncement.

SHEY NGONG
Was that the reason for the recent shouting and ululations?

NSANGONG
You heard them, Shey. You heard the people rejoicing in your misfortune.

SHEY NGONG
That is what happens when there is plenty of everything. The louse and the jigger have no need for brains.

NSANGONG
My ear does not follow your tongue, Shey.

SHEY NGONG
When people overfeed like pigs and soak themselves in palm-wine, they take pleasure in desecrating their gods.

NSANGONG
You speak the truth, Shey. When there is too much in the belly, the head becomes an empty shell. *(Bugle sound followed by Messenger's entrance.)* You friend has arrived.

MESSENGER
(Mock greeting) Holy one, the lion of Ewawa has pronounced that the farm-lands of your revered wives now belong to Kibanya's wives.

SHEY NGONG
By whose order?

MESSENGER
Order? But I just told you. By the pronouncement of the lion of Ewawa. The one you have challenged to a wrestling match.

SHEY NGONG
The leopard does not wrestle with a goat.

MESSENGER

I am glad to hear that. The rat does not play with the cat. I am glad you are beginning to see reason.

SHEY NGONG

I am the leopard. I am the cat.

NSANGONG

How far can you carry this fight, Shey? The forces against you are overwhelming.

MESSENGER

Yes, plead with your friend. May be he will have an ear for what your tongue says.

SHEY NGONG

The gods and the ancestors will fight their battle with the Fon. I am only their servant.

MESSENGER

Now that your wives have lost their farm-lands what are the gods and your ancestors doing? *One of the marks, Earth-goddess, suddenly becomes agitated and then pronounces.*

EARTH-GODDESS

The sun shines on the hills
The sun shines in the valleys
The sun shines in the depths of the streams
The sun shines.

MESSENGER

What was that?

NSANGONG

We are undone.

SHEY NGONG

The land has pronounced.

MESSENGER

What?

SHEY NGONG
The sun shines on the hills, in the valleys and in the depths of the streams.

NSANGONG
A drought! A drought! We are undone.

SHEY NGONG
Hurry, fellow, and tell your master the pronouncement of the land.

MESSENGER
You mean the gods have spoken?

NSANGONG
Do you or do you not have eyes and ears.

SHEY NGONG
You waste time. Hasten to the wise one and recount the happenings here.

NSANGONG
Go quickly.

MESSENGER
Very well. I will.

NSANGONG
I begin to believe in you, Shey. I will follow him and keep my ears close to the ground.
Exits. Shey Ngong smiles broadly and begins a victory chant accompanied by slow but complicated foot-steps.

Aya ooù, aya-oo ooù
è è è a la'a keu dore bi'an dore
iyéé iyie
Aya ooù, ayaoo ooù
èèè ngong'e keu dore bi'an dore
iyèè iyie
Aya oo, ayaoo
ééé beunwi'a keu dore bi'an dore

iyèè iyie
Ma'nfor subisu'oo yi n'ang bané
Ayaya, ayaya
Keuo leeh nji'i ngo'oh
loghe nfaa loghe ngaaboh
Ayayo ayayo keu shwa'a keu bi'e
Chong kuru ngu
Wasé' nja
O O chong
Wase' nja
O O chong
Wasé nja wa nda bone wasè, nya
Chong noo mulu'u
Wase nja
O O Chong
Wase nja wa nda bone wase nja
Chong. jeu'achu'u
wase nja
O O chong
Wase nja
O O O chong
Wase nja wa nda bone wase nja
Bibibi wulai
Wulai
Bibibi Wulai
Wulai
Achia wole?
Achia wole.

The he returns to his invocation

SHEY NGONG

Oh! Nyombom!
I am only your servant;
I am only your spokesman.
But if the sun shines.....
Sudden commotion and several female voices in great agitation and anger.

VOICES

Shey! Our husband!
Father of our children!
Shey, our husband! Are you sitting there quietly
When our farms have been seized from us?
What shall we eat? What shall our children eat?
What shall you eat, Shey? We know you are in there.
Speak up, Shey. Or shall we come into the sacred presence in
Our present condition? Speak up, Shey!

SHEY NGONG

Peace, wives! Peace!
Do I need to remind you that you stand on sacred ground? Peace! Peace!

VOICES

We await the words from your mouth, oh husband! Our ears are famished.

SHEY NGONG

Peace, wives! Peace! Is Kwengong, my first wife with you?

VOICES

We are all here, husband! We are....

SHEY NGONG

Kwengong?

KWENGONG

My ears are on the ground, husband.

SHEY NGONG

Kwengong, let the others go back home and wait there. You come inside. If the Fon wishes to wrestle with the gods, he must know how tough his belt is. Do you hear me, wives?

VOICES

We hear you well, father of our children. We go home to wait there.

SHEY NGONG
I thank you, wives. Kwengong, come inside.

KWENGONG
Here I am, husband.

SHEY NGONG
Wife, what did you people go to the palace to do?

KWENGONG
We wanted to bask ourselves in the sun that shines on the lucky ones.

SHEY NGONG
Lucky? Are you sure they are lucky, wife?

KWENGONG
When manless men like Kibanya have their caps topped with the red feather by the Fon himself, how else can I describe them?

SHEY NGONG
And you approve?

KWENGONG
But how could I, husband? It is the provocation that is driving us mad. And now our farm-lands are gone.

SHEY NGONG
I have told you not to torture your mind about the farm-lands. The gods of the land have already pronounced judgement.

KWENGONG
What is it?

SHEY NGONG
A drought. There will be a drought.

KWENGONG
But Shey, we are in the middle of the dry season. How long shall we wait to see this judgement come? What shall we, your wives, do?

SHEY NGONG

Let Kibanya and his wives step into your farm-lands if they have the guts. Manless man that he is!

KWENGONG

The Fon's watch-dogs will give him protection. He is now a title-holder. He wears the red feather on his cap.

SHEY NGONG

If that red feather still had any value, would Kibanya ever have been decorated? In the past, when Ewawa was still Ewawa, did people beg for the red feather or was it the council of elders which recommended to the Fon that so and so should be decorated because of such and such a service rendered to the land?

KWENGONG

The times are changing, Shey. The times have changed. Look at you! What is your reward? After how many years of loyal service to the gods and the land? The farmlands of your wives have been made over to the wives of the lowliest of the low. Why? Because he pays respect to the Fon. But you...

SHEY NGONG

Wife, I will not pay respect to a man who respects only palm-wine and food. When does the Fon really rule? How often has he consulted the council of elders or even implemented decisions by that revered body for the common good of all the land?

KWENGONG

But the people adulate the Fon because he gives them titles.

SHEY NGONG

What is the worth of a title if it must be bought? Those clamouring for the red feather are only making the Fon richer. Today, with a few goats and fowls even the lowliest of the low are beginning to file into the royal presence. How do you have a land in which everyone is a title holder?

KWENGONG

Is that why you refuse to apply?

SHEY NGONG
I spit on the red feather when people like Kibanya are crowned by the Fon himself. Where have our values of old gone? I spit on the red feather and I spit on the distributor of the red feather.

KWENGONG
If he hears that you will not live, my husband.

SHEY NGONG
The Fon never dies. He reigns eternally. That is our Fon's misguided obsession. *(Agitated male voice off)* What is that now? Who is there? What is happening?

VOICE
(Off) Shey oh! Shey oh! The palm-bush!

SHEY NGONG
(To Kwengong pointing at the Earth-goddess mask) Quick, get into that mask.

KWENGONG
Who? Me?

SHEY NGONG
Yes. You! Get into it quickly. (*Raising voice*) Come inside and tell me what is wrong with the palm-bush.

TAPPER
(Holding empty gourd upside down) See, Shey! See! No wine! No wine! No...

SHEY NGONG
Will you stop whining? Why no wine?

TAPPER
The palm-bush! The palm-bush! The palm...

SHEY NGONG
Speak up, fellow! What happened to the palm-bush?

TAPPER

The Fon has seized the palm-bush. His watch-dogs are there now. Getting drunk on the wine I tapped. Look at my clothes! All torn! In tatters!

SHEY NGONG

Your clothes were never whole, my man. But did you try to fight them?

TAPPER

I thought I could drive them out. In fact, I thought it was some joke. But... but...

SHEY NGONG

You are not a cow that can knock out a horde of flies.

TAPPER

They were many, Shey. Three of them. And I was alone.

SHEY NGONG

Never try to fight another's battle for him. They could have killed you. And what would I tell your wife and children?

TAPPER

Shey, they beat me up severely. I found them in my hut, where I store palm-wine. They were already drunk. And they had finished a whole pot of wine which I tapped yesterday. When I asked them what they wanted, they laughed and said the palm-bush had reverted to the Fon, its rightful owner.

SHEY NGONG

They said that?

TAPPER

Laughing. And laughing, asked me to inform you that your spy, Nsangong, had been caught.

SHEY NGONG

By whom? For what crime? On whose orders? Is the fellow mad?

TAPPER
I think so, Shey. The Fon is mad.

SHEY NGONG
Where is Nsangong now?

TAPPER
I was coming to that, Shey. When those three rogues threw me out of the bush, I took the road leading here because I knew you would be waiting. Half way through, I met with Tashi. You know Tashi, don't you? It was he who gave me the details. The things that are happening in this land are pregnant, he said. Imagine a respectable man like Nsangong, tied with ropes to a kolanut tree as if he were a cow and whipped by worthless thieves. Yes. They whipped him thoroughly until he began to bleed in several places. Then some people in the crowd intervened and carried him away to his compound. He could no longer walk. But, I tell you, Nsangong is a man. During all that time that he was being tortured, he never opened his mouth. Not even a sound of anguished pain or despair. That man is a man. It was his courage that encouraged some people to intervene and so saved his life, Tashi concluded. What did the rest do? The festivity continued, I asked? How could the festivity continue. Can you hear any drumming or singing? The feasting stopped, suddenly. The people have all dispersed.

SHEY NGONG
Returned to their homes?

TAPPER
That is what Tashi said, Shey. And I met with other men, women and children returning to their homes.

SHEY NGONG
The people abandoned palm-wine and food on their own account and returned to their homes? Are my ears hearing right? What about the notables and his watch-dogs? Did they leave too?

TAPPER
But how could they? They are living on the sweat of everyone else. How could they?

SHEY NGONG

It is strange, very strange that the people left palm-wine and went back to their homes. Palm-wine is the curse that is ruining this land. It is the curse.

Earth-goddess begins a giddy dance which rises in tempo until she begins to pronounce.

EARTH-GODDESS

The ground trembles in the valleys!
The ground trembles where the streams flow!
The ground trembles where the palms grow!
The ground trembles!

Rising sound of thunder rumbling in the ground.

TAPPER

What is this now? What is happening?

SHEY NGONG

Quick! Hurry and tell me what is going on.
Tapper exits.

TAPPER

(Off) Shey oh! Shey! The palm-bush below the palace is going down!

SHEY NGONG

Going down how? The palm-bush has developed feet? How can it be going down?

TAPPER

I mean going down! Going down! You don't understand? Yes! Falling! It has disappeared, Shey. *(Reappearing on stage)* A palm-bush disappearing in the dry season! Unbelievable, Shey! This is unbelievable.

SHEY NGONG

The land has pronounced judgment! The gods be praised.

EARTH GODDESS

The sun that rises must always set!
The Fon never dies!
The Fon reigns eternally!
The sun that rises must always set!

SHEY NGONG

(To Tapper) You heard it yourself. The sun that rises must always set.

TAPPER

Shall that really come to pass? Can the elephant really fall, Shey?

SHEY NGONG

Have you become doubtful of our gods and ancestors even after the trembling of the earth?

TAPPER

Not that, Shey. But where shall we get palm-wine for your evening invocations and libations?

SHEY NGONG

There must be palm-wine in the palace, since you say the Fon's watch-dogs drove you out of the sacred palm-bush. I wonder if the tremor reached there.

TAPPER

Shall I go and find out?

SHEY NGONG

Go for the palm-wine first. We will see about the palm-bush later.

TAPPER

How do I do that? The disease that attacked the cow cannot spare the goat. I do not want to suffer like Nsangong. We have all heard of people being beaten up or made to disappear by his watch-dogs. Today, it happened before the very eyes of the people. Tashi says the terrible sight nauseated many and others sent blades of grass deep down their throats. Even tappers went away leaving their pots and calabashes behind.

SHEY NGONG

Is that so? And now that palm-bushes are going down, this might be the beginning of the cure for the curse that has gripped the land in its claws.

EARTH GODDESS

The curse remains!
The plague remains!
The pot is whole!
The calabash is whole!
The curse remains.

SHEY NGONG

You hear that? You must make haste to the palace and bring palm-wine for the incantation.

TAPPER

How do I do that? They almost killed me in the bush; and I do not want to suffer the fate of Nsangong.

VOICE

(Off) Shey Ngong? Shey Ngong? Have you heard what happened to your friend? The rat does not play with the cat.

SHEY NGONG

Who is the rat, you knave? *(Signals Tapper to get into Kibaranko mask)* Come inside and say your proverb.

GWEI

A messenger does not receive the blows meant for the sender of the message. The Fon has sworn to sack your grove. *(Making for the gourd by the sacred pot)* Let me have a little wine before... *(Kibaranko begins to rumble)* What is that?

SHEY NGONG

Do you realise that you are on scared ground?
Kibaranko's rumbling intensifies while Earth-goddess begins to keen. Gwei tries to flee but discovers that he cannot move.

GWEI
Let me go! Let me out of here! Let me go, Shey!

SHEY NGONG
Is anyone holding you? Go! No one stops you.
The rumbling and keening intensify, reducing Gwei to a complete state of fear.

GWEI
I beg you, Shey. Holy One, let me go! I beg you, Holy One. Let me leave this place in peace.

SHEY NGONG
Let the Fon come sack the grove! Let him come and... He has drunk wine until it has gone into his head.

GWEI
That is true, Holy One. The Fon is drunk.

SHEY NGONG
If he hears that your head will fall.

GWEI
In private, Shey! I said it in private, Holy One. Everybody says the Fon is mad. But in private.

SHEY NGONG
And in public you sing his praises. The Wise One! Father of the land! Founder and Guardian of Ewawa! The Wise One! Shepherd of the land! Father and Mother of all the children! Curer of the sick! Keeper of the poor! And all the time he is seizing people's farm-lands and palm-bushes for himself and his notables.

GWEI
Out of fear, Holy One! Out of fear!

SHEY NGONG
You even adulate him. You worship him! You worship a man!

GWEI
Out of fear, Holy One. I have already said so.

SHEY NGONG
Is it out of fear that you now call me Holy One?

GWEI
Out of fear, Holy One.... I mean Shey!

SHEY NGONG
How can the whole land be afraid of one man? And you, what crimes have you committed on his behalf? What happened to Nsangong?

GWEI
It was not me, Holy One... I mean Shey!

SHEY NGONG
Yet you were quick to bring me the news. Have you heard what happened to your friend? The rat does not play with the cat. Talk!

GWEI
I swear by Kibaranko that it was not me. *(Kibaranko rumbles furiously)* I mean I swear by the gods, by Earth-goddess. *(Earth-goddess keens furiously.)*

SHEY NGONG
You see how you perjure yourself? How do people disappear in the land? Where do you keep them?

GWEI
They are taken to Ekpang, Shey.

SHEY NGONG
The bad bush?

GWEI
Yes, the bad bush.

SHEY NGONG
And killed? You kill people in the bad bush on behalf of the Fon?

GWEI
Very often it is the notables who order. Especially Nformi Nyam and Nformi Eleme.

SHEY NGONG
For what crimes. What are their crimes that you take their lives?

GWEI
For talking ill of the Fon or his notables.

SHEY NGONG
For that alone, you take a man's life? What is your gain? How much do you get paid?

GWEI
My wife did not have a plot to till, Shey. How were we to survive? My father's wives had been seized; and when he went to the Fon to complain, we never saw him again. He never came back. He disappeared, Shey! After that, it was easy to take his palm-bush.

SHEY NGONG
And instead of taking up arms to fight to avenge the death of your father, you allied with the Fon?

GWEI
How was I to fight alone, Shey? With what force? I would have disappeared too.

SHEY NGONG
So you took the easier road. And now your wife has a farm and you a palm-bush, not so? Now you lick the oil dripping from the Fon's fingers as he eats chicken. While he and his notables stuff their bellies with chunks of meat, you dive for the bones. Get up and go, knave! Slave that you are!

Gwei flees while Tapper emerges from Kibaranko mask very amused.

TAPPER
I wonder why they have not come for you all this while.

SHEY NGONG
Stop wondering and go for the palm-wine.

TAPPER

Not me, Shey. Let Kibaranko go. Kibaranko will do it.

SHEY NGONG

(Indicating spot next to sacred pot) Stand here.
Kwo'o! Kwo'o! Kwo'o!
The lion announces his presence with roaring! *(Tapper begins to rumble)*
The dog does not eat because he is hungry!
The leopard prowls among the goats
And they scatter into the dark night!
(Scoops liquid from sacred pot and makes rumbling Tapper to drink after which he becomes more agitated, ending in frenzy and howling.)
The lion spreads terror among the cattle and sheep!
(Tapper enters Kibaranko mask)
When the elephant flaps his ears and sounds his trumpet
The forest is in disarray for he has gone berserk!
(Howling Kibaranko exits in terrifying frenzy.)

KWENGONG

(Emerging from Earth-goddess mask) There are no restrainers. He will devastate the whole palace.

SHEY NGONG

You said that was the only cure, remember.

KWENGONG

Earth-goddess! Not me! Earth-goddess pronounced!

SHEY NGONG

And we must execute. Go quickly. The women must do something to avert the drought pronounced by Earth-goddess. Go, before darkness falls all over the land.

KWENGONG

I go, father of children.
Exits.

SHEY NGONG

Oh, Nyombom!
Creator and guardian of the land!
And you illustrious ancestors!

Grant me courage.
Bestow upon us the wisdom to steer
This land back on the right path.
Give Kibaranko the strength to sack
The palace where the notables of this land
Have turned themselves into suckers of blood and wine.
(Distant alarm)
Kibaranko in action!
Let their heads be crushed like pumpkins
And their brains be licked by the dogs!
Let their bones crack and their members
Be torn each from the other until they lie
Scattered in the devastating fire!
Let smoke rise from the roof-top
And the palace lie desolate!
Kibaranko, perform your task!

MESSENGER
Shey! Shey Ngong! How can you do this, Shey? How can...

SHEY NGONG
Calm yourself, fellow. How can what?

MESSENGER
You send Kibaranko out without restrainers? He is devastating the palace. Imagine, Shey, all palm-wine calabashes and pots broken and scattered in the courtyard! The whole place is smelling of palm-wine and flies are boozing all over the place.

SHEY NGONG
They too must drink. The appetite for wine does not belong to humans only.

MESSENGER
It was terrible, Shey. The Fon and the notables of the land were all drunk, in various degrees.

SHEY NGONG

Naturally! Is there a single day in this land that they are not drinking? The sun cannot rise and set in this land without someone taking a title or some other celebration.

MESSENGER

As I was saying, Shey, we were all in various stages of drunkenness when suddenly we heard the howling of Kibaranko and saw the Fon's wives and children running in total confusion and fear. That was the signal for each man to save his head. The Fon staggered from his throne and fell. When he saw that the notables were all running he cried for assistance. 'Save me from his wrath or I am dead. Save me, I say!' It was only then that Nformi Nyam and Nformi Eleme turned back and dragged him into the inner chamber, blocking the door behind them.

SHEY NGONG

I thought they had more guts than that. They should have faced Kibaranko.

MESSENGER

Shey, that is the only reason they have not come for you yet. They dread the Kibaranko. Yes! When Kibaranko saw that he had missed his target, he seized the throne, swung it round and round and let it crash on the ground, splitting in two. I raised the alarm from my hiding position behind the kolanut tree and took off with full speed. Shey, it was terrible.

SHEY NGONG

Pride drove the goat to wrestle with the leopard. Any way, it was all my fault.

MESSENGER

How your fault?

SHEY NGONG

If I had not insisted that he should be crowned, because the late Fon had confided in me, the elders would never have accepted.

MESSENGER
Is that so? I now see why he has been hesitant to do you in. The notables have hollered for your skin but he has prayed for patience. Now he has run out of it himself.

SHEY NGONG
As soon as he smelled, tasted and felt power, he turned against me. The disease that will kill a man begins like an appetite. Let him come and sack the grove.
The howling of Kibaranko is heard returning to the grove.
MESSENGER
If he catches me here, I am dead.
Messenger flees. Shey Ngong scoops potion from pot and moves towards entrance chanting.

SHEY NGONG
The eagle flies and flies
But always returns home!
The prowling lion comes back to its den for rest!
After devastating the forest
The elephant goes down to the river for a drink!
The farmer spent all day in the fields,
But returned home at dusk and went to sleep!
(As Kibaranko makes entrance, Shey Ngong empties the contents of the sacred horn on him. He begins a giddy dance and then collapses)
He has not brought back wine for my invocations.
(He unmasks Kibaranko and gives Tapper some herbs to chew. Tapper begins to stir.)
You did not bring the palm-wine.

TAPPER
The Fon has seized the palm-bush. His watch-dogs are there now. They beat me severely. My clothes are in tatters.

SHEY NGONG
You are no cow to brush away the flies from your body with your tail.

TAPPER

Eh? But I did! I scattered all the pots and calabashes and the Fon fled. Shey, the Fon ran for his dear life. I am telling you, Shey, the Fon is a man and he ran for his dear life. The Fon ran, Shey!

SHEY NGONG

Was he in the bush? My ear does not follow your tongue.

TAPPER

He was not in the bush, Shey. How could he? However, he ran for his life and I split the throne in two.

SHEY NGONG

What are you talking about fellow? A goat in the den of a lion? How did it happen?

TAPPER

I don't know, Shey. But the goat drove out the lion from his den and set the place on fire.

SHEY NGONG

Your mind is not correct, fellow. (*Distant chanting of female voices*) What is that now?

TAPPER

Women singing. Only women singing. The whole land is full of women. Not a single man left.

SHEY NGONG

Except the one who scattered the palm-wine pots and calabashes.

TAPPER

And split the Fon's throne in two.

KWENGONG

(Off) Father of children, shall I come?

SHEY NGONG

(To Tapper indicating Kibaranko mask) Get in there.

TAPPER
Who is it?

SHEY NGONG
One of my wives. Quick! *(Raising voice)* Come inside, wife.

KWENGONG
(Noticing Kibaranko) He returned? He came back here? No one would have believed that he would ever find his way back here. Even when there are restrainers, the Kibaranko has been known to become so wild that he strays into the forests and hills. And only pregnant women have been used as bait for his recapture. This is strange that he came back on his own.

SHEY NGONG
Nyombom and the spirits of the ancestors work in more ways than we think. What was the chanting for?

KWENGONG
Will you believe it, father of children?

SHEY NGONG
What is it, wife?

KWENGONG
The sun of the land has set! The elephant has fallen! The lion of Ewawa is no more!

SHEY NGONG
What are you talking about, wife? One of his watch-dogs was here and said he narrowly escaped the wrath of Kibaranko!

KWENGONG
But not the wrath of the women.

SHEY NGONG
How did it happen? How did it, wife?

KWENGONG

When I left you here to return home, I discovered upon arrival there that the place was deserted. The doors were all closed for fear of the Kibaranko.

SHEY NGONG

Where were the other women?

KWENGONG

I asked, and the children said that they had left a message for me to meet them at the twin-streams.

SHEY NGONG

At the twin-streams? It is not yet time for planting. Why at the twin-streams at this time of the season?

KWENGONG

They had decided to take very drastic action against the desecrator of the gods and ancestors.

SHEY NGONG

Go on, wife.

KWENGONG

When I got to the twin-streams, there was a large gathering of women, mostly the elderly ones. They were all naked, stark naked. It seemed that they had been performing some rites. Upon my arrival, they raised a great shout and one of them placed a pot full of some potion on my head. Go to the Fon! Go to the palace! they shouted. And make him drink! Then I knew what I was carrying.

SHEY NGONG

And you went?

KWENGONG

I went. I got to the palace just as Kibaranko was departing. I walked straight into the inner court. Of course, the whole place was deserted. Not a single body around. When I opened my mouth to speak, I could not recognise my own voice.

(Lights fade out. Then spotlight on Kwengong, a pot on her head. When she speaks her voice is warped.)

Chila Kintasi! Chila Kintasi!
Come out and receive the wares
The women over whom you wield
Great power have sent you!
Come out, I say, and receive the goods
Sent by those you dishonour so!
Another spotlight showing Fon completely dazed.

FON

Woman, who showed you in here? Who gave you leave to step into this place?

KWENGONG

Earth-goddess needs no one's leave
To walk where her feet will, Chila Kintasi.

FON

Watch your tongue, woman! Earth-goddess indeed! Your wretched husband, the self-made priest of inexistent gods and sower of bad words against our royal person, is still too smart from the venom of my power and you dare to insult our royal presence by profanely pronouncing our sacred name?

KWENGONG

The only husband Earth-goddess honours, Chila Kintasi,
Is the whole land of Ewawa.
Here are the wares the women commanded deliverance to their Fon!
Here are the fruits they urged me feed the crocodile that swallows its own eggs!
Receive them, oh Fon, and rejoice!
And may they make your belly swell with fat!
May they make you call another feast before the sun goes to sleep!

FON

(Looks curiously into pot and then turns away suddenly, holding his nose.)
Urine! Urine? What is the meaning of this abomination?

KWENGONG

Not urine, Chila Kintasi,
But the savoury juice from

The vaginas of those upon whom
You wield power, Fon.
Drink! Oh Fon!
Drink the liquor from the vaginas
And feel the power of power!

FON

I will die first.

KWENGONG

Then you will die indeed, Chila Kintasi.
Your own mouth pronounced judgement.
Die and deliver the land from the
Abominations of drunkenness and gluttony!
(The Fon begins to reel until he collapses.)
Die! Chila Kintasi, die!
And save the land from merry-making!
Die, Fon! So that we may think!
The people need your death to think!
Die! Die! Die!
(Fon lies still. Lights fade out, then on in the grove.)
I seized the pot and broke it on his head. Then I heard the women chanting in the courtyard. As I emerged, their questioning eyes met mine. I nodded and they raised a great shout making a passage for me; and I came straight here.

TAPPER

(Emerging from Kibaranko mask) Shey, it is time for action. None of his blood must be allowed to succeed.

SHEY NGONG

So what will happen?

TAPPER

The palace must be burnt down. No more Fons in this land! They neither rule with the head nor the heart. I say, no more Fons!

KWENGONG

But we need someone to rule!

TAPPER

Yes! The council of elders led by the chief priest of Nyombom. No more Fons!

SHEY NGONG

Has madness seized you, fellow?

TAPPER

I say no more Fons in this land. That's all!
Goes over to the sacred pot, scoops the potion and drinks. Then he begins to rumble and howl. Kwengong takes refuge in the mask of Earth-goddess.

SHEY NGONG

What do you think you are doing?

TAPPER

(Getting into Kibaranko mask) The palace must be burnt down. No more Fons in this land of Ewawa! No more grabbing of people's farm-lands and palm-bushed! No more piecemeal distribution of the red feather! No more!
Storms out of the grove knocking Shey Ngong to the ground.

SHEY NGONG

What has come over him? Why, is everybody mad?

KWENGONG

(Emerging from mask) He is not mad, father of children. I have been thinking it over. The people must have a right in deciding who rules over them and what person rules.

SHEY NGONG

Woman! What are you talking about? Have you ever heard of a snake without a head?

KWENGONG

Of course, the land will have a head. Only that the people will decide who that will be and for how long. And the affairs of the land shall be decided by all the people in the market place.

SHEY NGONG
Woman! What kind of people discuss matters of import in the market place? It will be like a gathering of fowls. Each one quacking away and not listening to the other.
Alarm and shouts of desperation are heard.

KWENGONG
He has set the palace on fire.

SHEY NGONG
I don't know what came over him.

KWENGONG
The apprentice learnt his master's lessons too well, I think.

SHEY NGONG
They might do him harm, I fear.

KWENGONG
Who? The only men left in the land are the women. And they do not want any more Fons. Get the antidote ready. He will soon be here.

SHEY NGONG
You better return to your Earth-goddess.
The howling of Kibaranko is heard as Kwengong gets into mask. Shey Ngong scoops potion from sacred pot and begins to chant.
The eagle flies and flies
But always returns home!
The prowling lion comes back to its den for rest!
After devastating the forest,
The elephant goes down to the river for a drink!
The farmer spent all day in the fields
But returned home at dusk and went to sleep!
As Kibaranko makes entrance Shey Ngong empties the contents of the sacred horn on him. He begins a giddy dance and then collapses on the ground, a bugle in his hand.
What have we here? The Fon's bugle!
He unmasks Kibaranko, gives Tapper some herbs and he begins to stir.
I see you brought back something.

TAPPER

Palm-wine? I need palm-wine.

SHEY NGONG

There is none. Even for my libation and invocations. You forget that you scattered all the pots and calabashes?

TAPPER

What did I bring, then? When the spirit of Kibaranko takes you, it is hard to remember anything.

SHEY NGONG

(Holding bugle up) This. The Fon's bugle. That is what you brought back.

TAPPER

My body is terribly hot. My throat is sore. My feet too.

SHEY NGONG

Because you were playing with fire. Where did you get it?

TAPPER

How would I know, Shey? The spirit of Kibaranko is like the whirlwind. It is madness.

KWENGONG

(Emerging from Earth-goddess) I hope no one was hurt.

SHEY NGONG

Have you not heard him say he remembers nothing?

KWENGONG

What is the Fon's bugle doing in your hand?

SHEY NGONG

He brought it from the palace, after setting the place on fire. And to think that this same bugle has sounded here twice today!

TAPPER

Keep it and become Fon, if you wish. The Fon's notables and offspring have all escaped. I mean those who were not consumed by the fire.

KWENGONG

He cannot be Fon. The women have decided. No more Fon's in the land!

TAPPER

So what will happen?

KWENGONG

The people will rule through the council of elders led by Shey, here. The day that he takes the wrong decision, that same day, the people shall meet in the market-place and put another at the head of the council of elders.

SHEY NGONG

And the affairs of the land shall be debated in the market place.

TAPPER

Wonderful idea! So that all the people shall see clearly that the fowl has an anus. Wonderful idea! No more secrets in the land!

KWENGONG

(To Tapper) Sound the bugle and let the people assemble in the market-place.

SHEY NGONG

No. Not the bugle. We must break clean from the past. Take the sacred gong of Nyombom and let it resound in all the nooks and corners of the land. From today, this bugle will stay here in the sacred grove, a living symbol of our enslavement by the Fon and his notables. Take the sacred gong to the people and let its sound vibrate through their very souls, a symbol of their liberation.

TAPPER

Playing a rhythm on the gong and moving into audience.
People of Ewawa!

People of this land!
As the sun rises at dawn
So shall we meet
In the market-place
To decide on the destiny of this land.
No more shall we allow
One person to rule our land for us!
From this moment, palm-wine shall no longer flow
In this land of Ewawa.
It shall be used sparingly
In libations to the gods and ancestors!
In preparing medicinal herbs for the sick!
People of Ewawa, have you all heard?
Have you heard the pronouncement?
The pronouncement of Earth-goddess, Nyombom?
Have you heard the pronouncement of the land?

CHORUS

We have heard o o o o!

The End

Part VI

The Rape of Michelle

Part VI

The Rape of Michelle

Dramatis Personae
(in order of appearance)

RUFINA: A beautiful woman in her thirties who owns a chicken parlour.

MICHELLE: Her coquettish fourteen-year-old daughter.

MIKINDONG: A college teacher over whom Rufina and Michelle are vying for attention and love.

ENO: Mikindong's friend.

NGENGE: Another of Mikindong's friends.

POLICEMAN

AKWEN: Mikindong's wife and a strikingly beautiful woman in her twenties.

ZENDE: A lawyer.

COURT USHER

MAGISTRATE

REGISTRAR

PROSECUTOR

OBALI: Zende's friend.

NDI: Another of Zende's friends.

Scene I

Rufina's chicken parlour. The furniture is typical of such places in Yaounde and around the country. There is Rufina, the land-lady who is about thirty and very pretty; and Michelle, her beautiful daughter at about age fourteen who often passes for her junior sister.
Present are Mikindong, a young college teacher, and his two friends, Eno and Ngenge, all of them belonging to the same age group. Very remarkable throughout this scene is Michelle's coquettish behaviour towards Mikindong.
When the scene opens Mikindong, Eno and Ngenge have just finished eating chicken and are complimenting Rufina for her cooking, as Michelle is tidying up the table while the clients are picking their teeth and washing down the chicken with gulps of beer.

ENO
(To Michelle) That was really delicious. Is that your hand-work?

MICHELLE
I am never allowed to touch the chicken whenever our teacher, Mr Mikindong, comes here. Some people forget that others deserve equal treatment. But I will have my turn.
Enters Rufina from the kitchen.

RUFINA
What is the child complaining about? I thought I was helping you!

MICHELLE
I am not complaining. But you only help me when teacher comes here.

MIKINDONG
Michelle, you mean you can roast chicken well? I always thought you were still too young to be able to do it.

MICHELLE
I beg you not to insult me. Too young to do it.

NGENGE
How can you say that of a grown woman like Michelle?

MICHELLE
I am not a woman. I am a girl. And I know how to do it.

ALL THE MEN
Really!

MICHELLE
You men are something else. I mean that I know how to roast the chicken.

ALL THE MEN
A-a-ah!

RUFINA
Stop teaching the child your dirty ways.

ENO & NGENGE
Child, indeed!

ENO
You heard her say just now that she is already a woman!

MICHELLE
I said girl, not woman.

NGENGE
What is the difference? A girl is a woman and a woman is a girl.

RUFINA
Michelle, take the tray to the kitchen.
Michelle exits.

NGENGE
She your little sister?

MIKINDONG
No, no. She is... (*Stops short when he notices Rufina looking at him sternly*).

RUFINA
She is my little sister.

NGENGE
She will be as beautiful as you are.

RUFINA
Who is beautiful? Are old women ever beautiful? *(To Mikindong)* Enh, teacher?

MIKINDONG
What?

RUFINA
I am asking if old women are ever beautiful. *(She sits on the arm of Mikindong's chair).* Especially when there are young girls around.

MIKINDONG
What do you mean? I come here for two things: the taste of your chicken and the fact that we are neighbours.

RUFINA
You think I haven't noticed? The way you flirt with Michelle is just disgraceful.

MIKINDONG
Oh, come on! Michelle is just a little girl.

RUFINA
And me? I am just an old woman, not so?

ENO
If he doesn't like you, I can always take his place.

NGENGE
And I don't mind having Michelle either. I prefer mine very succulent.
Enters Michelle.

MIKINDONG
Michelle, my friend wants you.

MICHELLE
Have you looked at me well? I think I know what I want.

RUFINA
Didn't I say it? It's you she wants. Go and tidy up the kitchen.

MICHELLE
Osh! Am I a house-girl? Whenever teacher comes here you always treat me like a nobody. I will have my turn.

ENO
Mr Oga, you're in for it.

NGENGE
Why don't you make up your mind and give us a chance too?

MIKINDONG
Please bring the bill.

MICHELLE
Are you running away?

RUFINA
Don't be so rude to my customers. Let me remind you that this house is mine.

MIKINDONG
I say, bring the bill.

RUFINA
If you think you can talk to me like that, you better go and look for your own place.
(*She hands the bill over to Mikindong who settles it quickly and gets up. Eno and Ngenge empty their glasses and also stand*). I have never seen such insolence.

MICHELLE
Pay me for all the work I have been doing and I will leave.
The three men leave hastily.

RUFINA

Every time my customers come here you want to show them that you are young and more beautiful. But I am telling you that if I ever hear that you and teacher have done anything... that day you will go.

MICHELLE

But it's you who say he likes me!

RUFINA

I don't care. But I am telling you now that I like him. If he doesn't like me and prefers you, we will see.

She exits. Michelle slumps into a chair and weeps.

Curtain.

Scene II

A cell at the Police Station. The teacher, Mikindong, is in detention. When the curtain opens he is seen sitting on the floor which is wet. Barest clothing, feet unshod. He is very dejected and anxious. He is startled by the door opening. A policeman enters.

POLICEMAN

Teacher, how are you feeling this morning? It is a bright and warm day, isn't it?

MIKINDONG

You do not mean to provoke me, do you?

POLICEMAN

Oh no! Don't get me wrong. I am rather bringing some sunshine into this cold hole of yours.

MIKINDONG

Well, out with it. Am I going to be released?

POLICEMAN

I don't know about your being released. I don't know if it can happen. Michelle's mother is determined to see you serve a good term in prison. She is always in the Commissioner's office.

MIKINDONG

I am not even going to be released on bail?

POLICEMAN

No. No bail for a rapist.

MIKINDONG

I am no... No use. You won't understand. No one will ever understand what happened.

POLICEMAN

What did you do that for?

MIKINDONG
Please, leave me alone. I see the kind of sunshine you brought.

POLICEMAN
The sunshine is still out there. A real beauty queen, if you ask my opinion. Says she is your wife. Why did you do it? With such a beautiful wife?

MIKINDONG
I say you will never understand. just leave me alone.

POLICEMAN
Shall I usher in your wife? I bet you must be dying of cold. A man with such a beautiful wife raping a mere child!

MIKINDONG
A mere child! I say you will never understand. Stop torturing me, and let her in, please.

Policeman goes out and soon returns with Akwen, a strikingly beautiful woman in her twenties. She is carrying a basket. She is angry, but when she sees the state in which Mikindong is, her features soften and she becomes anxious for his sake.

AKWEN
Is this how things are? Why don't they even let you wear some warm clothes?

POLICEMAN
Madam, this is cell, not a hotel room.

AKWEN
And you will freeze my husband to death because this is no hotel room? (*Searches her basket and brings out a pullover and socks*). Here, put these on before you catch pneumonia.

POLICEMAN
Madam, I wish to remind you that your husband is a criminal and that this is a police cell, not hotel room.

MIKINDONG
Give him something; some money for beer.
Akwen fishes out her purse. She takes out some coins and stretches her hand towards the policeman who peers into her hand and shakes his head.

POLICEMAN
Madam, I will not do you a favour for nothing. You think I am alone on duty? There are three others out there. You saw them with your own eyes. What you are giving me cannot even buy a bottle of red wine.

AKWEN
Alright, here is something for all of you. And, please, treat my husband well.
Mikindong now wears the pullover and socks.

POLICEMAN
It all depends on you, Madam. Our treatment of your husband depends on you. You can even bring him a blanket and a tiny mattress, if you wish. But I have told you, there are four of us on duty. Yes, everything depends on you.

AKWEN
Please, I will do anything to make him comfortable.

POLICEMAN
Now you begin to understand. Bring the things late at night. When there are not many people again in the station. Your husband is not just anybody and he deserves good treatment. That is why he is in this cell alone. Go to other cells and you will see fifty people. They pack like sardines. But as I say, it all depends on you. Don't stay too long. Or you will put me into trouble. The law says that criminals must never be left alone with visitors.

Exits.

AKWEN
Here, eat something. Let me pour you a cup of coffee. It will warm you up.

MIKINDONG

Thank you. But I can't eat anything. No appetite.

AKWEN

It rained last night. I was so cold and could not sleep. Why did you do it? Hardly six months married. And now this. Dear, why did you do it? And to a mere child! Look at me. Am I not a woman?

MIKINDONG

Please, please, please...

AKWEN

And what is going to happen to me? They say her mother is bent on sending you to jail for as long as the law demands. The minimum is seven years...

MIKINDONG

Please, stop it! Stop it!

AKWEN

And since you are a teacher, you will get the maximum for corrupting youth put under your charge.

MIKINDONG

Akwen, stop it! I say, stop it! If you came to torture me, just go away.

AKWEN

But why did you do it, dear?

MIKINDONG

You will never understand. Nobody will understand. Did you contact Mr Zende?

AKWEN

Yes, I saw him. He has been very kind. In spite of the fact that her mother has been fighting to delay the legal process, he managed to get a date fixed for the hearing. That will be in another three days. He is coming to see you tomorrow morning.

MIKINDONG

You have done very well. Can I ask you a favour?

AKWEN

Yes?

MIKINDONG

Promise that you won't join the police in torturing me whenever you come here again. Promise me that, or I won't see you again when next you come.

AKWEN

I promise, dear. But it is the loneliness and the embarrassment which I can't stand. I promise.

POLICEMAN

(Off) Madam, your time is finished. I know you missed him last night. But it is not very nice in cell, is it?

MIKINDONG

You better go. I must have time to put my thoughts together before Mr Zende comes tomorrow.

AKWEN

Don't worry too much. God will show the way. I will try and see the presiding magistrate. I can't lose a husband only after six months of marriage.

MIKINDONG

Do you know who the prosecutor is?

AKWEN

Yes. It is a certain money-minded man called Traisel. I hear her mother gave him a lot of money to make sure that you were refused bail and not to worry about the case going to court soon.

MIKINDONG
They say she is always in the Commissioner's office. When you bring the things in the evening, give those boys out there a good bribe.

POLICEMAN
(Off) Madam, have you not finished the thing? Where were you before he did what he did?

MIKINDONG
Go now. Don't let us antagonise them.

AKWEN
I will come again in the evening. Keep calm.

Curtain.

SCENE III

Following day. Police cell as in Scene II. Mikindong is wearing the pullover and socks brought by his wife the previous day. He is sitting on a thin mattress on which there is a folded blanket. He is fairly composed. The door opens and the Policeman enters.

POLICEMAN
Teacher, I am sure that you had a good sleep.

MIKINDONG
Yes. I slept well. You people are very kind.

POLICEMAN
I told your wife that everything depended on her. And she did her duty. And now you are happy. And we are happy. That is how life should be. You make me happy. I make you happy. One hand washing the other. And that is how things should be.

MIKINDONG
Again, I say, thank you. If I ever get out of this thing, I will be able to show real gratitude to you.

POLICEMAN
Is it true that the case is coming up soon?

MIKINDONG
I am hoping so, but one can never tell. Money can turn the scales; especially as you say her mother is always in the Commissioner's office.

POLICEMAN
Don't mind the foolish woman. She thinks it is the Commissioner who does the work here? When are you going to court?

VOICE
(Off) Brigadier, the man's lawyer is here.

POLICEMAN
I am coming.

Exits and soon returns with Zende, the lawyer.

ZENDE
Good morning, Mr Mikindong. I hope you had a good rest. I see they are not treating you badly at all.

MIKINDONG
They are very kind people.

ZENDE
Yes, they usually are. When they want to.

POLICEMAN
Don't mind the lies people tell about the police. We are not beasts but human beings. But we too must eat.

ZENDE
Okay, go and buy yourself a packet of cigarettes.

POLICEMAN
I am doing this only for you. You know what the regulation here is. I am doing this for your sake only.

ZENDE
Thank you so much for being so considerate.

POLICEMAN
We don't smoke. And this money cannot even buy a bottle of red wine. There are three other policemen outside. You saw them yourself.

ZENDE
Okay, go and have your drink. And thanks for co-operation. My client, the teacher, will never forget you.

Exit Policeman.

MIKINDONG
I don't know how to thank you for all the trouble.

ZENDE
Part of the profession. We are in court the day after tomorrow. Cost me thirty thousand francs to the Registrar.

MIKINDONG
My wife told me so.

ZENDE
Did you do it?

MIKINDONG
No. I did nothing to her.

ZENDE
Now you better tell me the truth. Unless I know the truth, I cannot help you. We are not in court yet, remember.

MIKINDONG
I did nothing to her. If I had done it, I would not be here now.

ZENDE
Where would you be?

MIKINDONG
At home. In the comfort of my home.

ZENDE
Your fortune is hanging in a balance. The minimum sentence for rape is seven years; and you are telling me that you are here because you didn't rape her?

MIKINDONG
She was the one who wanted to rape me!

ZENDE
Mr Mikindong, I am a very busy man. Stop wasting my time and tell me the truth.

MIKINDONG
I have told you the truth.

ZENDE
What about the medical certificate? What do you say to that?

MIKINDONG
You know yourself that money can fetch anything. That certificate was bought.

ZENDE
And the girl's screams? And the witnesses? What do you say to that?

MIKINDONG
That is the part of the story which I still don't understand. Her screams. She must have felt insulted.

ZENDE
You mean she offered herself and you refused to take her?

MIKINDONG
Exactly so.

ZENDE
What about the witnesses? Her mother, she wants to see you in jail.

MIKINDONG
That is another story. She too offered herself; but I wouldn't take her.

ZENDE
You mean she is so hot after you because you rejected both she and her daughter?

MIKINDONG
Yes.

ZENDE
What are we going to say in court? Who will believe your story, with all the evidence they have?

MIKINDONG
You know yourself that the law is what it is. Many innocent people get convicted while criminals go scot-free. All I ask of you is to make contacts with the presiding magistrate. I know he would like an envelope. My wife has promised to see him.

ZENDE
I agree with you. It is a question of seeing people. Luckily for you, the magistrate is a personal friend of mine. We are on very good terms. But the prosecutor, Traisel, is a beast. As far as he is concerned, you are already a criminal and condemned. I wonder how much money she gave him.

MIKINDONG
One hundred thousand. That's what my wife said.

POLICEMAN
(Off) Do you want me to be dismissed? *(Enters)* What are you still doing here?

ZENDE
You have been very kind. I am through with him. Remember, the game is yours to play.

MIKINDONG
I will remember. But remember your own role. Contacts.

POLICEMAN
That is the right word. Contacts. A telephone call from above to the magistrate! An envelope from below to the magistrate! And the deed is done. The case is closed or simply thrown out of court. Contacts!

ZENDE
I see you are a very practical philosopher.

POLICEMAN

Oh yes! We must be practical and realistic. You think the magistrate eats truth? You think the prosecutor eats truth? You think the commissioner eats truth? Nobody eats truth. But people need a drink now and again. They need money to do things. That is what I call practical philosophy.

ZENDE

More grease to your practical philosophy. I will see you in court.

Exits.

POLICEMAN

Teacher, let me tell you something. Whether you did it or not does not really matter. If you do not make contacts, you are going to stay in prison for a good part of your only life. And what will happen to your beautiful wife and your work? She will become the woman of some powerful man. But with money... you can move mountains.

MIKINDONG

Thank you so much for the advice. But how am I to get the money? That is why I wanted bail.

POLICEMAN

Do not ask me. You are even lucky that you have such a beautiful wife. She will get the money for you. But, tell me, why did you do it?

MIKINDONG

Are you at it again? Leave me alone. If you want to know why I did it, wait till we get to court.

POLICEMAN

I will wait.

VOICE

(Off) Brigadier! The Commissioner wants you in his office.

POLICEMAN

Coming! I will come back later.

Exits.

MIKINDONG
Good riddance.

Curtain.

Scene IV

The courtroom. To upstage centre is a table at which the Magistrate and his Registrar will sit when they enter. The Prosecutor will enter with the Magistrate; but will immediately take his place to the right forestage. Defence counsel is at left forestage with Mikindong and Policeman. Michelle and Rufina take their place among the audience on the right front row while Akwen is on left front row. Solemn atmosphere of a courtroom.

COURT USHER
Court!
Everyone stands as the Magistrate and his suite enter.

REGISTRAR
(Reading from a file after everyone has sat down). Case No. 777/81. The People against Mr Mikindong.

MAGISTRATE
Will the accused, please, stand up?

REGISTRAR
That you, Mr Mikindong, on the first Thursday of December in the year of Our Lord nineteen hundred and... at about ten o'clock in the morning, in the Magisterial District of Yaounde, did lure a minor, by the name of Michelle, into your house and raped her thereby committing a criminal offence contrary to Section 296 of the Cameroon Penal Code. Do you plead 'guilty' or 'not guilty'?

MIKINDONG
Not guilty.

MAGISTRATE
The accused may sit down. What is your case?

PROSECUTOR
I am Traisel for the prosecution.

ZENDE

I am Zende, defence counsel.

MAGISTRATE

Proceed with your case.

REGISTRAR

Michelle, you will come forward and swear on the Bible.
She is made to swear.

MAGISTRATE

Your names?

MICHELLE

Michelle.

MAGISTRATE

Michelle?

MICHELLE

Michelle.

MAGISTRATE

Michelle. Michelle who? You must have some other name.

MICHELLE

F F F Fo Fokam. But everybody calls me Michelle.

MAGISTRATE

Michelle Fokam, what is your occupation?

MICHELLE

What is 'roccupation'?

MAGISTRATE

What work do you do?

MICHELLE

I don't do any work.

MAGISTRATE

School? Do you go to school?

MICHELLE
I have finish school.

MAGISTRATE
Where do you live?

MICHELLE
In Osse, with my mother.

MAGISTRATE
The prosecution may proceed.

PROSECUTOR
Michelle, how old are you?

MICHELLE
I am fourteen years of old.

PROSECUTOR
Do you know that man?

MICHELLE
Yes, he is a college tutor and he use to come our house.

PROSECUTOR
He used to come to your house for what?

MICHELLE
To drink beer and sometimes to eat chicken. My mother has a chicken parlour.

PROSECUTOR
Have you ever entered his house?

MICHELLE
We live in the same quarter na! How can I not go to his house?

PROSECUTOR
What do you go to do in his house?

MICHELLE
Sometime my mother send me to h
is wife.

PROSECUTOR
When did you last go to his house?

MICHELLE
On one Thursday in the beginning of December.

PROSECUTOR
What did you go there for?

MICHELLE
I was going to salute his wife.

PROSECUTOR
Did you see her and greet her?

MICHELLE
No.

PROSECUTOR
Whom did you see?

MICHELLE
I saw him.

PROSECUTOR
And what happened?
Michelle is silent.

MAGISTRATE
Michelle, tell the court what happened.

MICHELLE
He was wearing only a small knicker and was reading a book lying in a long chair. Then... then he call me to come and sit by him and I refuse. Then... then he stand up and come and hold my two hands and talk softly to me...

PROSECUTOR

What did he say?

MICHELLE

He... he said that he love me too much.

MAGISTRATE

Yes?

PROSECUTOR

Go on!

MICHELLE

Then... then... he take me over to the long chair and ... and... start to rub his body against my body.

MAGISTRATE

Yes?

PROSECUTOR

Go on!

MICHELLE

Then... then... he start to remove my dross and when I refuse he slap me and throw me on the ground... and... and... tear my dross... and pull my legs apart... and enter into me. And... because I feel much pain... I started shouting for people to come and help me. Then... then... people come... and my mother come and take me to Police Station... and from there to the hospital where doctor examine me.

PROSECUTOR

Here's the doctor's medical report which bears testimony to the fact that this child was raped.

MAGISTRATE

Will the accused, please stand up? Mr Mikindong, do you know this child?

MIKINDONG

Your Worship, I do.

MAGISTRATE
How did you come to know her?

MIKINDONG
We live in the same neighbourhood and her mother runs a chicken parlour. I go there fairly often to have a drink.

MAGISTRATE
So you came to know her in her mother's chicken parlour?

MIKINDONG
Yes.

MAGISTRATE
Has she ever entered your house?

MIKINDONG
Yes. She comes once in a while either just visiting or to run an errand for my wife.

MAGISTRATE
So, you're married?

MIKINDONG
Yes. That is my wife.

MAGISTRATE
How old are you?

MIKINDONG
Twenty-eight, your Worship.

MAGISTRATE
Do you exercise any profession?

MIKINDONG
I am a teacher by profession, your Worship.

MAGISTRATE
Where do you teach?

MIKINDONG
In the Government Secondary School, Osse.

MAGISTRATE
And your wife, does she work?

MIKINDONG
She is also a college teacher.

MAGISTRATE
Where was your wife on that first Thursday of December 19..?

MIKINDONG
She had gone to our former place of work to get our salaries from the bank.

MAGISTRATE
So you were alone in the house?

MIKINDONG
Yes, I was alone because the houseboy had gone to the market.

MAGISTRATE
Your wife was not at home. Your houseboy had gone to the market. So, you were in the house alone; with Michelle. And you raped her?

MIKINDONG
No, your Worship. I did not rape her.

MAGISTRATE
Here is the medical report which bears witness to the fact. Here is a certified true copy of her birth certificate which bears testimony to her age. There are witnesses who came to her rescue after you had ravished her. What do you say?

MIKINDONG

I will just tell this court what happened in my house on that day and it be left for the court to judge. On that day, after eating breakfast, and because I did not have classes, I sat in a chair in the parlour and began to read.

Scene suddenly transformed into Mikindong's sitting-room. Fairly well-furnished. Mikindong is reclining in an easy chair-for-three reading. He is wearing shorts and his torso is bare. There is a knock at the door and Michelle enters. She is wearing a 'kabba' which makes her look like a full-grown woman.

MICHELLE

Good morning, Teacher. No school today?
She walks across to where he is and stands over him.

MIKINDONG

No school today, Michelle. Good morning. And how is your mother?

MICHELLE

She has gone to the market.

MIKINDONG

So, who is in the house?

MICHELLE

Nobody.
She sits in the same chair and begins to stroke Mikindong's chest.

MIKINDONG

What do you think you are doing? (*Pushes her off.*)

MICHELLE

Nothing.
She begins to stroke his legs while giggling.

MIKINDONG

Stop that, Michelle!

MICHELLE

Lies on him and begins to tickle him. Then she begins to whimper.
Honey, love me! Honey, love me!

MIKINDONG
Who taught you that kind of rubbish?

MICHELLE
Moves up to him and throws her arms around his neck; at the same time planting a kiss on his lips.
It is not rubbish. Honey, love me! That is what my mother usually tells her many men. And now I am telling my own man. Honey, love me!

MIKINDONG
Freeing himself from her and backing away around the stage while she pursues him.
If that is what your mother taught you, it is dirty. You are still too tender for such things.

MICHELLE
Me? Too tender? Look! *She takes the 'kabba' right up, exposing a pair of firm cherry-like breasts.* Is this what you call tender?

MIKINDONG
Michelle, put down your dress and stop fooling!

MICHELLE
Still pursuing him and now more earnest.
Honey, love me! Please honey, love me! I am very hot. Love me, honey!

MIKINDONG
Stop fooling, Michelle. And get out of here.

MICHELLE
Not before you have done it to me. There is a devil in me! Please come! Come! Come!
She lies down on the settee and looks at him with begging eyes.

MIKINDONG
Going over to her as if in response. Then, without warning, he gives her a sound slap across the face.

Get up and take your filthy body out of my house! Daughter of a bitch!

In the same spirit Michelle falls down and begins to scream. She rolls across the floor and rips off her panties.

MICHELLE

Leave me! Leave me! I say, leave me! I am dead! Oh, I am dead! Leave me! Leave me! Leave me!

Mikindong is completely embarrassed and frightened. As he is running over to the door in confusion, she gets up and, still screaming, begins to struggle with him. Scene transforms again into court session as before.

MIKINDONG

Then the neighbours came bursting into my house. And she kept screaming; and everyone concluded that I had violated her. Her mother went for the police immediately; and I was arrested and locked up.

MAGISTRATE

Do you have anything to say?

PROSECUTOR

I certainly do, Mr Magistrate. Now, Mr Mikindong, do you expect this court to believe the story you have just narrated?

MIKINDONG

I said it was left to the court to judge.

PROSECUTOR

Do you expect this court to believe that that plaintive cry, 'Leave me! Leave me! I am dead! I am dead!' was sheer pretence? Do you expect this court to believe that this little girl ripped off her own pants from her own body, tearing it to pieces in pretence? Do you expect this court to believe that a naked man struggling with a little girl did not intend to violate her? That is, if he did not actually rape her? Mr Magistrate, Sir, before you lies a medical certificate delivered by a practising medical doctor to the effect that this little girl, Michelle, was raped on the first Thursday of December in the year 19... This poor girl was trapped in the home of a man into whose care has been entrusted the education and moral upbringing of our young citizens. Mr Magistrate, Sir, this court should, and must set an example on this rapist arraigned before you. I demand maximum sentence.

MAGISTRATE

Does the accused have anything else to say?

ZENDE

Your Worship, Sir, I should like to ask the plaintive a few questions. Michelle, what did you go to do in Mr Mikindong's house at that time of day?

MICHELLE

Nothing. I just wanted to find out if his wife had returned back.

ZENDE

Did you find out? Did you ask about her?

MICHELLE

No.

ZENDE

Why not?

MICHELLE

I... I forgot.

ZENDE

Who is your mother?

MICHELLE
That is my mother.

ZENDE
What does she do for a living?

MICHELLE
She has a chicken parlour.

ZENDE
Have you lived with her all your life?

MICHELLE
Yes.

ZENDE
Is she married? Who is your father?

MICHELLE
I don't know my father. She is not married.

ZENDE
Did you go to school?

MICHELLE
Yes.

ZENDE
Did you complete your primary education?

MICHELLE
I finish, but fail.

ZENDE
Where do you sleep?

MICHELLE
With my mother.

ZENDE

On the same bed?

MICHELLE

No. In the same room.

ZENDE

Am I right to presume that when people come to drink and eat chicken, you help your mother in serving them?

MICHELLE

Yes.

ZENDE

Does your mother ever receive men visitors in the room in which both of you sleep?

PROSECUTOR

Mr Magistrate, Sir, I object to that question.

ZENDE

I repeat. Does your mother ever receive men in the room in which both of you sleep?

MICHELLE

Yes.

ZENDE

Do some of these men ever sleep with your mother on her bed in the room in which both of you sleep?

PROSECUTOR

Mr Magistrate...

MAGISTRATE

Michelle, answer.

MICHELLE

Yes.

ZENDE
Michelle, can you now tell this court how that teacher raped you? Tell us what he did to you on that fateful day.
Michelle does not say anything.

MAGISTRATE
Michelle, describe to this court what that man did to you.
No reaction.

ZENDE
Your Worship, Sir, I am satisfied. This little girl is not as little as my learned colleague has made this court to believe. I am inviting this court to look at her carefully: her dress, her gait, her manners. I am also inviting this court to look at her mother. Michelle's birth certificate says her mother was seventeen when she had her. Michelle herself is fourteen this year. Rufina has brought up her daughter in her own footsteps. We have a saying that when mother-cow is chewing grass, its young ones watch its mouth closely.
Two days ago, Your Worship, I was in Rufina's chicken parlour. I was with two other friends.

Scene switches to Rufina's chicken parlour. Zende, Obali and Ndi enter. Rufina, who has been sitting in a chair, stands up and ushers them into chairs.

RUFINA
Michelle, bring some glasses.

Michelle walks in dressed very smartly and wearing a beautiful hairdo. She walks about coquettishly and, as she shakes hands with the three men, reveals various aspects of her coquetry.

ZENDE
This must be your small sister. How are you, my girl?

MICHELLE
Am I your girl?

OBALI
If you are not now, you can be shortly.

MICHELLE
Well, we will see.

RUFINA
Any chicken?

ZENDE
No. We are in a hurry. We just want a quick drink.

MICHELLE
Can you not give your girl a quick drink too?

ZENDE
Go ahead. What do you drink?

MICHELLE
Let me see. Can I take a beer?

ZENDE
Please yourself.

MICHELLE
Thank you, honey.

NDI
Did you hear that? She is already honeying you.

ZENDE
We better go before the love fever catches me.

Zende settles the bill and, as they are leaving, Michelle holds his hand and leans coquettishly against him.

MICHELLE
You will come again?

ZENDE
For sure! For sure!

Blackout. Back to the court scene.

ZENDE

Your Worship, Sir, one last thing. A medical certificate can be bought anywhere, any time. I am asking this court to throw out the charges brought against my client.

MAGISTRATE

If defence counsel doubts the authenticity and validity of the medical certificate, then we will have the medical officer who issued the certificate into the witness box. But when the medical certificate was first tendered in court, there was no objection from defence counsel. However, it has been brought to my notice that the defendant was refused bail. In the light of the evidence before this court, I hereby order his immediate release on bail. Meanwhile, judgement will be given in two weeks from today. For now the court is going on recess to resume in the afternoon.

COURT USHER

C o u r t!

Everyone stands as the Magistrate and his suite leave.

Curtain.

Epilogue

Home of Mikindong. Furnished as in Scene IV Flashback. Festive mood following release of Mikindong from Police custody and his appointment that same day as Principal of one of the secondary schools in the city. Present are Mikindong, Eno, Ngenge, Akwen who is constantly serving drinks and chewables to the men.

NGENGE
Chei! Oga, you have been vindicated. Mr Principal, all to your little self. But that woman and her daughter are something else.

ENO
Real devils, if you ask my opinion. Your appointment is sure proof of your innocence. You know, before anyone is appointed in this country, there is always an investigation into the man's character. Massa, the case is finished.

MIKINDONG
We cannot be too sure that the case is over until judgement is delivered. This appointment might even put one into more problems.

AKWEN
What problems, dear? You have my love and you are principal. You know, I am even beginning to suspect that she might have known that this was coming and so decided to spoil your name. All sorts of people go to chicken parlours; and she might have overheard your name being discussed.

NGENGE
That is really possible, Akwen. But why would she want to spoil a thing like that?

ENO
What a question! I am surprised that you people have not yet realised that Mikindong is replacing her country-man as Principal of that college.

EVERYBODY
Ah yes! You are right! You are damn right!

MIKINDONG
I never looked at it that way. And, I didn't know about this at all.

NGENGE
Now I know that she is a real devil. If anyone ever sees my foot in her place again, let them cut it off. Can you imagine that she presents Michelle as her small sister?

AKWEN
She doesn't want to be thought of as an old woman. That is why she and her daughter have been fighting over my husband. I don't really know what you men want.

MIKINDONG
But we only went there for the chicken and a drink! Nothing else.

AKWEN
Don't I cook for you in this house? Can't you drink at home as you are doing now? But, of course, you must go to chicken parlours where mothers and their daughters will fight over you and throw you into jail. And I have to suffer trying to get you released.

NGENGE
Don't be angry, Akwen. You know your husband is an honest man.

AKWEN
Indeed, he is!

MIKINDONG
Let us not quarrel over that now. Haven't we suffered enough? Even now, we don't know how the case is going to turn out. Please, let us not quarrel.

A knock at the door and Zende, the lawyer, and Magistrate enter.

AKWEN
Oh! It's Mr Zende and the Magistrate! Please come right in and make yourselves comfortable. You are very welcome. Please, Mr Magistrate, come and sit down.

ZENDE
Good evening, Mrs Mikindong and Gentlemen. We thought... Mr Magistrate and I... that we should just stop by and congratulate Mr Mikindong for his appointment. Congrats, Teacher! Can you imagine? Two great events in one day!

AKWEN
Thank you very much, Mr Magistrate. I am just overwhelmed by events.

MAGISTRATE
Madam, I am really delighted to be here for this celebration. When Mr Zende stopped by my place and announced that your husband had been appointed principal, I felt it a duty to come and shake hands with him.

AKWEN
Oh! Mr Magistrate, let me get you some champagne. There is something to celebrate.
Exits.

MAGISTRATE
With all this celebration and the champagne popping all over, you think they can still put together something reasonable?

ZENDE
I might just have to remind him.
He moves across to where Mikindong is sitting while Akwen serves the Magistrate some champagne.

MIKINDONG
You put up a most brilliant performance in court today.

ZENDE
Nothing out of the ordinary, really. It is my profession, you know? But let me warn you that the battle is only just beginning.

MIKINDONG
But why didn't he pass judgement?

ZENDE
That is why I came here with him. It is now that the real work must begin.

MIKINDONG
But why should a man suffer so much and lose so much money even though he is innocent?

ZENDE
That is the problem. Until a revolution takes place, we will continue to function through the telephone call from above and the envelope from below, as your friend, the policeman, put it. And, you know, now that you have been appointed principal he is expecting a sizeable envelope. He now knows that you have everything to lose.

MIKINDONG
Oh my God! I said it! However, I will do everything possible. How much do you think he will be willing to accept?

ZENDE
I told you before that we are friends. I have been talking to him this evening as we were driving here; and he might just accept half-a-million.

MIKINDONG
What?
The attention of the others is attracted.

ZENDE
Any time you are ready, just stop by my chambers. We must be on our way now.

MAGISTRATE

Mr Mikindong, again I congratulate you most heartily. In fact I do so from the bottom of my heart. That is not a job that one should lose by going to jail. Mrs Mikindong, thank you very much for your kindness. Good night.

MIKINDONG

Oh God! What a life!

AKWEN

What is it dear? Are you okay?

MIKINDONG

No. The Magistrate! The Magistrate!

The End

Part VII

Shoes

Characters

FIRST SOLDIER: Commanding Officer

SECOND: Captain and second in command

THIRD: Chief Warrant Officer

FOURTH: Sergeant

VOICES: Young Woman
                      Man
                      Old Woman/Old Women
                      Crowd

This play is set anywhere in a military dictatorship

The Beginning Was ...

Four soldiers, their weapons at the ready storm playing area from different directions and then converge CS. Silence followed by wild laughter.

FIRST
Terrorists!

SECOND
Vandals!

THIRD
Traitors!

FOURTH
Subversives!

They burst into wild laughter again and then do a jig.
SOLO: ebeesee, ebeesee!
CHORUS: Wonderful!
SOLO: ebeesee, ebeesee!
CHORUS: Wonderful!
SOLO: Small gondele, big, big bobbi!
CHORUS: Wonderful!
SOLO: Big gondele, small, small bobbi!
CHORUS: Wonderful!
SOLO: We soja dem di jam noting!
CHORUS: Wonderful!
SOLO: Woman na so dem buku fo ya!
CHORUS: Wonderful!
SOLO: Small gondele, big, big bobbi!
CHORUS: Wonderful!
SOLO: Big gondele, small, small bobbi!
CHORUS: Wonderful!

Another burst of laughter.

FIRST
Intoxicators and propagandists!

SECOND
Power mongers and vandals!

THIRD
Ignorant manipulated traitors!

FOURTH
Jealousy na im go kill dem all.

FIRST/SECOND
Terrorist vandals!

THIRD/FOURTH
Subversive traitors!

FIRST
Troops attention!
At ease! How many did we capture during the operation?

FOURTH
Who cares? All the baggas should have been shot on battle field. Especially with that stampede. Even two hundred could die.

SECOND
You are right, Sergeant. Our boys of the sacred choir would have demonstrated their expertise in forcing it down the throat of whoever would want to listen.

THIRD
What you fo do with the bodies?

FIRST
Bobbies? You don't know what to do with bobbies?
SECOND
You squeezam small, small. Then you suckam like picken who has not seen his mammy for one whole day. After that you take your belt and lasham well, well. That is what you do with bobbies.

THIRD
Yes, that is all you know. Woman palaver and torture. Who call bobbi? I said what you fo do with the bodies? Die body or corpse, that's what I mean.

FOURTH
That is easy, man. Load them on trucks and dump them in shallow graves in the forest.

SECOND
Which forest?

FIRST
What do you mean, which forest? There is a lot of forest all over the place: east, south, centre; centre, south, east. Everywhere is forest.

THIRD
And when the parents and relatives come?

FIRST
Show them the empty cells and mortuary. Nobody dead. Nobody arrested. Soldier no kill nobody. Soldier no carry loaded gun. Soldier is there to protect vandals and subversives.

SECOND
And if they insist.

FOURTH
Insist? Who born dog? Then we teargas and horsewhip them. Nonsense! Insist indeed.

FIRST
And my question.

SECOND/THIRD
What question?

FIRST
How many did we capture during the operation?

THIRD
Who cares to count? Four or five truck loads. Something like that.

FIRST
Any girls?

SECOND
Plenty. You know they are more easily affected by the gas. And since we surrounded them completely it was by far better to catch a girl.

FOURTH
Na who no like bobbi we-i sabi book? I will show them.

FIRST
Who? The girls or the bobbies?

FOURTH
Those half-cooked subversives who think they know all the book in the world. Now they allow themselves to be manipulated by those jealous, greedy and ambitious vandals who call themselves Manjong

and Mfu leaders. People who cannot control their own wives and children now think they can manage affairs of the land.

THIRD

Why do you talk as if to say you are angry? You know say we in the military we don't have any hand inside politics matters.

SECOND

Yes, we are just there to execute orders, not to play politics.

FOURTH

When the other man and his people chopped and chopped for over twenty donkey years nobody said anything. Now my own man, the General comes, he has not even done half-time and people are already shouting. Dat one na jealousy pure and simple.

FIRST

You shut your big mouth, Sergeant! Too much size-mut na-im di kill dis country. We have a job to do, that's all. Troops attention! At ease! Now let's get the shoes in one nice heap. Fall out!

Fourth is examining shoes to see if any of them can match.

FIRST

Hei, you! Sergeant! What the hell do you think you are doing?

FOURTH

Nothing, my Commandant. I just wanted to see if any of them can match. Imagine, Commandant, so many shoes but none to wear.

FIRST

This is no joking matter, fellow. You are a looter. You have looted before! You were going to loot again.

FOURTH

No, Commandant! It is a lie. I was not looting. I have not looted. I just wanted to see if ...

FIRST
Shut up! So I am a liar, Sergeant?

FOURTH
No, my Commandant. You are not.

FIRST
They give you free uniform and free gun for you to protect the land and the people and these become your licence for looting and brutalizing and ra ...

FOURTH
But you started the r-r-r, my Commandant.

SECOND/THIRD
Aiye ye ye! We heard nothing! We saw nothing!

FIRST
Sergeant, first you insult me by calling me a liar. Now you accuse your Commandant of ... of ...

THIRD
Rape!

SECOND/FOURTH
Aiye ye ye! We heard nothing! We saw nothing!

FIRST
Chief Warrant Officer, is your Commandant capable of...of ...

THIRD
No, my Commandant! You can never r ... r ...

SECOND/FOURTH
We heard nothing! We heard nothing!

FIRST

Sergeant, you stand accused of looting and of intending to loot. Guilty or not guilty?

FOURTH

Not guilty, my Commandant. The owner of the radio-cassette would have willingly allowed me to take it. Only that he was not there. I swear that he would have allowed me to take it.

SECOND

But Sergeant, you forced your way into the room. You broke the door. The owner was not there, and you looted.
Miming role of Fourth.
Open this door! Open up, you vandal, or I break the door.
Where are you, vandal? Subversive over-sabi bookshops! Come out and I will show you something. Standard Seven is better than big, big cerfticate. Big cerfticate, no work to do. So you become subversives and vandals and terrorists.

FIRST

I say, Captain, where did you learn your buffoonery? You should be in the national theatre or university theatre.

SECOND

Na lie dat, Oga. National theatre no get salary and university theatre is only bandits and subversives.
Aha! What do we have here? Radio-cassette.
Presses the play button and female voice rings out.
Freedom! Freedom! Everywhere there must be freedom!
Stopping it.
I knew it! Vandals and subversives! This is the evidence!
I have found the proof! I don see-am.
Sergeant, put that thing back.

FOURTH

This is the evidence. The Commandant must know. He must.

SECOND

I said put the radio-cassette back.

FOURTH
The Commandant must know. This is the evidence.

SECOND
For the last time ...

FOURTH
You are the people protecting vandals and subversives, not so? I will not. A son of the soil will never, never allow traitors to take power from us. And, Captain, you are protecting people who want to destroy the land. The Commandant will know.

FIRST
And did you ever let the Commandant know? You sneaked away to your place with the radio-cassette. Somebody's private property, you loot. Everybody's common property, you embezzle. That is how you turn the whole land against yourself, and when people talk you say they are jealous.

THIRD
But, my Commandant, everybody's common property is nobody's private property. So therefore ...

SECOND
He can practise stomachtological auto-development with impunity and arrogance.

FIRST
That is why the whole land is in chaos because of people like you. Where is the radio-cassette?

SECOND
He gave it to an ashawo in return for sexual favours.

FOURTH

(Slapping Second) Take this.

SECOND
You too, take this!

FIRST
This is the height of indiscipline; a junior officer assaulting his seniors!

SECOND
All in the name and defence of sons of the soil.

FIRST
Sergeant, so long as you are in the army you are going to obey army law and discipline. If you want to play politics you must hang your uniform and then go into politics. Until you do that you are still in the army. I hear you have been teaching civilians military discipline. Let us see how this works on you.

FOURTH
I am sorry, my Commandant. Very, very sorry for what I did, Captain.

SECOND
You? Sorry for what? The land is yours. We are all your slaves. So why are you sorry?

THIRD
This is the first time his mouth has said the word "sorry" ever since he joined this patrol.

FIRST

Sergeant, why do you take pleasure in tormenting peaceful citizens? People are already in the peace and tranquillity of their homes at night. You boldly walk up to the door.

Open up, quick! Military patrol! Military control!

FOURTH

Good evening, soldier. Do you need any help?

FIRST

Shut up, you vandal. Do you need any help? It is you vandals giving us no sleep. Four days now my mouth has not even seen a toothbrush, I cannot even change my dross, I cannot even sit down to drink a good beer with friends and you want to help me?

FOURTH

But, soldier, what have I done to deserve these harsh words? You found me in my house.

FIRST

So I don't have a house eh? That is why for over four days now water has not seen my mouth. That is why my back has not seen water because I don't have a house. Thank you.

FOURTH

I did not say you do not have a house, Officer. Only that you found me ...

FIRST

Shut your mouth before I make you eat shit, vandal. Let me see how ugly your body be. Undress!

Trousers!

FOURTH

Trousers? Before my wife and children?

FIRST

So I don't have a wife and children, thank you. That is why every week I have only thirty minutes with my wife and children. I said trousers.

What is the famous song?

THIRD

ebeesee, ebeesee!
Wonderful!

FIRST

No, not that one. The one the vandals sing on the roads during their marches.

THIRD

Soldier di sofa, Commandant di chop money.

FIRST

That is it. Mr Civilian, ready go! Left, right. Left, right. Left, right! Song!

FOURTH

I don't know the song, Officer.

THIRD

Soldier di sofa, Commandant di chop money.

FIRST

Quick march! Left, right. Left, right. Left, right.

On the roads you march for hours without tiredness. Chief Warrant Officer, bring water quickly.

Now, vandal, down and do the roll about. You know what this revolver can do to you? I said down, vandal, and take a swine-bath.

That is treatment we give to vandals and power mongers. You may now go back to your wife and children. If election come and you don't vote for General he will still declare himself General; and I will come back and give you more hot coffee of military discipline. *(No longer acting)*

You can go and tell the General. I want those shoes in a neat pile by the time I come back. And, Sergeant, let me not hear that a single one has been looted.

Exits.

SECOND

Sergeant, you no go wear your uniform? If he comes back and sees you like that he might repeat the treatment.

FOURTH

I will tell the General. I swear to God Almighty that the General must know.

THIRD

But that is what he said. Go and tell the almighty General. You are instead swearing by the Almighty God.

FOURTH

You have started again?

SECOND

Leave him alone, Officer. Sergeant, please, wear your uniform and save us the embarrassment.

FOURTH

Whatever you people are plotting against me in this patrol, the General will know.

SECOND/THIRD

We-e-e-eh! Please save us from your General.
Fourth laughing.

THIRD
What is so funny, Sergeant? What is killing you with laughter?

FOURTH
That song fittam well, well.

SECOND
Fit who? What song?

FOURTH
Soldier di sofa, Commandant di chop money. The song fittam gang.

SECOND
Why do you say that?

THIRD
All the money that Supreme Military gives for our feeding how much does he spend?

FOURTH
One sardine and one bread, two times a day. Is that all we deserve?

SECOND
Maybe Supreme Military does not give him what we deserve. The temptation to line one's pockets with money which belongs to others is now universally applicable in the land.

THIRD
Those of us on the ground are in real trouble. Now the Commandant has gone to have a good meal which he will flush down with wine and even champagne. He will take a bath, change his clothes, play with his children and even sleep with his wife or his "spare tyre" before coming back to give us orders.

FOURTH

While we only get relief after one week. Book is good, lie no sweet.

SECOND

But you are the very people singing that Standard Seven is better than big, big diploma.

THIRD

It is also true, Oga. What do you do with big, big certificate these days? Many people have to hide their big, big certificates and show the small, small ones in order to enter army or police. That is the only job left in the land; army or police.

FOURTH

That is something that has surpassed my intelligence, this army and police business. With the very friendly neighbours we have and all the friendship agreements that have been signed.

SECOND

As far as I know, there is no threat of war with any of our friendly and brotherly neighbours.

THIRD

Are you sure, Captain? What about the one whom the choir boys have always accused of supporting marches and demonstrations in this area?

FOURTH

Ah forget. Even that one has finally come out in support of the General. Didn't you hear that he sent a big load of military gifts to the General when he started having serious problems with his own people?

THIRD

People say that he was asking the General to advise him on how to deal with the marches and demonstrations in his land.

SECOND

So at last the General has something to export in return for support and friendship, the art and science of defusing marches and demonstrations. So his policy of recruiting into the army and police is yielding profit, especially as it is highly recommended in the international trading places in London, Paris, Beijing, Tokyo and Washington.

THIRD

But why are they so interested in the army and police?

FOURTH

Because we buy guns, bullets, grenades, teargas and other military equipment from them.

SECOND

Sergeant, you are beginning to think like a real soldier. Not some ethnocentric, fanatic politician. You see, all those big countries producing military equipment need markets for their products. So they start financial problems in the land by refusing to buy what we produce.

THIRD

Either they refuse to buy our cocoa or coffee or they pay very little for it.

FOURTH

So our fathers and mothers have no money to buy small things like oil and salt, or to pay school fees or buy books for their children.

SECOND

Even to pay taxes. People cannot find the money to pay. So the economy of the land is threatened. People can no longer buy goods and services. Industries are forced to close down; more and more people are thrown out of their jobs; more and more children can no longer go to school. And those who are leaving school cannot find jobs because enterprises are compressing or closing down.

FOURTH
How does the army and police business come inside, since people cannot find work in other areas?

SECOND
As more and more people lose their jobs and unemployment continues to mount, there is social malaise resulting in accusations, agitations, demonstrations and marches against the rulers of the land.

THIRD
So, in order to stop these problems the rulers of the land turn to the army and the police for self-preservation not so? Hei! the Commandant is coming.

First enters.

FIRST
What is this talk about self-preservation? Who has been releasing state secrets? Sergeant? You? Did you tell them about the medical reports?

FOURTH
No, my Commandant, I told them nothing. I know nothing.

FIRST
But you knew! You knew that bullets ... Oh no! I am just from the hospital and those doctors have made their reports. Written out everything in black and white.

SECOND
If they get into the hands of the leaders of Mfu and Manjong...

FIRST
What I dread most is the private and the international press.

FOURTH

And Amnesty International. They are the ones who started making so much noise about leaders of Mfu and Manjong being beaten.

THIRD

Didn't I tell you? Don't shoot! Don't shoot! I pleaded. But you opened fire kpa-ka-ka-ka-ka!

FIRST

So it was you again, Sergeant?

FOURTH

My Commandant, the General gave orders that ...

FIRST

The General! The General! Always the General! Yet it was the same General who went on radio and television and declared practically on oath that the demonstrators had only been dispersed with teargas because they were wielding sticks and throwing stones. Zero dead, he declared. And yet ... and yet...

SECOND

You saw corpses?

FIRST

Who said corpses? Who saw corpses?

THIRD/FOURTH

Aiy ye ye ye! We said nothing! We saw nothing!

FIRST

Good. You see only what I say I have seen. And you say only what I say.

CHORUS

We see only what you say you have seen, and we say only what you say.

FIRST

Who gave you orders to shoot, Sergeant? Was it you, Captain?

SECOND

I did not know that anyone was carrying bullets. I did not give orders to anybody to shoot anything.

THIRD

Sons of the soil, defenders of the land, had ammunition.

SECOND

And what are we?

THIRD

Strangers in our own land, I suppose.

FOURTH

It is just that ... just that ...

FIRST

Will you shut your big mouth, soldier?
Chief Warrant Officer, you and Sergeant may leave this area now until you are summoned back.

THIRD

By your orders, my Commandant.
Third and Fourth salute and exeunt.

FIRST

Captain, what I saw in the hospital...

SECOND

Any dead?

FIRST

Four. All of them had bullet wounds although one or two must have died as a result of the stampede.

SECOND

What about the wounded? Are there many?

FIRST

What kind of question is that. Does this pile of shoes not tell you a story.

SECOND

Yes, it does. A tragic story. But then one is always hoping that things are not as bad as they appear I don't even know why we attacked them.

FIRST

We have all become hypocrites and pretenders and liars. Falsehood is now the main menu with which the rulers feed the ruled in the land.

SECOND

So there are many wounded?

FIRST

Many had been treated and sent home, the doctors said. But I saw seven who had been operated because of bullet wounds. There is this girl lying there in a comma with a big wound in the back of her head. Somebody must have hit her hard with the butt of a rifle. I don't know if she can survive.

SECOND

She must be the one I hear they showed on television. They said she had tried to escape by jumping from the military truck which was transporting those who had been captured. They said that she was the only one who had received injuries.

FIRST

Liars! They pushed her off the truck. Some ethnofascist was bent on killing her.

SECOND

What is enthno ...?

FIRST

Any fool drunk with tribalism is an ethnofascist.

SECOND

I hear the father talked on television.

FIRST

Don't mind the fool. He was grinning from ear to ear as if his daughter was lying on her bridal bed. And the way these television people treat patients on the danger list is just sickening. I felt like vomiting. He said the General was taking charge of all expenses. Now the doctors say no one has passed around ever since the interview was broadcast. And they need spirit, disposable syringes, cotton and more drugs for the poor girl.

SECOND

Holy Mary in heaven! Things have got to the level where the hospital cannot provide cotton wool and syringes? Wonders will never end in this land.

FIRST

And while this is happening white elephants are mushrooming in the land of our Moses. What is the use of airports and skyscraper hotels in a land where there are no motorable roads?

SECOND
If they hear that you will receive one hundred strokes on your bare bottom.

FIRST
You mean like those leaders of Mfu and Manjong who were treated like highway robbers?

SECOND
Exactly!

FIRST
Summon the two. I should like to know what happened from the original mouth of a son of the soil.

SECOND
Chief Warrant Officer! Warrant Officer? You and Sergeant to report at once.(*Third and Fourth enter*).
Troops attention! Present your arms! At ease!

FIRST
Sergeant, what is this about leaders of Mfu and Manjong being whipped?

FOURTH
My Commandant, who are they? Every vandal deserves a hot cup of black military coffee.

SECOND
You call the heads of Mfu and Manjong vandals?

FOURTH
Orders are orders! Who cannot start a Manjong house. They all have their eyes on the General's throne. And must be stopped at all cost.

THIRD
And what will happen when people assemble in the market place?

FOURTH
We will break them with teargas, grenades, water cannon and even...

FIRST
Soldier, your enthusiasm blinds you from seeing beyond your nose. When you break the people with water cannon and teargas and...

FOURTH
Horsewhips and even real bullets. Let them try.

SECOND
Sergeant!

FOURTH
My Commandant!

FIRST
You want war? You want to see the land totally destroyed. Can you stand the brunt of war?

FOURTH
It is the vandals who want war. Those who want the General's throne; it is they who want to destroy the land, my Commandant.

THIRD
What arms do they have apart from their placards?

SECOND
Harmless placards: Liberty! We want freedom! We want justice! We want jobs! Give us freedom!

FIRST

That is all you ethnofascists know, eating, fighting and fornicating.

FOURTH

Have you heard that? You have all heard him? This time Sah, you go see-am. Insulting the General and all his people as useless thieves, drunkards and fornicators. This time we go hear.

By your orders, my Commandant!
Exits.

SECOND

Hei, Sergeant! Where are you going?

FIRST

To the General, of course.

THIRD

He must be thinking that the General is God.

SECOND

How is he going to see the General?

FIRST

Ever since this crisis erupted I have tried in vain. Booked audiences, written memos, sent telexes and phoned. All to no avail. The General is in a meeting. The General has gone to his home town. The General is not available. The General has gone to his village. The General has gone on a private visit to the white man's country. The General is in his home town. The General is not available. The General is in the village.

SECOND

If the General is not in his home town he is out of the land on a private visit. I wonder if he ever does any work.

FIRST

What could be more fundamental? Any authority with democratic pretensions must regard these as basics. These are inalienable human...

FOURTH

Rights eh? I knew that some people are only pretending to be loyal. They are the real people encouraging the rebellion. Dangerous crowds of people armed to the teeth with stones and sticks and clubs are now carrying harmless placards.

SECOND

Sergeant! What impudence! Where has our good military discipline gone?

THIRD

To politics and stoma ... stoma ... ma ...

SECOND

Stomachtological auto-development in the name of a cause in which no one has any faith.

FOURTH

Which stomach? Look at my own and tell me how much is inside that you think I eat. I am only doing my duty as a good soldier, protecting the authority of the land.

SECOND

You mean the authority of the General?

FOURTH

The General is the land and the land is the General. But a good soldier must eat to be fit for action. My Commandant, no rations today?

THIRD

So you have a Commandant?

FIRST
Last week he presided over a meeting of the war council.

THIRD
My Commandant, is there a war? I never knew there was a war council in this land.

SECOND
Watch your size forty-six mouth, soldier!

THIRD
By your orders, my Captain.

SECOND
There is a war council in this land, my Commandant? What war? Against whom? I mean which of our neighbours ...?

THIRD
My mother warned me. If you go to the army and get killed, I will take my life, she threatened. Now war has come and I must leave my wife. Poor wife! Poor mother! I wish I had listened to you. But the army is the only place where there are jobs. Or the police. And now war is coming.

SECOND
My Commandant, will I be able to take my family to the village? At least they will be safe there with my parents. Please, my Commandant, two days will be sufficient.

THIRD
For me I need only one day, my Commandant. If you can let me go tomorrow I shall be back the day after tomorrow.

SECOND
You are a junior to me and so cannot go first. My family is even more important than your own.

FIRST

Look at the people who call themselves soldiers, quaking and quivering like old women when they smell war.

SECOND

Who is quivering and quaking? I only want to take my family to the village, that is all.

THIRD

And I want to see my mother for the last time, that is all.

FIRST

When it comes to fighting unarmed civilians you show your fangs like starved Indian cobras. But when you hear about war you start sweating in your armpits and pissing in your pants.

SECOND

No one pissed, my Commandant.

FIRST

Speak for yourself, Captain. Just take a look at Chief Warrant Officer. He is wet in the lower regions.

THIRD

I am sorry, my Commandant. I have been on guard over these shoes for too long. No rest, no food no break. But ... but my Commandant, which land ... I mean which of our neighbours has declared hostilities against us? It cannot be the one whom Sergeant said had sent military gifts to the General?

FIRST

What do you mean?

SECOND

The war council! You said the General presided over a war ... Oh, my God!

FIRST

The demonstrating placard wielders, that is all.

SECOND/THIRD

Ah! Only that!

SECOND

The army is the best place. It is the only profession.

THIRD

Especially with air-cover, helicopter-grenade-attackers.

SECOND

And back-cover from police water-canon delivery tanks. Come, Officer and give me another hug.

SOLO: ebeesee, ebeesee!
CHORUS: Wonderful!
SOLO: Ebeesee, ebeesee!
CHORUS: Wonderful!
SOLO: I go fo war I see something!
CHORUS: Wonderful!
SOLO: Small mami, big, big bobbi!
CHORUS: Wonderful!
SOLO: Small work big, big money!
CHORUS: Wonderful!

FIRST

(Barks out) Attention!

For this show of indiscipline and complete disrespect for military hierarchy, your food rations for today are suspended.

SECOND/THIRD

Food rations suspended! But my Commandant ...

SECOND
The shoes, my Commandant! Guarding these shoes is hard work. Hard work!

THIRD
Yes, guarding shoes is hard work, my Commandant.

FOURTH
Guarding shoes is hard work.
Guarding shoes is hard work! A letter from the Supreme Military, my Commandant!

FIRST
(Reading) Report to the General's Office, Supreme Military Headquarters immediately.
Deep silence followed by sarcastic laughter from Fourth.

SECOND
The General wants to see you at last, my Commandant.

THIRD
I don't like this. I don't like it at all, at all.

FOURTH
Some people think that because they command others they cannot be commanded by others. So, therefore, they can insult those in power the way they like.

SECOND
Sergeant!

FOURTH
Some people think that because we are junior in their eyes, so therefore, we are junior everywhere.

FIRST
Captain, you take command until my replacement is sent; and Sergeant's rations are suspended if they ever come.
First exits.

FOURTH
What are rations? A tin of sardine and a rotten piece of bread. Any time I want to eat, I know what to do. Any time I am thirsty, I know where to go. Rations, indeed!

THIRD
Who does not know? Harassing innocent civilians and looting their property just because you are a soldier.

FOURTH
And so? And so? Supreme Military gave him big money for ration. He put it in his pocket and gave us one sardine and one bread just because he is Commandant. Nonsense! I told the General everything. Everything!

SECOND
What will the General do to him, Sergeant? Cut off his neck?

THIRD
It will not be the first time. All those people who are said to be killed by robbers and gangsters, including people of God, and even his own wife, are there not rumours that the hand of the General is inside?

FOURTH
Do you hear what he is saying? Have you heard what slanders he is vomiting? It is good, really good that I was sent to this patrol. I now know that all of you are against the General. That is why they order you to deal with those vandals and subversives and you come and loiter here pretending that you are guarding shoes. Shoes, indeed!

THIRD
Old boy, I said rumours. To God in heaven did I call someone's name? And you know it is the Commandant who posted us here to guard these shoes. I have been asking myself why a man should be

guarding old tattered shoes like these. *(mirthlessly)* Shoes and men in arms! How strange!

FOURTH

Shoes! And three men armed to the teeth! Strange, indeed!

SECOND

Don't forget number four, in fact, our number one! Shoes and four men in arms!

FOURTH

Na lie, Oga! If your Commandant comes back then I am not a son of the soil and my mother is a fornicator.

THIRD

And you a bastard.

SECOND

Sergeant! Your tongue.

FOURTH

By your orders, my Captain.

SECOND

Attention! Present your arms! Attention! About turn! Quick march. Left, right! Left, right! Left, right! Song!

SOLO: ebeesee, ebeesee!
CHORUS: Wonderful!
SOLO: ebeesee, ebeesee!
CHORUS: Wonderful!
SOLO: Small gondele big, big bobbi!
CHORUS: Wonderful!
SOLO: Small mami big, big bobbi!
CHORUS: Wonderful!
Exeunt.

...And Never Shall Be Again

SECOND
Warrant Officer? Chief Warrant Officer?
Sergeant? Warrant Officer? Chief Warrant Officer? Sergeant!
Third and Fourth come running.
Oh ho oo! I see you have been enjoying yourselves. You both stink of alcohol and, Sergeant, you are visibly not normal; not to say drunk.

FOURTH
No, my Captain. I am not drunk.

SECOND
And Chief Warrant Officer, where is the object of your assignment?

THIRD
The shoes! The shoes! The shoes!

SECOND
Yes, Officer. The shoes!

FOURTH
Hei! What happen here? Where Commandant's shoes go?

SECOND
Attention!
Now if you don't tell me what happened to that heap of shoes I will shoot both of you before I am court-martialled.

THIRD
Please, my Captain, don't shoot me. You know we have always fallen and risen together in this patrol. It was Sergeant's idea. He

should ... should ... he should bear ... bear ... bear the sentence for this.

FOURTH

Liar! You talked first. I am not even me inside because Commandant himself said no ration for me.

THIRD

This man is a liar from birth, Captain. He is the one who said he knew a place very near-by where we could get something to pacify the brass-band in ...

FOURTH

Because your stomach was making music like a brass-band. And then you yourself said that the Captain had gone to his house to eat and even fornicate. If na lie let lightning strike me. Captain, he even say that ... that it is only the juniors who always suffer and do monkey work while ... while ba ... baboon di chop. Na lie?

THIRD

I swear to God, this man is a born liar. This me? That I said what? That Captain do what?

SECOND

Whatever you said, I want those shoes or I shoot both of you. Especially you, Sergeant. How did Supreme Military know about the shoes, their disappearance?

THIRD/FOURTH

What! Supreme Military! The General knows?

THIRD

Stop pretending, Sergeant. You are the one. You went and made the plan. Then came back and fooled me to go with you, and your people came and took the shoes.

FOURTH
Honest to God, I am not inside this one, I swear. But, my Captain how do you know that ... ?

SECOND
Silence! *(mockingly)* Captain how did you know that ... ? The radio. That's how! And Supreme Military have even issued a press statement.*(Adopting voice of newscaster)*

The following is a press statement from the General's Office. A group of marauding vandals, very heavily armed with clubs, sticks, stones and rocks, recently over-powered a light patrol of soldiers and made away with very sensitive military material including shoes.

THIRD
Thank God, we are saved. Thank God, we are free.

FOURTH
You see what I was saying, Captain? It is not here. We are saved. We are free.

SECOND
Silence! Don't you dare to interrupt or I will shoot you before I finish delivering the press statement. If it is not here, where are the shoes? Answer!

THIRD
Since we were not away for long ...

FOURTH
Yes, hardly one hour. Not even one hour at all, at all.

SECOND
Silence! You were drinking. You got drunk and slept off. You were away for more than one day.

THIRD

Never, never, Captain!

FOURTH

At all, at all. You too can exaggerate, my Captain. It is true that I tried to sleep with one titi-ngon but she said that she was seeing moon. So sleep, at all, at all. Drunk, a calabash of wine can be drunk?

THIRD

Lies.

SECOND

Silence! You will see stars, not moon. So I am lying? So Supreme Military is lying. So the General is a liar. After you have been shot you will both appear before the military tribunal to answer charges of libel and disrespect for the supreme organs and institutions of the land. And you will have to face the firing squad all over. Lies, indeed. Since I am lying, what is today?

You don't know? Tell me what day today is.

THIRD

Today is ... is... today is ...

FOURTH

Today! Yes, today is today.

THIRD

Yes, today is today, of course. Simple. Today is today, Captain.

SECOND

You are making a fool of me? You are calling me a fool, not so? This will simply precipitate your execution.

THIRD/FOURTH
Like precipitated democracy...

SECOND
Silence! The demon be crazy with you. I order you to listen to the radio before I finish you.

(Adopting voice of newscaster)

The whole area has been sealed off and a house to house search is being carried out.

FOURTH
We found only some chewables and drinkables, Captain. No military material.

THIRD
No shoes either. Only chewables and drinkables. People nice, even. No vandals.

SECOND
Silence! You contradict Supreme Military statement.

(Reverting to voice of newscaster)

The area is known to have a very large number of vandals and it is feared that the material stolen might be used to destabilize the land and so compromise the peace for which the General, Supreme Commander, has laboured so untiringly and so relentlessly.

You don't have mouths anymore?

I say, have your tongues been plucked out?

THIRD
True, Captain, vandal is no good.

FOURTH
Very, very true, my Captain. Vandal is no good.

SECOND

Consequently, a state of emergency has been declared in the area in order to protect innocent and law-abiding people and their property.

Now, soldiers, you fall out and I want those shoes back here in the same nice, little heap.

THIRD/FOURTH

By your orders, Captain!
Sudden shrill female voice off.

FEMALE VOICE

Leave me! Leave me, I say. Help! Please, help me. These soldiers will kill me. I don't know anything about shoes. Leave my wrapper. Help! Help! I say, leave my wrapper. I beg, officer, take my shoes and leave me alone. I say I don't know anything about shoes. Leave me! You will tear my pant you this brute. What shoe can be hidden there? Leave me! I say leave me. Help! Help! Help! Help me e e e e e!

SECOND

How many patrols are in this area.

THIRD

I thought only us, but now I am not sure.

FOURTH

I am afraid for the people. I think the General has sent in his personal security guard.

MALE VOICE

Shoes? I know nothing about shoes. Leave me alone. I say I know nothing about shoes. Oh, my coat and my shirt. Yes, take mine. Take my shoes and leave me alone. A a a h! They will kill me! You are knocking my toes off. Help! Help! Help! Help me e e e e!

SECOND

You see how important those shoes are? We are all going to be court-martialled and shot. I wonder why they haven't come for us yet.

THIRD

All this because Sergeant's mouth is always dribbling with saliva. Eating and drinking and ...

SECOND

Silence!

Boot steps of many people running off. Sarcastic laughter of old woman off.

FEMALE VOICE

Come take you chop no my bikkin. You di lun weti again? Soja man witi long, long gun di lun woman na lun? Na only nyong girl wuna di fanam? Shoes, shoes! Wus kana shoes soja dem go chakara country so and den beat Chila dem and chakara nyong girl dem lass?

More old women's voices.

Wusai dem dey? Shoes! Shoes! Shoes! Wuna come take shoes. Wuna come take lass. Shoes! Lass! Shoes! Lass! Wuna come take shoes. Wuna come take lass!

THIRD

The Kil'u women. Very old and very dangerous women.

SECOND

They carry arms?

FOURTH

Yes, bamboos. Long bamboos.

SECOND

What do they do with the bamboos?

THIRD

Nothing. They just walk with the bamboos. Like walking sticks, you know.

SECOND

Why were the soldiers running?

THIRD

Captain, you know what it means for an old woman to expose her nakedness before your eyes?

FOURTH

A curse beyond measure.

THIRD

The end of your manhood. What is the use being a soldier without your manhood?

SECOND

Where have they been? I never heard about them before.

THIRD

They have always been around. Kind of the Mountain of Elephants. Sleeping volcano if you see what I mean.

FOURTH

But why the volcano eruption only now?

THIRD

You should know, Sergeant. Since the day you people whipped leaders of Mfu and Manjong and Kwifon did not react, the Kil'u erupted. The pronouncements of Kil'u are law in the land. If Kil'u says today is market or nobody's nose should smell the outside air, that is law.

SECOND
How I wish the Commandant were back! There must be something else to this matter than just shoes. An alibi, yes. The shoes are an alibi.

FOURTH
You are right, Captain. Only Ali Baba and the forty thieves can do this type of thing.

THIRD
What thing?

FOURTH
The shoes disappearing.

SECOND
Yes, the General has an alibi. Ali Baba and his forty times four hundred hoodlums can now take their revenge on the people in this part of the land.

FOURTH
Are you sure, Captain? I have been wondering about those shoes myself. All useless. None of them could match. You remember how the Commandant punish me because I wanted to see if any can match.

SECOND
You begin to think like a man, Sergeant, a real man. You remember I asked you what is today?

THIRD
And he answered that today is today.

FOURTH
Yes, today is today; and I stand by what I say.

SECOND

You are becoming a man, Sergeant. Try again. I mean ... like ... like ...

FOURTH

Ah! You mean money-wise?

THIRD

Salary-wise, to be more exact.

FOURTH

I understand you, Captain. One end of the month is already joining with the other end to make number two without salary. This is bad oh!

THIRD

And our rations, they don't come any more. They forget us, Captain. Maybe you send a message just to remind them.

SECOND

They don't forget us, Warrant Officer. The money they can find is barely enough to keep the General's personal security. That is why ...

THIRD/FOURTH

They send another patrol to do damage in our sector after they withdraw our Commandant.

SECOND

How I wish he were back!

FOURTH

I now understand what you were saying before about, what you call it? Social ma ... ma ...

SECOND

Malaise. Social malaise, agitations and demonstrations.

THIRD
That is why they only employ in the army and police. And now, no salary and no rations.

FOURTH
And if we open our mouth to ask for salary and rations they will send the General's personal security to ... to...

SECOND
You are now a man, a real man...

THIRD
Hei listen! Someone approaching.
First enters in civilian dress, carrying a travelling bag.

SECOND/FOURTH
The Commandant! The Commandant himself! Our Commandant is back!

SECOND
Troops, attention! Present your arms!

FIRST
Don't worry boys, relax. I am glad to see you all. I was afraid that you might all be under military custody awaiting sentence. Except Sergeant, of course.

SECOND
My Commandant, Sergeant has become a man, a real man. Are you on leave?

FIRST
You mean because I am not wearing a uniform. I am no longer your Commandant. I resigned. Left the army.

SECOND/THIRD/FOURTH
What? Resigned? Left the army? Not possible.

FIRST
Sure possible! All the foreign radio stations carried the news last evening. It is unfortunate that when you are on patrol events pass you by.

SECOND
What will become of us? We have all been longing for your return.

FIRST
Ssshii! Listen! What is that?
Distant shouting of crowd.

VOICES
We want freedom! We want jobs! We want our salaries! Give us freedom! Liberty now! Freedom! Liberty! Freedom!

SECOND
Another demonstration.
Sudden outburst of gun-fire and then pandemonium.

FIRST
Well, I am going to join them. Maybe I will be shot. Maybe I will die. But the people are sure to win. It doesn't matter how long it takes and how many get killed. I smell freedom and liberty for all. I am standing up to be counted.

SECOND
My Commandant, you cannot leave us. I will follow you.

THIRD
Captain, we have always fallen and risen together. If you are going with Commandant, we fall and rise together.

FIRST
You cannot come with me in your present state.

SECOND/THIRD
We are not staying. We will throw away the uniforms and give our arms to Sergeant.

FOURTH
Who do you think is staying? We have been four men in arms being used like play things, like toys even, by a small nyama-nyama group of very corrupt thieves and self-seekers, to humiliate, to torture and to kill our own brothers and sisters, the suffering people, in the name of a law and a land which they manipulate at will and in which they have no faith.

THIRD
Haba! Sergeant don vex.

FOURTH
My Commandant, I am very sorry for all the misunderstanding. Please, don't throw me away. I am coming with you.

SECOND
You see what I was saying, my Commandant. Sergeant is our man.

FIRST
Sergeant, take my hand. I am glad you now know that we were all being manipulated. You are our man.

I think I have enough clothes in my bag to go round. I suggest we go into the bushes over there. We will dig a hole and hide your uniforms and arms inside. We might be needing them in future for the liberation struggle.

SECOND
Commandant, please give us military order for the last time.

THIRD/FOURTH
Yes, military order for the last time from our Commandant.

SECOND
For the last time.

FIRST
Alright, alright. However, before I humour you, let me warn that out there, with the people, we must abandon the wanton violence against others that was our way of life in the army. From this moment we must demonstrate a deep respect for human life and the basic rights of each and every individual.

THIRD/FOURTH
We are ready, Commandant. We promise that we are with you.

FIRST
Good. Troops, attention!
Present your arms! At Ease! Now listen carefully to the words of this song.
People di sofa General di chop money!
Soja di sofa General di chop money!
People and soja di sofa, General di chop money! OK?
Troops, attention! To the right turn! Mark time!
Left, right! Left, right! Left, right! Left, right! Song!
Forward march! Left, right! Left, right! Left! Left! Left!

Exeunt.

The End

www.ingramcontent.com/pod-product-compliance
Lightning Source LLC
Chambersburg PA
CBHW012041290426
44111CB00021BA/2934